Hidden Addictions

Hidden Addictions

Marilyn Freimuth

JASON ARONSON
Lanham • Boulder • New York • Toronto • Oxford

Published in the United States of America
by Jason Aronson
An imprint of Rowman and Littlefield Publishers, Inc.

A wholly owned subsidiary of
The Rowman and Littlefield Publishing Group, Inc.
4501 Forbes Boulevard, Suite 200, Lanham, Maryland 20706
www.rowmanlittlefield.com

PO Box 317
Oxford
OX2 9RU, UK

British Library Cataloguing in Publication Information Available

Library of Congress Cataloging-in-Publication Data

Freimuth, Marilyn, 1951-
  Hidden addictions / Marilyn Freimuth.
    p. cm.
  Includes bibliographical references and index.
  ISBN 0-7657-0079-4 (cloth : alk. paper)
  1. Obsessive-compulsive disorder. 2. Compulsive behavior. 3. Substance abuse. 4.
Drug abuse. I. Title.
  RC533.F745 2005
  616.85'227—dc22

                                                             2004027394

Printed in the United States of America

♾™ The paper used in this publication meets the minimum requirements of American
National Standard for Information Sciences—Permanence of Paper for Printed Library
Materials, ANSI/NISO Z39.48-1992.

Contents

PART II

Preface

After ten years working as a psychologist in private practice, I would have been confident to say that I had not treated an addicted person. Two things happened to change that. First, I began receiving referrals from an addictions counselor adept at helping people give up even the most longstanding of addictions. When emotional problems threatened their continued sobriety, he would refer them to me for psychotherapy. As these new patients related their histories of interpersonal conflicts, low self-esteem, unpredictable behavior, and emotional outbursts, a thought began to take shape in my mind: "This can't really be the first time I've treated patients who have addictions." With a new ear, I began listening to these patients in early recovery. As they related their experiences, I began to hear bits and pieces of stories I heard from patients years before—patients I never considered as having an addiction problem.

Then a second event happened. Around the time these thoughts were taking shape, a thirty-seven-year-old divorced woman, mother of two, and CEO informed me that she thought she had a drinking problem. Beginning eighteen months before, she had started sipping wine in the evening as she read. For the past nine months, she finished a bottle almost every evening. I would never have thought this successful, articulate, and funny woman had a drinking problem. Her revelation led me to wonder who else in my current practice might be addicted. There was a twenty-two-year-old recent college graduate whose meteoric rise in his company suggested a bright professional future. He had come to see me for social problems. In one session, he revealed, in an unselfconscious manner, that the only way he got out of his apartment on the previous weekends was by smoking marijuana. With my nascent sensitivity to addiction problems, I inquired further about his substance intake and found that he socialized primarily in bars and would drink until quite drunk. Sometime during the evening he might take a Valium or two as well.

As I continued listening to my current patients, I found, to my surprise, that more than one-third could be described as having substance use related problems. While none were substance dependent, several would qualify for a formal diagnosis of substance abuse. Many others could be described as at-risk for developing an addiction. They were using substances in a more moderate manner, but the mood altering properties of the substances were affecting their lives, including psychotherapy, in a negative manner.

I wondered why I had not recognized addiction-related issues in my patients before this time. It was true that I had no courses on addictions in graduate school. Was it just a matter of needing specialized training? After talking informally to a number of colleagues about the prevalence of addiction in their practices, I doubted the answer was as simple as providing better education. A number of younger colleagues had received training in addictions during graduate school or on an internship, and yet they, like my older colleagues, spoke of treating few or no addiction problems. If an addiction was being treated, it was because patients in psychotherapy presented addiction as their primary concern. Some providers had referred these patients for specialized treatment, while others, who had decided to treat these patients, often spoke disparagingly of how little the patient benefited from psychotherapy. Other professionals said they were happy not to have such patients in their caseloads, given that "addicts" act out and are difficult to treat.

The frequent successes of my addiction counselor colleague suggested that treatment outcomes could be quite positive for this group. Plus, I was enjoying working with my patients in early recovery as well as those whose addiction problems had now emerged. I began to wonder if these negative attitudes toward addictions were more widespread than the few psychotherapists I spoke to and if such attitudes in any way influenced one's ability to recognize addictions.

I did not believe that my colleagues treated as few addiction-related problems as they indicated. I suspected that they, like me, did not recognize what they saw in psychotherapy as indicative of addiction. I know that what I had expected to see, based on media portrayals and DSM-IV criteria, was someone with deficient coping skills whose functioning was severely compromised. But this was not turning out to be the case. The patients I was treating were often quite functional despite frequent and intense use of substances.

This series of experiences led me to wonder what psychotherapists need to know in order to better recognize and treat addictions. I began reading some of the extensive literature on addiction treatment. These books and articles, for the most part, assumed that addiction was the presenting problem; a patient came to treatment explicitly asking for help or a significant other identified addiction as the patient's problem. None of the literature captured what I was looking for: What will the psychotherapist hear or see that is a clue that substance use needs to be explored? How does one bring up addictions with patients who come to psychotherapy for psychological distress but, in the process of intake or during treatment, show signs of an addiction or addiction-related problem? Books on addiction assessment were no more useful in answering my questions. Like the treatment literature, assessment was directed at patients where addiction was an explicit part of the referral question. These books further assumed that the provider wanted to do a formal addiction interview or administer screening instruments on a routine basis.

I did come across a relevant body of literature that examined assessment of addictions in the medical setting where there is concern that addictions often go unrecognized by physicians. However, the assessment procedures were limited in focus (mostly alcoholism) with the goal being to develop the briefest screening tool possible. I could not find what I was looking for: how to listen to the clinical dialogue for clues that undisclosed addictions are present and how to ask questions in the context of a psychotherapy session that elicit the appropriate information.

When I could not find the answers I sought in the existing literature, I decided I would need to discover them myself. I began to take notes on patients whose substance use turned out to be a problem, how this information came to be revealed in the treatment, and how I approached our discussions of the topic. At the same time, I began a small research project aided by my students at the Fielding Graduate University. In one study, we interviewed psychotherapists who defined themselves as relatively naïve about addictions. Our questions were directed at better understanding the factors that prevent therapists from recognizing addictions in their patients. A second study involved interviewing psychotherapists and addiction counselors, who consider themselves experts in the addiction field, about the signs and symptoms they have used to identify addictions. From these interviews, we distilled a list of indicators that can help a psychotherapist listen in a new way for addiction issues. These interviews with master clinicians provided other information that can be of use in psychotherapy, such as how to distinguish problem use and abuse from dependence and how to ask questions that are likely to reveal an addiction problem. Finally, I began reading autobiographical as well as fictionalized accounts of how people develop and recover from addiction in order to see if their experiences of living with and without addiction held clues to improving assessment practices.

This book synthesizes what I have learned. The goal here is to help health-related professionals of various theoretical orientations understand how to assess for and recognize addictive behaviors and their consequences. In contrast

to other texts on this topic, the focus here is on the types of patients that psychotherapists are most likely to see, that is, patients who come into treatment
asking for help with depression, anxiety, low self-esteem, marital problems,
or just a general sense that life is not working.

Addictive behaviors are defined broadly to include substance-based addictions and those that arise from excessive behaviors, also known as process addictions. Process addictions came to my attention through my work with patients in early recovery. Frequently, these patients reported a history of
problems with "overdoing it." Common examples of excessive behavior include eating, gambling, spending money, and sex. These behaviors were not
always a part of their history. Quite often excessive behaviors emerged during psychotherapy as substance use ceased. It became clear to me that if
someone plans to work with addicted patients, it will be necessary to recognize both substance-based and process addictions.

This book is intended for professionals and graduate students in the mental health fields who, whether they currently know it or not, work with persons who have or may develop addictions. This book will help them to recognize a patient's addictive use of a mood-altering substance or behavior and
its impact on the process and outcome of psychotherapy. Those in the health-
related fields will also find much of value. Along with a discussion of the relative merits of different screening tools, such as those preferred by the busy
physician, they will learn about interview questions that are effective in elic-
iting information essential to making a diagnosis. This book can also be a
valuable resource for those in training to treat addictions; not only will counselors learn about the major assessment tools and individual/cultural differences in assessment outcome, they will also become more cognizant of how
mental health issues interact with addictive disorders.

In the process of presenting ways to assess for diverse types of addictions,
this book provides the reader with a wide range of knowledge about addictive
behaviors: how substance effects mimic psychological symptoms, the nature
of tolerance and withdrawal, the similarities between substance-based addictions and those which are behavior-based, and individual differences in the
way addictions are presented in psychotherapy. Close attention is paid to the
reasons why addictions often go unrecognized in psychotherapy. This allows
the reader to identify those most relevant to him or her. Finally, the reader can
use this book as a resource for learning about structured as well as interview-
based methods of addiction assessment. The goal here is to provide the reader
with knowledge about addictions and their assessment in a way that is clinically useful. To this end, the assessment process is presented in a manner that
can be seamlessly integrated into the ongoing dialogue between patient and
treatment provider.

1

What Is an Addiction?

Joseph is addicted to pornography. Karen can't stop using cocaine. Gary gambles excessively. Tony compulsively uses the Internet. Mary Ellen is an alcoholic. Christopher is addicted to exercise. Josy is a compulsive shopper. Brittany is addicted to love. People can become overly involved with many different kinds of substances, behaviors, and experiences. Is any excessive behavior an addiction? Are addictions more than bad habits? What distinguishes an addiction from a compulsion? Answers to these questions can help the clinician to know what to look for in order to recognize whether a patient's problem includes a current or potential addiction.

Drugs and alcohol are understood to be something people can become dependent upon. But what about all those other excessive behaviors that people get attached to but that do not involve an intoxicating or mood-altering substance? Gambling is the most common. Sex, food, exercise, buying, work, even computers and the Internet have been studied in the professional literature. When these behaviors become problematic or excessive, they are referred to as process addictions.

DSM-IV AND ADDICTIONS

Looking into the *Diagnostic and Statistical Manual of Mental Disorders-IV* (DSM-IV) (American Psychiatric Association 1994) to better understand and diagnose addictions will provide no clarity because *addiction* is a term that has been completely dropped from its nomenclature. Behaviors once described as addictive now belong to the general category of Substance-related Disorders, which is divided into two types: dependence and abuse. Substance

3

Dependence (DSM-IV code 304), like addiction, carries with it the sense that the person is unable to control substance use. Dependence, in turn, is distinguished from abuse (DSM-IV code 305), which involves intentional misuse or overuse that is creating some negative consequences.

Gambling, which in its addictive form is labeled pathological gambling (DSM-IV code 312.33), has no conceptual connection to the substance-related disorders. Pathological gambling belongs to a totally separate diagnostic category called "impulse control disorders not elsewhere classified." This category also includes kleptomania, pyromania, and other behaviors that have no obvious connection to addiction.

Eating disorders (DSM-IV code 307) have their own category with the major subtypes being anorexia and bulimia. Some have argued that bulimia and binge eating (a diagnosis understudy) are addiction-like given that both involve excessive consumption along with an impaired sense of control. These forms of eating disorder are correlated with substance use disorders (Wilson 1991) as well as other process addictions. For example, obese women binge eaters are more likely to have a problem with excessive buying than obese women who are not binge eaters (Faber, Christenson, de Zwann, and Mitchell 1995). (Assessment of eating disorders, as a type of process addiction, will not be covered in this book for two reasons: (1) Emphasis here is on facilitating a clinician's skill in recognizing addictions that are not obvious. For most patients, the negative consequences of overeating will be apparent. (2) Questions have been raised about whether an addiction model applies to eating disorders [von Ranson, McGue, and Iacono 2003]).

Sexual disorders belong to yet another diagnostic grouping. Under the heading "sexual disorders" there is no diagnosis that captures the notion of sex addiction. There is a diagnosis for hypo- or under-sexuality, but none for excessive sexual behavior. Paraphilias, where the object or aim of sexual desire is not socially acceptable, may have some elements in common with sexual addictions (see chapter 6).

With the proliferation of computers, a new form of process addiction has been defined that involves an excessive use of this technology. Quite often this includes use of the Internet for sexual purposes and this is referred to as cybersex addiction. Similar to addictions to exercise, work, or shopping, computer-based addictions have yet to be recognized as problems meriting their own diagnostic category.

Some argue that the term "addiction" should be confined to the problematic use of substances that have psychoactive effects. The DSM-IV apparently adheres to this viewpoint. Substance-related disorders are in one diagnostic category with substance dependence being most similar to what, in common parlance, is an addiction. Gambling, the only process addiction to be mentioned,

Table 1.1. Addictive Behaviors and DSM-IV Diagnostic Categories

DSM-IV Category	
Substance-related disorders	Substance Abuse and Dependence
DSM-IV Category	
Impulse control disorder	Pathological Gambling
Common Parlance	
Process addictions	Other types of behavior potentially enacted in an addictive manner: eating, sex, shopping, exercise, work, computer use
DSM-IV Category	
Anxiety disorder: Compulsion	

is considered separately as an impulse control disorder. There is no discussion of the diagnostic status of other process addictions, such as excessive and repetitive computer use, sex, or buying; presumably all would be classified as compulsions, which in the DSM-IV are a type of anxiety disorder.

DSM-IV: DEFINING SUBSTANCE ABUSE AND DEPENDENCE

In commonsense parlance, an addiction involves a behavior done in excess, for example, too much alcohol, gambling, or shopping. But what defines "in excess"? Is six hours a day on the Internet excessive but four hours is not? Two people can consume the same amount of alcohol on a daily basis and one will show no deficits and the other will be unable to carry on with daily routines. Excess is difficult to define given that the effects of a behavior will vary based on a person's gender, size, age, culture, and other life circumstances.

Instead of defining dependence based on quantity of use, early versions of the DSM focused on the hallmark signs of physical dependence: tolerance and withdrawal. *Tolerance* involves the same response or diminished effects when increasing a substance's dosage. *Withdrawal* refers to acute symptoms that appear with sudden cessation of substance. Originally, it was assumed that certain drugs, with repeated use, would necessarily create physical dependence. Prolonged use of heroin, Valium, and alcohol, like most drugs with depressant or sedating effects, was known to create tolerance and withdrawal. Thus, the original model of addictions developed out of dependence on these types of drugs.

About the same time that *substance dependence* replaced *addiction* as a diagnostic term, the centrality of tolerance and withdrawal for diagnosing an addiction was called into question. Researchers were surprised to observe that Vietnam veterans who used heroin or opium daily could stop cold turkey without major adverse consequences once they returned home (Robins, Davis, and Goodwin 1974). Furthermore, as the range of drugs that people used expanded, it was found that many substances (e.g., hallucinogens and inhalants), even when used frequently and in large quantities, failed to create the two classic signs of physiological dependence. These observations led to a major modification in the criteria that define substance dependence. Current diagnostic practices include withdrawal and tolerance as but two of seven signs of substance dependence. That only three of the seven criteria need to be met to make a positive diagnosis means that tolerance and withdrawal are no longer necessary to diagnose an addiction.

If neither the amount of substance use nor physiological dependence defines addiction, then what criteria are used? As the DSM evolved, attention turned to providing precise descriptions of the range of symptoms common to a given diagnostic category. What stands out with addictive substance use is the person's relationship to a substance. Where substance abusers "like" or "want" chemical-induced changes, those who are substance dependent or addicted "need" these effects. One often hears addictive behavior described as being "out of control." However, G. E. Vaillant's (1995) classic research into the natural history of alcoholism indicated that a construct such as "out of control" was not conducive to reliable assessment. Focusing on alcoholism, he argued that a better predictor would be the negative consequences of this behavior. Following Vaillant, current diagnostic practices define substance-related disorders not in terms of quantity or subjective indicators, such as "feeling out of control," but in terms of observable behaviors and negative consequences. When developing these criteria for substance-related disorders, the goal was to create a set of general attributes that could apply to the abuse of or dependence on a wide range of substances.

Substance Abuse

Substance abuse is characterized by a maladaptive or harmful pattern of substance use that manifests itself in recurrent adverse consequences. Adverse consequences are defined in terms of social problems and hazardous use. Negative social consequences include unfulfilled role obligations, legal troubles, interpersonal problems, and declining school or work performance. Hazardous use entails endangering oneself and others, such as by driving or operating machinery while under the influence, failing to look after one's children properly, using unclean needles thus increasing risk of HIV infection, or being more likely to have unprotected sex when intoxicated. In the ICD-10 (World Health Organization 1997), the equivalent of substance abuse is called harmful use. Harmful use omits social consequences and instead focuses on substance-induced damage to health. The damage may be physical (e.g., ulcers from alcohol, hepatitis from drug injections) or psychological (e.g., drug-induced depression or anxiety).

DSM-IV Criteria for Substance Abuse

A. A maladaptive pattern of substance use leading to clinically significant impairment or distress as manifested by one (or more) of the following, occurring within a twelve-month period:

 1. Recurrent substance use resulting in a failure to fulfill major role obligations at work, school, or home (e.g., repeated absences or poor work performance related to substance use; substance-related absences, suspensions, or expulsions from school; neglect of children or household).
 2. Recurrent substance use in situations in which it is physically hazardous (e.g., driving an automobile or operating a machine when impaired by substance use).
 3. Recurrent substance-related legal problems (e.g., arrests for substance-related disorderly conduct).
 4. Continued substance use despite having persistent or recurrent social or interpersonal problems caused or exacerbated by the effects of the substance (e.g., arguments with spouse about consequences of intoxication, physical fights).

B. The symptoms have never met the criteria for substance dependence for this class of substances (American Psychiatric Association 1994, 182–83).

Initially, substance abuse was conceptualized as a precursor to substance dependence, but the two often have distinctly different courses. While a few people move from abuse to dependence, the majority of those diagnosed as substance abusers remain abusers or overcome their problem. Those most likely to move from abuse to dependence have a family history of addiction (Schuckit et al. 2001).

Substance Dependence

Like substance abuse, substance dependence is characterized by negative consequences. Its distinguishing feature is a cluster of behavioral, psychological, and physiological symptoms that convey the sense that the person is out of control and, hence, dependent on the substance. The DSM-IV requires that the phrase "out of control" is observable so that there can be agreement on its meaning. Out of control is inferred not from self-reported feelings but from actions, such as: 1) continued use despite negative consequences, 2) the substance taking on a central role in the person's life, 3) attempts to cut back have been unsuccessful, and 4) using larger amounts than intended. The ICD-10 (World Health Organization 1997) refers to the "dependence syndrome" that has the same general criteria as substance dependence but with an additional component—experiencing a strong desire or compulsion for the substance.

DSM-IV Criteria for Substance Dependence

A maladaptive pattern of substance use leading to clinically significant impairment or distress, as manifested by three (or more) of the following occurring at any time in the same twelve-month period:

1. Tolerance
2. Withdrawal
3. The substance is often taken in larger amounts or over a longer period than was intended.
4. There is a persistent desire or unsuccessful efforts to cut down or control substance use.
5. A great deal of time is spent on activities necessary to obtain the substance (e.g., visiting multiple doctors or driving long distances), use of the substance (e.g., chain-smoking), or recover from its effects.
6. Important social, occupational, or recreational activities are given up or reduced because of substance use.
7. The substance use is continued despite knowledge of having a persistent or recurrent physical or psychological problem that is likely to have been caused or exacerbated by the substance (e.g., current cocaine use despite recognition of cocaine-induced depression, or continued drinking despite recognition that an ulcer was made worse by alcohol consumption) (American Psychiatric Association 1994, 181).

While the goal of the DSM-IV is to provide a list of operationally defined and observable criteria for abuse and dependence, the current criteria still leave room for subjective judgments. What counts as a "great deal of time" when it comes to obtaining a substance? How many times does one need to try to cut back on drug use for it to qualify as "persistent"? The rationale for keeping some subjectivity is addressed as follows: "These concepts are stated in relatively generic terms to be guidelines for the clinicians and researchers, using a general approach to optimize the commonsense modifications of the criteria that are needed in different cultural settings, for divergent subgroups of patients and depending upon other relevant information for the patient"

(Hasin et al. 2003, 251). The impact of individual differences on assessment is the topic of chapter 8.

The Range of Substance-Related Disorders

The diagnostic categories of substance abuse and dependence provide a set of generic criteria that can be applied to consumption of specific chemical substances. The DSM-IV lists eleven substance groups: alcohol, amphetamines, cannabis, cocaine, hallucinogens, inhalants, nicotine (dependence only), opioids, phencyclidine, and sedative/hypnotics/anxiolytics. Caffeine is included on this list but there is no diagnostic code for abuse or dependence (see appendix A). There is a twelfth catch-all category known as "other or unknown substance-related disorders" that allows for the diagnosis of abuse or dependence for substances that fall outside the eleven groups. Two common examples include nitrous oxide and anabolic steroids. This twelfth category also allows for the diagnosis of a frequently overlooked form of substance abuse: the misuse of prescription medications.

Taking a prescription drug on an ongoing basis in any way other than prescribed is considered equivalent to substance abuse. Misuse includes regularly using a medication for purposes other than prescribed or in an amount greater than prescribed. Medications that are most often abused include opioids prescribed for pain relief, depressants prescribed to alleviate stress or sleep disorders, and stimulants given to curtail attention problems. Misuse of prescription stimulants is documented in Elizabeth Wurtzel's autobiography (2002). Harvard graduate and best-selling author of *Prozac Nation* by age twenty-six, Wurtzel was prescribed Ritalin by her psychiatrist to alleviate difficulties completing her writing assignments. One day she discovered that Ritalin's effects could be heightened if she chopped it up and snorted it. Thus began an odyssey of lying about lost prescriptions to get more of the drug from her psychiatrist while also procuring Ritalin and cocaine through illegal means. Snorting turned to intravenous injections ending ultimately in a breakdown, hospitalization, and recovery. Prescribed medications for weight control have recently become another source of abuse. Following a weight increase, a typical side effect of antidepressants, a psychiatrist or general practitioner may prescribe a weight control medication that the patient then uses in excess.

Parallel to substance-related disorders is a list of substance-induced disorders, including intoxication, withdrawal, and a wide range of substance-induced mental disorders (e.g., substance-induced mood disorder, anxiety, sleep disturbance). As will be presented in chapter 9, many of these symptoms overlap extensively with psychological disorders, and this poses a challenge when making a differential diagnosis.

DISTINGUISHING ADDICTIONS FROM COMPULSIONS

When reading the literature on excessive exercise, spending, or Internet use, these behaviors are identified as addictions in some articles and as compulsions in others. This dual naming reflects a larger debate regarding the nature of addictions. Is gambling really an addiction? Why not refer to it as compulsive gambling? Is alcoholism the same as compulsive drinking? Is it better to understand excessive computer use as a computer addiction or as compulsive use of the computer? Is one addicted to shopping or is shopping a compulsive behavior? For that matter, why does one call excessive hand washing a compulsion rather than an addiction to washing hands? Phenomenological descriptions of addictions have the same driven, out-of-control quality that characterizes a compulsion. The obsessive thinking that accompanies many compulsions is also observed with addictions. An individual ruminates about the next opportunity to use while worrying about the consequences at the same time. Obsessions and compulsive behaviors are classified as anxiety disorders, a diagnostic category totally distinct from substance dependence or pathological gambling, the two addictive behaviors included in the DSM-IV.

Despite the ease with which the words *addictive* and *compulsive* are interchanged, authors of the DSM-IV contend that it should be fairly easy to distinguish the two:

> Some activities, such as eating (e.g., Eating disorders), sexual behavior (e.g., Paraphilias), gambling (e.g., Pathological gambling), or substance use (e.g., Alcohol dependence or abuse) when engaged in excessively, have been referred to as "compulsive." However, these activities are not considered to be compulsive as defined in this manual because the person usually derives pleasure from the activity and may wish to resist it only because of its deleterious consequences (American Psychiatric Association 1994, 422).

Compulsive cleaning or checking to see if the stove is turned off is not intrinsically pleasurable. Rather, compulsions "are repetitive behaviors (e.g., hand washing, ordering, checking) or mental acts (e.g., praying, counting, repeating words silently) the goal of which is so to prevent or reduce anxiety or distress, not to provide pleasure or gratification" (American Psychiatric Association 1994, 418). Compulsive behaviors are said to be ego-dystonic and as such, enacting them is experienced as a source of distress (even though the behaviors are intended to reduce stress associated with some imagined negative outcome). When obsessive thoughts accompany compulsive behaviors, they are experienced as unrealistic or irrational; a woman obsessed with cleaning knows the house is not dirty. In contrast, addictive behaviors, whether drinking, snorting cocaine, gambling, or shopping, are behaviors that are primarily gratifying. A sense of well-being, excitement, or "rush" accompany the behavior. Addictive behaviors are ego-syntonic. Distress only occurs when they create negative consequences for the person's life (e.g., compromised health, arguments with friends). When addictive behaviors are accompanied by obsessive thoughts, they take the form of craving or preoccupation with the behavior and/or are reality based; that is, the person struggles with realistic thoughts about the behavior's adverse effects.

The authors of the DSM-IV believe it is a rather straightforward matter to distinguish compulsive behavior from behaviors that are described as addictive. But is this distinction so obvious? Professional parlance continues to join the two. The National Institute of Drug Abuse (NIDA) begins its definition of addiction as follows: "a state in which an organism engages in a compulsive behavior, even when faced with negative consequences" (2003). Even the DSM-IV, in its discussion of substance dependence, refers to "compulsive drug taking" (American Psychiatric Association 1994, 176).

Arguing from a psychoanalytic perspective, Dodes (2003) concludes that addictions cannot be distinguished routinely from compulsions. He finds the notions that addictive behaviors are always a source of pleasure and desired while compulsive behaviors are motivated solely to relieve stress and are ego-dystonic too facile. With time, compulsions can become a source of positive feelings; a behavior that was initially motivated to avoid anxiety (i.e., negatively reinforced) can become a source of pleasure. "It is fairly common for compulsive actions to become not just accepted, but valued. Consider for example the case of someone repetitively arranging his desk. Over time, the person might find some pleasure in keeping the desk neat. The person might even take pride in the careful, ordered way he or she does things" (Dodes 2003, 183).

On the other side of the argument, addictive behaviors are not necessarily solely pleasurable but can, like compulsions, occur to relieve negative affective states. At first there may be pleasure in a behavior—the person enjoys having a drink or playing slot machines—but for some, the motivation shifts from enjoyment to a means of coping. When a behavior functions as a coping mechanism or a way to alleviate negative affects, it is more likely to become addictive (Cooper, Frone, Russell, and Mudar 1995). A man initially snorts cocaine to be sociable. He finds it energizing and pleasurable. At some later point in time, when he faces a deadline at work, he remembers how focused he felt on cocaine, tries some again, and discovers that the project is finished more quickly than he imagined. Soon, whenever faced with stressful deadlines at work, he feels he must use cocaine in order to be effective. The rush that comes from feeling high leaves him with a positive feeling, but afterward he can't sleep and, while completing the task at hand, he is less effective at work the next day. This behavior is on its way to becoming addictive. In the same manner as alcoholics, pathological gamblers, and those addicted to the Internet, this man continues using cocaine despite his knowledge that the activity's enjoyment is losing salience.

Others have recognized the close link between addictions and compulsions (Carnes 1996; Goodman 1998), noting that they often co-occur and have common symptoms, etiologies, and family histories. While addictions and compulsions may be difficult to distinguish once they are developed, their clinical course is quite different.

Distinguishing Compulsive and Addictive Attributes of Excessive Behaviors

Compulsion: ego-dystonic to start, behavior driven to reduce anxiety or avoid imagined harm, over time the behavior can become valued/pleasurable. Obsessive thoughts, when present, are not limited to the excessive behavior and its consequences.

Addiction: ego-syntonic to start; in its pre-addicted form, the behavior is performed for pleasure or for its arousing/sedating effects but later may be motivated to manage negative affective states which include but are not limited to anxiety. In some cases, there is evidence of tolerance and/or withdrawal.

Rule out that excessive behavior is not symptomatic of a more primary disorder (e.g., manic episode, organic disorder).

Other distinctions between compulsions and addictions emerge during the therapy process. Compulsive behaviors, because they are ego-dystonic, are a source of distress and, as a result, are likely to be talked about in therapy. On the other hand, potentially addictive behaviors that begin as pleasurable and are experienced as normative/ego-syntonic are less likely to be discussed and only become a topic for therapy when negative consequences emerge. Dodes' discussion of the case of Caroline illustrates how compulsions are more likely to be a topic in psychotherapy than addictions. As Caroline's binge eating (which Dodes considers an addiction) improved, she began talking about spending money on new clothes, jewelry, and furniture for her apartment. Her manner of talking did not indicate that spending was a problem. Dodes writes, "At first, I had no idea this was happening. Caroline would mention to me how beautiful her new sofa was, but not that she had overdrawn her account to buy it" (2003, 189). Once this addictive buying was addressed and ceased, a new excessive behavior emerged which Caroline experienced as distressful and immediately reported it in therapy—compulsive cleaning.

There is another feature distinguishing addiction and compulsions, but it can only be applied after successful treatment. As one psychotherapist I interviewed reported, "One rarely hears of a patient lamenting the absence of a compulsion but often those with history of addiction mourn its loss."

EXCESSIVE BEHAVIORS: ADDICTION OR COMPULSION?

Research has addressed whether the characteristics of process addictions better suit the model for obsessive-compulsive disorders (OCD) or addictions. Blanco, Moreyra, Nunes, Saiz Ruix, and Ibanez (2001), after reviewing the experience of pathological gambling, its demographics, neurophysiology, and co-occurring disorders, conclude that gambling has more in common with addiction than OCD. Gambling and substance abuse co-occur at a high rate (up to 50 percent of pathological gamblers were substance abusers), and both disorders are more common in men, and respond to similar treatment strategies. Like substance dependence, gamblers develop a tolerance and will wager more and more money to get the same level of arousal. When not gambling, many describe withdrawal symptoms, including irritability and difficulty concentrating (Petry 2002). Although gamblers have repetitive, obsessive thoughts related to gambling, unlike compulsions, gamblers do not have the excessive doubt common to those with OCD (Blanco et al. 2001).

Christenson et al. (1994) studied repetitive, excessive buying to see if this behavior best fit the symptoms of an addiction or OCD. When participants described their experience associated with buying, 67 percent of the depictions resembled OCD. These descriptions included reference to intrusive thoughts to buy and resistance to such thoughts. Unlike typical OCD, few in this group had any other obsessions or compulsions. Christenson et al. also looked at how often descriptions of buying behavior were similar to an impulse control disorder, such as pathological gambling. Attributes that excessive buying share with impulse control disorders included: "(1) repetitive problematic behavior, (2) urges or mounting tension preceding the behavior, and (3) release of tension or gratification following the behavior. . . . Buying was also often ego-syntonic, a typical feature of impulse control disorders, and the opposite of the phenomenological experience of compulsions, which are by definition ego-dystonic" (Christenson et al. 1994, 10). Descriptions of excessive buying fit the profile of an impulse control disorder in 96 percent of the cases. Further evidence for a link between excessive buying and addictions comes from a study (Mitchell et al. 2002) showing that excessive buyers have higher lifetime histories of substance dependence or abuse and, like substances, buying, initially done for its enjoyment, can with time be used to self-medicate unpleasant affective states such as sadness, loneliness, anger, and hurt (Christenson et al. 1994).

While this research indicates that process addictions are best described as an addiction rather than as a compulsion, it is quite apparent from the degree of overlap that there is no definitive demarcation. Goodman's succinct summary of the relationship between impulsive behaviors, compulsions, and addictive disorders brings conceptual clarity to this overlap:

> All three types of disorders involve difficult-to-resist urges to engage in overt behaviors that entail harmful or unpleasant consequences. The primary function of impulsive behaviors is to produce pleasure or gratification. In terms of learning theory, it is motivated primarily by positive reinforcement. Meanwhile, the primary function of compulsive behavior is to reduce anxiety or other painful affects. In terms of learning theory, it is motivated primarily by negative reinforcement. Finally, addictive behavior functions both to produce pleasure and to reduce painful affects. It is motivated by positive reinforcement and negative reinforcement. Addictive behavior thus shares core characteristics with both impulsive behavior and compulsive behavior (Goodman 2001, 197).

With this in mind, Blanco et al. (2001) conclude that the conceptualization of excessive behaviors as an addiction or a compulsion need not be mutually exclusive. Instead, one may wonder if there are different subtypes with effective treatment depending on the type. For the clinician making an assessment, this would require carefully exploring the person's experience of the excessive behavior and its development to determine if it is best described as an addiction or compulsion.

THE ADDICTION CONSTRUCT

Current diagnostic practices give no conceptual unity to the problems that in common parlance are referred to as addictions. What is it about a behavior that characterizes it as addictive rather than intemperate or a bad habit? Is an addiction any behavior that begins as pleasurable but over time becomes excessive or motivated by anxiety reduction?

For Kohut "there is an unnamable quality that an addiction has, a quality of urgency, a no-delay-tolerating quality, wiping out all differentiations. For example, for an alcoholic alcohol is the important thing. It does not matter whether it is good or bad bourbon, good or bad wine" (1987, 118). When it comes to addictive relationships, one of Kohut's interests, the attachment to someone becomes more important than the quality of the relationship.

Shaffer provides a more developed definition. Among those working in the addiction field, the characteristics of an addictive behavior are: "(1) some element of craving or compulsion; (2) loss of control; and (3) continuing the behavior in question in spite of associated adverse consequences" (1999, 1445).

Goodman provides a slightly different approach. Addiction is "defined as a disorder in which a behavior that can function both to produce pleasure and to provide escape from internal discomfort is employed in a pattern characterized by (1) recurrent failure to control the behavior, and (2) continuation of the behavior despite significant harmful consequences" (1993, 226). Modeling the DSM-IV, he provides a menu of symptoms where any combination of three or more is indicative of addiction.

ADDICTIVE DISORDER

A maladaptive pattern of behavior, *leading to clinically significant impairment or distress*, as manifested by three (or more) of the following, occurring at any time in the same twelve-month period:

1. tolerance, as defined by either of the following:
   a. need for markedly increased amount or intensity of the behavior in order to achieve the desired effect
   b. markedly diminished effect with continued behavior of the same level of intensity
2. withdrawal, as manifested by either of the following:
   a. characteristic psychophysiological withdrawal syndrome of physiologically described changes and/or psychologically described changes upon discontinuation of the behavior
   b. the same (or a closely related) behavior is engaged in to relieve or avoid withdrawal symptoms
3. the behavior is engaged in over a longer period, in greater quantity, or at a higher level of intensity than intended
4. there is a persistent desire or unsuccessful efforts to cut down or control the behavior
5. a great deal of time is spent in activities necessary to prepare for the behavior, to engage in the behavior, or to recover from its effects
6. important social, occupational, or recreational activities are given up or reduced because of the behavior
7. the behavior continues despite knowledge of having a persistent or recurrent physical or psychological problem that is likely to have been caused or exacerbated by the behavior (Goodman 1998, 15–16).

Both Shaffer and Goodman define addiction without reference to any particular substance or behavior. This means that any behavior can potentially occur in an addictive manner. The addictive quality of the behavior rests with "*how* the behavior relates to a person's life" (Goodman 1993, 227). The two definitions are similar in their focus on struggles to control a behavior and its negative consequences, although Goodman provides more specifics that are useful to the clinician in operationalizing the criteria.

One significant difference in their descriptions of the addiction construct is that Shaffer mentions an "element of craving or compulsion" as a component of addiction (Shaffer 1999). Goodman, in following the practices of the DSM-IV, does not refer explicitly to craving/compulsion. Curiously, the DSM-IV section on Substance Dependence acknowledges that cravings are not a criterion while, at the same time, it defines a craving as "a strong subjective drive to use the substance" that is "likely be experienced by most (if not all) individuals with Substance Dependence" (American Psychiatric Association 1994, 176). The ICD-10 does not use the term *craving* but instead refers to a strong desire or compulsion to take a substance as one criterion defining the dependence syndrome. Thus, despite apparent differences, all agree that craving is an element of addiction.

Shaffer (1997) goes on to say that although certain behavior patterns can be labeled reliably as an addiction, this does not guarantee that there is such a thing as an addictive disorder. In other words, beyond the common behavioral descriptions, what evidence is there for similar processes underlying different manifestations of addictions? Flores (2004)) argues that the common denominator is affect regulation and attachment problems. Recently, there has been growing evidence that an impaired regulatory/reward mechanism, based on a neurotransmitter dysfunction, is shared by different types of addictions (e.g., Carnes 1996; Goodman 1998, chapter 5; Wasilow-Mueller and Erickson 2001).

The occurrence of tolerance and withdrawal has also provided a rationale to support an addictive process shared by diverse forms of excessive behaviors. Research supporting this position shows that tolerance and/or withdrawal can develop for process addictions such as gambling, exercise, and cybersex addictions (Chan and Grossman 1988; Petry 2002). Tolerance is represented by an increase in the frequency or intensity of behavior to get the same outcome; a person will shop longer and longer before feeling complete or the gambler spends increasing amounts of money before feeling satisfied. Withdrawal appears in the form of unpleasant feelings when the behavior stops. Those who exercise excessively experience lowered mood and agitation when their usual routine is disrupted.

Other evidence used to argue in support of an addictive disorder comes from the typical outcome of addiction assessment: a person is found to have several different, simultaneous addictions or a history of experiencing different forms of addictive behavior. Numerous epidemiological studies show that individuals have co-occurring substance addictions and/or a mix of behavioral and substance-based addictions. High rates of drug and alcohol dependence are found among those with sexual addictions. Eating disorders occurring along with drug addiction are common (Christo et al. 2003). Or one addiction is switched for another. In early recovery from alcoholism, a patient may begin smoking, drinking coffee, or attending Alcoholics Anonymous (AA) meetings in an excessive manner. For a further example, see the earlier description of Caroline, taken from Dodes (2003); as her binge eating came under control, she began to spend excessively.

Developing an answer to the question "What is an addiction?" is critical for assessment. In order to recognize an addiction, mental health providers need to construct their own understanding of a term that carries multiple meanings in common parlance and professional circles. Whether there is value in assuming there is a general addictive process that manifests in different behaviors will emerge out of clinical and research efforts. Does thinking about a certain set of behaviors as an addiction allow the treatment provider to develop a case formulation and treatment plan that ultimately helps the patient address the problem and move forward in life? The success of twelve-step programs with excessive sexual behavior, gambling, spending, eating, and substance-based addictions suggests that all of these problems can benefit from similar treatment. It also seems that the same is true for psychotherapy of these disorders: treatment approaches that have been effective with substance addictions are also effective for process addictions (e.g., Petry 2002).

SUMMARY

Rather than defining addiction with reference to the frequency and amount of substance use, the DSM-IV focuses on lack of control and negative consequences associated with substance use. Craving is acknowledged as part of addiction, but it is not listed as one of the criteria. These same criteria can be used to define process addictions. Thus, following Goodman (1993) and Shaffer (1999), any behavior or substance use is considered addictive when it has an element of craving, is experienced as being of out control, and continues despite adverse consequences arising from the behavior.

In developing an approach to addiction assessment within the context of psychotherapy, I will focus primarily on what the DSM-IV refers to as Substance-related Disorders. Of these, alcohol use problems are illustrated most frequently because it is the most common addiction and most likely to be intermingled with the problems psychotherapy patients present. Despite the DSM-IV giving no conceptual unity to the different kinds of "things" we can become attached to in an addictive manner, there is good evidence for an addictive process shared by diverse forms of excessive behaviors. In terms of assessment practices, this means that, with a few simple modifications, approaches to the assessment of alcohol are applicable to other substance-related and process addictions.

2

Lessons Learned from a Brief History of Addiction Treatment

Historically, addictions have been treated outside the context of psychotherapy. A person seeking psychotherapy for help with alcoholism or drug abuse would most likely be referred to one of two places: (1) Alcoholics Anonymous or another twelve-step program, or (2) an addiction psychiatrist or a specialized treatment center run by medical practitioners. The past twenty years have seen a diversification in the philosophy of treatments and the types of patients with addiction issues. Along with this diversification, psychotherapy has become a setting for treating addictions.

As a mental health professional interested in assessing and treating addictions, there is much to learn from the various philosophies and models that have shaped the addiction field. While often presented as factions competing to dominate the field, each is better viewed as a potentially viable way of approaching addiction assessment and treatment. Where once a person, usually a white, middle-aged man, would seek treatment for alcoholism as his only addiction, today addictions represent a heterogeneous set of problems affecting men and women of all ages and cultures with polysubstance use as the norm. A one-size-fits-all approach is no longer viable.

THE TWELVE-STEP APPROACH

In the United States, the twelve-step method has dominated the addictions treatment field. This philosophy first took shape in the form of Alcoholics Anonymous (AA), which was developed in the 1930s by a small group, composed mostly of men, for whom the medically based treatments of the era had been ineffective. Instead of turning to professionals, this small group relied on fellowship with other alcoholics. Their relationships with each other and be-lief in a higher power facilitated finding the new life they had been looking for. The success of their interactions spawned the twelve-step self-help movement.

The twelve-step philosophy holds that addiction is a disease that, much like diabetes, cannot be cured. Where the diabetic must avoid excessive sweets and take insulin in order to be healthy, the alcoholic or drug addict must completely avoid substances and attend twelve-step meetings in order to stop their addictive behaviors. To do otherwise risks a return to illness. Born out of dissatisfaction with professionally based treatments, the twelve-step philosophy states that those best prepared to help are in recovery from the disease of addiction. The twelve-step philosophy does not ignore the fact that many persons in recovery suffer psychological problems. In fact, "character defects" are recognized as a part of the twelve steps. However, it is believed that once a person becomes ab-stinent (i.e., stops the addictive behavior) through continued twelve-step work, he or she can perform the long-term work of becoming sober. Sobriety requires abstinence and "working the steps" to develop a new philosophy for living. Since its inception with alcoholics, twelve-step self-help programs have been de-veloped which address substance-based addictions other than alcoholism (e.g., marijuana, cocaine) as was well as process addictions (e.g., eating, love, sex).

The publication of E. M. Jellinek's *The Disease Concept of Alcoholism* in 1960 brought professional respectability to some of the assumptions of twelve-step philosophy. His research into alcoholism led to conclusions that mirrored those espoused in twelve-step programs. Addiction is a disease that a person does not create or control. Abstinence is the only successful outcome, at least for certain types of alcoholics (alphas) who have an inherited vulnerability for drunkenness. Subsequently, biological models have been forged that define just how the alcoholic and nonalcoholic differ on a physiological level.

By the 1970s, the twelve-step philosophy had been incorporated into a pro-fessionally based medical treatment for addictions. Known as twelve-step treatment, this approach begins with a period of detoxification, if needed, fol-lowed by a more extended stay at a rehabilitation facility. Usually treatment is offered on an inpatient basis, although intensive but shorter inpatient and/or outpatient programs are becoming more common. Daily attendance at twelve-step meetings is incorporated into the treatment plan and abstinence is required. While often occurring within a medical setting, those most likely to do the actual day-to-day treatment are persons with an addiction history.

Psychotherapy is not part of the twelve-step treatment process, although the model acknowledges that psychological problems can exist alongside an addiction. It is common for a patient entering or in addiction treatment to show signs of depression or anxiety. Psychotropic medication may be pre-scribed to alleviate these symptoms, which are assumed to be a response to the drug, the drug's withdrawal, and/or the intense life changes experienced during the recovery process. The traditional addiction treatment community argues that, in most cases, psychological problems will abate with a period of abstinence. Psychological treatment, however, is not ruled out completely. A referral to a psychotherapist is made to address any ongoing life problems that could contribute to relapse. Such referrals are likely if psychological symptoms, such as depression or anxiety, are ongoing and/or help is needed to address the many interpersonal, economic, and psychosocial problems that have developed during years of addiction.

Over time, it became apparent that one subgroup of alcoholics performed poorly in twelve-step treatment. Patients with a history of severe mental illness were more likely to drop out of treatment or, if they stayed the course, were more likely to relapse. For this dually diagnosed population, a sequential treatment plan, where addiction is treated first followed by psychotherapy for any residual emotional issues, has been replaced by more integrated and intensive programs (Carroll and McGinley 1998). Providers with a background in mental health work closely with addiction counselors to facilitate recovery that is informed by the disease model. Because of the destructive interactions between mental illness and addictive substances, the goal of lifelong abstinence for this group is considered essential.

Integrated treatments for dually diagnosed patients forever changed the addiction treatment field. For the first time, mental health providers had a role to play. The idea that the people best suited to treat addictions had to be in recovery from addiction themselves began to lose some ground. However, the role of mental health providers remained quite restricted. Because most treatments for dually diagnosed patients continued to draw heavily from twelve-step philosophy, the idea that "like should treat like" remained entrenched. Many psychotherapists felt that it would be illegitimate to treat addictions. As one psychotherapist has put it, "I was intimidated by the thought that they [addiction counselors] possessed some mysterious knowledge about addiction that was very different from what I knew about 'regular' psychological and emotional problems" (Gordon 1998, 72).

The way treatment evolved for dually diagnosed patients limited the role of mental health providers in another way. Most treatments were designed for patients falling on the more severe end of the mental illness spectrum who were diagnosed with schizophrenia, bipolar disorder, and other psychoses (thus, the origin of the acronym MICA [mentally ill chemical abusers]). This dual-diagnosis treatment model left a major gap in the psychotherapeutic treatment of addictions; the model does not fit patients with less severe psychological disorders who are likely to seek treatment from psychotherapists on an outpatient basis.

CONTRIBUTIONS FROM PSYCHOTHERAPISTS AND RESEARCHERS

Before twelve-step programs and twelve-step treatments, psychoanalytic principles most often informed treatment of addiction. Psychoanalytic theory assumes that addiction is a symptom, which means that once underlying characterological issues are resolved, there will no longer be a need for the addictive behavior. While this approach has had successes (Johnson 1992), the idea took shape in the twelve-step community that psychoanalytic treatments (interpreted as being synonymous with psychotherapy) should be avoided. This came about in AA meetings where those who had been in psychotherapy reported how years of treatment had done nothing to reduce their addictive behaviors.

Around the time that twelve-step treatment was gaining in popularity, a small group of researchers and psychologists began to question whether addiction was a disease and abstinence the only viable treatment outcome. Arguing that addiction was primarily psychologically and contextually determined, they contend that addictive behaviors are learned (e.g., Beck, Wright, Newman, and Liese 1993). As a learned behavior, people find alcohol rewarding. Some drink to fit in to a social group, as is often the case with adolescents; others drink to relax or avoid negative feelings. In either case, the behavior of drinking alcohol is strengthened through reinforcement. From a cognitive-behavioral perspective, addiction is a learned behavior, not a disease. Teaching a person new ways of coping will solve the need for the excessive behavior. This line of thinking led to a reconsideration of whether abstinence was the only viable outcome of addiction treatment.

If addiction is not a disease but a learned behavior, then those who are addicted to alcohol or another substance could conceivably learn to act differently in relation to that substance. They could be abstinent or they could learn to use it in a controlled manner. A self-help program known as Moderation Management arose to meet the needs of alcoholics desiring to return to controlled social drinking (Kishline 1994).

The traditional addiction treatment community found the evidence for controlled drinking, like that published by the Sobells (Sobell and Sobell 1973), to contradict what they had experienced. Those in recovery have many stories to tell about friends or acquaintances who tried an outcome other than abstinence. Many would use in a moderate way, even for lengthy periods, but inevitably the level of use would increase and return to the previous addictive pattern.

In the professional literature, a heated debate about controlled drinking ensued that ended with major questions about its viability (Pendery, Maltzman, and West 1982). The outcome of this debate was that twelve-step approaches to addiction treatment remained in the forefront while research in universities continued behind the scenes in order to identify the type of person for whom controlled drinking was most likely to be a stable and successful outcome (Rosenberg 1993).

During the 1990s, a new philosophy of addiction treatment, known as harm reduction, emerged. Arising out of the spread of HIV among injection drug users, the goal of harm reduction, as the name implies, is to reduce the negative consequences that arise due to addictive behavior. In the case of injectable drugs like heroin, harm reduction treatment is provided even if the user is not interested in ceasing drug use. An acceptable harm reduction goal would be to ensure that clean needles are made available. For the alcoholic treated within a harm-reduction model, an acceptable goal could be consuming less alcohol or making sure that if one gets drunk, a friend or spouse will provide a ride home. Any lessening of the harm resulting from substance use is considered a positive outcome in the harm-reduction paradigm. Thus, relapse for a substance dependent person is not considered a failure. Periods of abstinence mixed with relapse, if they result in an overall reduction in harm, represent one type of successful outcome.

Popularization of the harm-reduction model helped to facilitate the role of psychotherapy as a primary means of addiction treatment. Harm-reduction philosophy is easily incorporated into psychotherapy. Recently, several books on addiction treatment have been written that integrate harm-reduction principles and psychotherapy (Denning 2000; Marlatt 1998; Tartarsky 2002). A central tenet of harm reduction is that the "consumer" sets the goals. In twelve-step treatments, where abstinence is required, the goal is set by the therapist and the patient must agree or leave treatment. In contrast, with a harm-reduction approach, the therapist works with the patient to discover the best outcome. Treatment can include periods of moderate substance use or reduction in risky outcomes, even if the ultimate treatment goal is abstinence. For example, if patient and therapist agree, treatment can begin with a carefully monitored period of controlled use. The outcome of this trial determines the next step in treatment. Through the process of psychotherapy, the most workable outcome will be created jointly by patient and psychotherapist.

It would be a mistake to equate harm reduction with the controlled use movement. Controlled use or abstinence is an equally desirable outcome in harm reduction treatment; which is chosen will depend on what is best suited for the patient. As one set of harm-reduction providers described it, "abstinence is the endpoint on the continuum of harm reduction approaches" (Marlatt, Blume, and Parks 2001, 20).

PSYCHOTHERAPY AS A PLACE TO TREAT ADDICTIONS

Perhaps the most significant step on the road to making psychotherapy a place to treat addictions came with the publication of Miller and Rollnick's

(1991) now classic text on motivational interviewing. They made explicit what many had known implicitly—traditional addiction treatments are more about relapse prevention (i.e., helping a person stay sober) than helping a person get to a point where he or she is ready to cease or limit an addictive behavior. This emphasis on relapse prevention is most salient in twelve-step treatments where patients must stop their addiction as a prerequisite to receiving help. A man brought to treatment against his will, as a result of incarceration or a family intervention, will be required to undergo detoxification, where all substance use ceases, before treatment can begin. Abstinence is both the precondition and the goal of twelve-step treatment. In the case of twelve-step self-help groups, it is acceptable for an active substance user to attend a beginner's meeting. The twelve-step philosophy holds that by merely bringing the body, the mind will follow (i.e., a person will come to accept the goal of abstinence). However, the most developed aspects of the program and the core of twelve-step work (e.g., the steps) is directed at maintaining abstinence.

Miller and Rollnick's comprehensive overview of addiction treatments led them to realize that there were few structured treatment programs designed to help individuals decide to cut down on and/or give up their addictive behavior. To address this void, motivational interviewing was developed. Following the humanistic philosophy of Carl Rogers, motivational interviewing is designed to help people transition from wondering if they have a problem to doing something about it. The techniques of motivational interviewing can be an important adjunct to psychotherapy. Many substance users have a vaguely defined concern about whether a given behavior is excessive, but are not ready to acknowledge a problem or make a change. People in this position are likely to seek help from a mental health provider with the goal (which often will not be stated explicitly to the therapist) of finding out *if* there is a problem. Motivational interviewing can help with this process.

Psychotherapists have been looking for a model of addiction treatment that is more consistent with their philosophy of treatment. Motivational interviewing has provided this link. Many psychotherapists do not accept the twelve-step notion that addiction is a disease. Instead, addiction has been viewed more often as a symptom or a learned behavior where psychological and situational factors play a significant role in its development. According to the self-medication hypothesis of Khantzian (1997) and the self-psychology of Kohut (1987), addictive behaviors are attempts at emotional repair. For the cognitive-behaviorists, addiction is a learned behavior maintained by beliefs and the power of reinforcement. The biopsychosocial model assumes that psychological variables, interacting with biological propensities and social context, lead to addiction.

The often-cited opposition between the positions that addiction is a disease or a psychological disorder is losing ground with further research. Whether an addiction begins as a disease or not, it is critical that psychotherapists recognize that once an addictive process takes hold, it can have a life of its own. Long-term use of certain substances or the occurrence of excessive behaviors alters how the brain functions in terms of the response to and production of neurotransmitters. The reward center of the brain appears most compromised. Prolonged substance abuse alters the brain's set point, creating a resting level that is more negative than before drug use (Leshner 2001; Wasilow-Mueller and Erickson 2001). It is common for patients with severe addictions to say that the only time they feel normal is when they are using drugs. For some, addictive ways of behaving permanently alter physiological functioning, while for others, functioning returns toward normal once the addictive behavior decreases or ceases. This means that addiction cannot simply be treated as a symptom of some psychological processes. Rather, addictive behaviors need to be considered as a primarily problem and, as such, should be treated directly along with the psychological issues that contribute to their initiation and maintenance.

A further source of opposition between twelve-step approaches and psychotherapy is psychotherapists' discomfort with confrontational techniques that have come to be associated with twelve-step treatments. Techniques of motivational interviewing, arising as they do out of the work of Carl Rogers, are consistent with psychotherapy's emphasis on the therapeutic alliance as critical to the change process. For others, twelve-step programs are simply dismissed as a quasi-religious or cultlike group that is antithetical to psychotherapy. While psychotherapy has a history of standing outside addiction treatment, it is important that psychotherapists do not continue to foster this division. Twelve-step approaches need not be antithetical to psychotherapy; the incorporation of twelve-step work into psychotherapy benefits a patient's emotional growth in psychotherapy and recovery from addiction (Freimuth 2000).

It is important to recall that the traditional addiction community's avoidance of psychotherapy arose out of the frequency with which those attending twelve-step meetings criticized psychotherapy for not resolving their addiction problems. Contrary to these anecdotes of failed psychotherapy, the professional literature reports on successful resolution of addictions through purely psychological treatment, including psychoanalytic therapies (e.g., Johnson 1992; Smaldino 1991; Weegmann and Cohen 2002). In these reported successes, the therapist was well aware that addiction was the primary problem to be addressed. I wonder how often psychotherapy failed, not because the treatment was ineffective, but because the treatment provider did not recognize the presence of an addiction.

Caroline Knapp, in her autobiography *Drinking: A Love Story*, "trudged into the Mass. General once a week to see the shrink and then sat there on the blue sofa in his office like a lump, stagnant and sad and often mute" (1996,

138). She gives no indication that her "shrink" recognized her alcoholism or growing reliance on marijuana. While sometimes Knapp referred to being concerned about her drinking, the therapist never seems to define this as a problem. A patient of mine who read Knapp's book reported that when she brought Knapp's story to friends in AA, she often was met with the reply, "Yeah, why don't therapists pick up on addiction more often?" The negative reputation that psychotherapy has had within the twelve-step community seems to have more to do with poor diagnostic practices—the issue this book is designed to address—than some inherent limitation of psychotherapy to treat addiction.

SUMMARY

Only recently has psychotherapy been considered as a primary means of addiction treatment. In 1997, Miller and Brown published a seminal article arguing that psychologists should treat alcohol and drug problems. Psychologists and other mental health providers have the required skills, but they need to adapt these skills to this special population. Miller and Brown's article represented a radical departure from traditional addiction treatment by encouraging the fields of psychotherapy and addiction to unite.

This integration is essential for effective treatment given that emotional problems and addictive behaviors are too often intertwined. Statistics indicate that addictions occur more frequently than any other mental health problem (Grant and Dawson 1999). Regretfully, addiction treatment models say little or nothing about assessing those who do not identify addiction as their primary problem. Rather it is assumed that a person seeks treatment, expressing concern about substance use, or the person is brought to treatment by a significant other, such as a spouse or employer, who defines addiction as the problem.

This will not be true for the majority of people entering psychotherapy. Patients are unlikely to announce, or even know, that addiction is a concern. Instead, persons seeking psychotherapy come in asking for help with life problems that may be an unidentified consequence of their addictive behaviors. They have marital conflicts, problems with work, or troubles meeting people. Too often, the therapist joins the patient in failing to recognize that addiction is the problem (see chapter 3) with the outcome that psychotherapy has limited success or, more likely, fails.

3

The Need for Addiction Assessment in Health Care Settings

Ours is a culture of consumption, whether it is alcohol, drugs, sex, food, buying, or gambling (Starace 2002). Alcohol use is considered more normative than nonuse and a key part of many significant rituals. Advertisements on television and in magazines advocate taking pills to alleviate physical and psychological discomforts.

Reflecting these cultural values, close to half of the U.S. population uses alcohol each month, while 7 percent take an illicit drug, the most common being marijuana (Substance Abuse and Mental Health Services Administration 2002). Using psychoactive substances is not the same as abuse or dependence. Most people only drink or use drugs on designated social occasions and they maintain reasonable levels of consumption. For some, what begins as an intermittent and limited use of legal or illegal substances becomes abuse and dependence.

While no one intends to become addicted, the regularity with which this happens is noteworthy. Sixteen percent of the adults in the general population use drugs and/or alcohol at levels indicative of abuse or dependence. At this frequency, substance-related disorders are the most frequently occurring mental health problem in America (Brems and Johnson 1997; Grant and Dawson 1999; Reiger et al. 1990). The figure grows substantially larger by including binge drinkers and process addictions.

PREVALENCE OF ADDICTIONS IN PSYCHOTHERAPY PATIENTS

Given the high degree of substance use, abuse, and dependence in the general population, the overlap between substance use disorders and other DSM-IV diagnoses is striking and must be taken seriously by all who practice psychotherapy (Brems and Johnson 1997). The National Comorbidity Study, based on household surveys, shows that over 50 percent of individuals with alcohol dependence qualify for another psychiatric diagnosis, usually anxiety and depression (Kessler et al. 1997).

In mental health settings, the incidence of substance use disorders is two to four times higher than in the general population. This means that at least 30 percent of persons with mental health problems have a co-occurring substance use disorder (Kessler et al. 1997; Reiger et al. 1990). This is especially true for patients with symptoms of anxiety and depression (Evans 1998) where around one quarter will meet the criteria for at least one substance-related disorder. More specifically, 24 percent of those with an anxiety disorder and 32 percent with an affective disorder have one or more substance-related disorders (Reiger et al. 1990). The association is even stronger for other diagnostic categories. Among people diagnosed with bipolar disorder or schizophrenia, the lifetime prevalence for substance disorders rises close to 50 percent (Wolford et al. 1999) (see table 3.1.).

The co-occurrence of post-traumatic stress disorder (PTSD) and addiction is just beginning to receive attention from researchers. The figures suggest that up to 30 percent of patients being treated for PTSD have a coexisting addiction problem. In the case of women in treatment for chemical dependency, up to 70 percent have reported histories of physical or sexual abuse (Wasilow-Mueller and Erickson 2001). Recently, attention has also turned to an increased prevalence of alcoholism for those with attention deficit disorder (ADD) and attention deficit hyperactivity disorder (ADHD), borderline personality disorder, and binge eating problems (Lilenfeld and Kaye 1996). For adolescents being treated for substance use, common co-occurring psychological syndromes include conduct disorders, ADD or ADHD, learning disabilities as well as adjustment problems (Tarter 2002).

Table 3.1. Lifetime Prevalence Rates for Substance-Related Disorders in Persons with a Mental Health Diagnosis

<u>Schizophrenia 47%</u>
<u>Anxiety Disorders 24%</u>
Panic Disorders 36%
Obsessive Compulsive Disorders 33%
Phobias 23%
<u>Affective Disorders 32%</u>
Bipolar Disorder 56%
Unipolar Depression 27%
Dysthymia 31%
<u>Antisocial personality Disorder 84%</u>

Data from Reiger et al. 1990.
Underlined terms are major diagnostic categories, and those underneath are subtypes.

These figures, high as they are, do not include behavioral or process addictions such as gambling, or addiction to exercise, shopping, sex, or the Internet. Prevalence rates for process addictions are less readily available. One recent statistic for gambling derived from admissions to a primary care setting shows that 6 percent of patients making a physician's visit have a gambling problem (Pasternak and Fleming 1999). Co-occurring disorders are common among those with process addictions. Those who shop excessively have a higher rate of substance use (Mitchell et al. 2002) and eating disorder involving over consumption (e.g., binge eating and bulimia) (Faber et al. 1995). Up to 75 percent of problem gamblers are depressed, 12 percent have made suicide attempts, 46 percent meet criteria for mania, and 20 percent meet standards for ADHD (Talmadge 2003). Dysthymia, major depression, and anxiety disorders have been reported in close to half of those being treated for sexual addictions. Of the anxiety disorders, social phobias were most common (Goodman 1998). These figures on the frequency of psychological disorders among those with process addictions, when combined with the 30 percent figure for those with co-occurring mental health problems and substance use disorder, further emphasize the need for mental health practitioners to be skilled in recognizing evidence of addiction.

Dual diagnosis is the term used most frequently for describing the co-occurrence of an addiction and psychiatric disorder. In most cases, this label will be a misnomer because patients will have more than two diagnoses. A person rarely abuses just one substance; most are polysubstance abusers. Among persons being treated for alcoholism, 57 percent meet the criteria for drug dependence. Eighty percent of cocaine users also abuse alcohol (alcohol alleviates cocaine "jitters"). Polysubstance use is the norm for adolescents (Brown University Digest of Addiction Theory and Application 2002). Similarly, a patient diagnosed with a DSM-IV psychiatric disorder who also misuses psychoactive substances can have several psychiatric diagnoses. Having more than two diagnoses also occurs because psychiatric and substance-related diagnoses coexist with one or more process addictions. For example, up to 50 percent of pathological gamblers have a substance-related disorder (Petry 2002) as well as a co-morbid psychiatric condition. As these statistics indicate, despite the name, many dually diagnosed patients have more than two diagnoses.

BEHAVIORS AT RISK FOR ADDICTION

Within the traditional addiction treatment community, a person has the disease of alcoholism or not. This dichotomous approach to assessment is mirrored in the assessment of most other addictions; behaviors are recognized as problematic only if they meet diagnostic criteria. This dichotomous view omits a wide range of behaviors that are at risk for becoming addictive. As an alternative conceptualization, a continuum model of addiction incorporates varying levels of a behavior. One end of this continuum is marked by nonuse or nonoccurence, and the other end is anchored by addiction and dependence. In between the extremes are at-risk or subclinical levels of a behavior that, in the case of substance use, are described as occasional, experimental, or recreational use. The habitual occurrence of behaviors in this midrange is distinguished from addictive behaviors because the resulting problems are minor and the negative consequences occur on an intermittent, rather than continuous, basis.

In light of how addictions develop, a continuous rather than dichotomous model makes sense and has important implications for prevention. Behaviors that have the potential to become addictive start in more moderate forms. An alcoholic does not begin by drinking until blacking out. Initially, he or she drinks to be social. A man addicted to exercise does not begin exercising by striving for the rush of running twenty miles every day. He begins exercising in order to be healthier.

Certainly, not all who drink or work out become addicted. The origin of any addiction does not lie in the substance or the behavior itself. Genetics, environment, and developmental factors all contribute to whether a moderate behavior becomes excessive. One factor influencing the development of addiction that has significance for psychotherapy is the person's relationship to the behavior. As Shaffer emphasizes, "it is the relationship of the addicted person with the object of their excessive behavior that defines an addiction" (1997, 1577). An addiction is most likely to develop when this relationship is characterized by the objects ability to "reliably and robustly shift subjective experience" (Shaffer 1997, 1576).

A treatment provider's ability to recognize subclinical levels of addictive behaviors is critical because, upon entering treatment, these at-risk behaviors can complicate accurate assessment of the presenting problem. As developed fully in chapter 9, symptoms of depression can be masked or lessened for the patient addicted to cocaine. The anxiety of a person who drinks a few glasses of wine each evening will be muted. When substance use is more than intermittent, side effects develop that mimic psychological disorders. At higher amounts and frequency, cocaine use enhances anxiety while alcohol exacerbates depression. Because of alcohol's depressant effects, a patient whose depression seems in need of medication may in fact be suffering from more moderate levels of depression.

One approach for defining a behavior as being at-risk relies on the diagnostic criteria described in chapter 2 for addictive disorders (Goodman 1998) or substance dependence. Meeting more than one criterion but less than the number needed for a diagnosis points to the possibility that the behavior is at-risk of becoming addictive. A behavior is problematic if it is negatively affecting the quality of a patient's life and/or altering what he or she talks about in the clinical dialogue. For example, the full extent of a patient's anxiety will not be recognized if he or she is drinking alcohol regularly as a way to relax. Another way to define a behavior as problematic is to assess its purpose. Is a patient using substances or enacting a behavior for purely social reasons or as a way to shift subjective experience (e.g., enhance good feelings and/or manage emotional discomfort)? When behavior or substance use occurs primarily for its psychoactive effect, addiction is more likely (Cooper et al. 1995; Khantzian 1997). In such instances, psychotherapy becomes a place to address alternative means of managing these feelings as a way to ensure that the current behavior does not become addictive or that one addictive behavior is not replaced by another (Christo et al. 2003).

Thinking about addictive behaviors as occurring along a continuum means that psychotherapists need to think broadly when considering the goals of addiction assessment. The sole purpose is not to determine if substance use or a behavior is occurring at an addictive level. By paying attention to at-risk behaviors, an addiction assessment also helps the provider determine (1) the extent to which a presenting problem is muted or exacerbated by behaviors with psychoactive effects, and (2) if currently moderate behavior could progress into an addiction.

THE UNDERDIAGNOSIS OF ADDICTION

Individuals with addiction related problems are seen more often in general health and mental health settings than addiction treatment centers (Weisner and Matzger 2003). Given this fact and the high incidence of addiction in the general population, why does research show that addiction is one of the most commonly missed diagnoses? Among college counselors, who are expected to be attuned to substance use problems, half of the intake reports did not mention concerns about alcohol use even when a student's self reported use was worthy of concern (Matthews, Schmid, Conclaves, and Bursley 1998). Primary care physicians routinely fail to recognize alcohol problems in up to 90 percent of their patients (Johnson et al. 1995). Another study found that out of 187 patients who had been identified by researchers as alcoholics, only 4 were identified correctly by emergency room physicians and 29 by psychiatrists (Ananth et al. 1989). In general, it is believed that only one in ten alcoholics are correctly diagnosed in health care settings.

In outpatient mental health settings, the actual number of patients whose use of substances and mood altering behaviors is influencing their lives or treatment is unknown. Nor is there any exact data on the frequency with which outpatient providers fail to recognize addictive disorders. Indirect evidence however suggests that mental health providers overlook addictive behaviors with great frequency. The extent of the problem is hinted at in two studies that examine whether the MacAndrew Alcoholism Scale-Revised (MAC-R), a scale developed from MMPI-2 items, is a valuable tool for assessing alcohol problems in outpatient settings. Psychotherapists were asked to identify all their patients who qualified for a substance use problem. The MAC-R was quite good at recognizing this patient group; there were hardly any false negatives, which means that only a few patients, identified as addicted by their psychotherapists, were not recognized as such by the MAC-R. The more striking result was the large number of false positives on the MAC-R. In other words, many patients had MAC-R scores indicative of a substance use problem but were not so identified by their clinicians (Rouse, Butcher, and Miller 1999; Stein, Graham, Ben-Porath, and McNulty 1999). This high rate of false positives may reflect the scale's inaccuracy. A more likely interpretation is that the scale is accurately picking up addiction issues that clinicians failed to recognize.

Certainly it is easiest to recognize an addiction if a person enters therapy saying, "I want help with my addiction problem." But all too often potential psychotherapy patients do not recognize that their presenting problems are reliably linked to the use of some substance or mood-altering behavior. Behaviors that are destined to become addictive initially are ego-syntonic and a source of pleasure or relief. This means that a patient will come to therapy for help with an interpersonal problem, work stress, low self-esteem, or lack of life satisfaction that, in their subjective world, has no reliable link to addictive behavior. The National Household Survey (NHS) supports this conclusion. NHS provides a unique perspective on addictive behaviors because it surveys a large sample of the general population rather than only those in addiction treatment or medical facilities. Participants are asked about the frequency and quantity of use for a wide range of substances and any serious problems that result from them. These data reveal that the vast majority of persons whose substance use meets diagnostic criteria and would benefit from treatment are unaware of having an addiction (Substance Abuse and Mental Health Services Administration 2002).

Professionals often resort to blaming the victim in order to explain why addictions frequently go unrecognized. Failure to recognize addiction in one's patients is attributed to the patient's denial. Denial leads the alcoholic to minimize the extent and dangerous effects of drinking. It follows that if the patient won't recognize the depth of the problem, then the therapist cannot know either. Minimizing or denying the degree of the problem is most common in the later stages of addiction when there are likely to be other observable signs of addiction that facilitate recognition of the problem.

As I will argue in chapter 4, denial probably does little to explain the frequency with which practitioners overlook addictions. This is because most persons who seek psychotherapy will be in the early stages of addiction before denial has developed. Rather than denial, one of several explanations for why an addiction is unrecognized stems from professional diagnostic practices. The more common psychiatric diagnoses (e.g., depression, anxiety, or schizophrenia) are based on direct observation or report of signs and symptoms. A patient's account of hallucinations is followed by an inquiry about other signs of schizophrenia. A patient who reports work-related problems and increasing uncertainty about his future should have a therapist whose questioning distinguishes the problem as anxiety or depression. The diagnosis of addictions requires an added step. A substance-related problem is not inferred from the problematic behavior itself (e.g., how much one drinks or gambles). Rather, to diagnose an addiction requires a therapist to assume that what the patient reports is *not* a symptom of the problem but a negative consequence of the problem. This point is best illustrated with an example. A new patient enters therapy reporting sleep disturbances, appetite changes, and loss of interest in others. Psychotherapists, who are much better trained to recognize psychopathology than addictions, will assume that these concerns are symptoms of the problem and simply conclude that the patient suffers from depression. This could be a misinterpretation given that each of the previous symptoms is a negative consequence of excessive substance use.

Summary

Addictive disorders and behaviors at risk of becoming addictive are prevalent among psychotherapy patients. Patients who chose psychotherapy are unlikely to report an addiction as part of the presenting problem. As a result, psychotherapists can draw inaccurate conclusions from a patient's reported symptoms. For some patients, signs of addiction will be misinterpreted as evidence of a psychological problem rather than the negative consequences of an addictive disorder. Given the many ways in which addictions can be veiled, it becomes the treatment provider's responsibility to take a more active role in assessment. However, there are many factors acting against psychotherapists' sensitivity to addictions. In some cases, it will be the therapist who contributes to the lack of recognition (see chapter 4), while at other times the nature of the addictive process itself will serve to mask its presence (chapter 9).

THE BENEFITS OF ACCURATE ADDICTION ASSESSMENT

The cost of leaving an addiction untreated is high. Before addressing reasons why this happens so frequently, I would like to review the benefits of routinely completing a thorough screening for addictions:

1. *Lives will be saved.* Some deaths will be a result of drunk driving. Other deaths will occur because of HIV contracted during intercourse while

under the influence of a substance. The suicide rate among alcoholics is 20 times the norm. Death is 2.5 times more likely in any given age bracket for those who abuse substances. In a one-year period in New York City, cocaine was used immediately before one out of every five completed suicides (Marzuk et al. 1992).

Cocaine's contribution to an accidental overdose is realistically portrayed in the novel *Rachel's Holiday* (Keyes 1998). Rachel's alcohol and cocaine use is spiraling out of control despite the increasing concern of those around her. Her abuse comes to a dramatic conclusion one evening as she tries to come down from her cocaine high. Finding that she can't sleep, she takes a few sleeping pills. The pills are not working fast enough and she takes some more. As her consciousness becomes hazy, she loses track of how many pills she has taken. Rachel has no intent to kill herself; luckily her life is saved only because her roommate returns to the apartment.

2. *Increase a patient's awareness of potentially addictive behaviors.* How many drinks did you have the last time you went out? After asking this kind of question, patients are often surprised to discover the quantity of alcohol they consumed. A similar lack of awareness accrues to connecting drug or alcohol use to its negative consequences. A mother who smokes marijuana to relax at the end of the day never relates her memory lapses to drug use but rather hormonal changes or her stressful day. Such lack of awareness means that a new patient may come into a therapist's office talking about the consequences of his or her addictive behavior (e.g., family disputes, unhappiness, problems at work). Simply asking a few questions may stimulate the new patient to wonder if current life problems are in any way related to substance use. For some, these questions bring to light the beginnings of a substance use problem, which, if left unnoticed, could develop into abuse or dependence.

3. *Patients learn that addictions are a topic for psychotherapy.* Most people begin wondering if their substance use is problematic or not up to ten years before seeking alcoholism treatment (Randall et al. 2002). During this time, a person may enter psychotherapy for other life problems. A neutral inquiry into mood altering behaviors and substances informs the patient that, along with other personal concerns, addictions are talked about in the therapeutic setting. This knowledge can uncover a person early in the addiction cycle. A patient may be using drugs or alcohol periodically to alleviate stress or enhance positive feelings. No one plans to become addicted, but, over time, addictive behaviors create changes in physiology that make it difficult to stop. In the case of alcohol, such early intervention can mean that problem drinking does not develop into alcohol dependence.

A neutral inquiry into addictive behaviors also facilitates a patient's acknowledgment of a problem later in treatment. As one of my patient's reported, "I know that I would not have 'fessed up to you at the end of my drinking if you had not raised the issue ('how much do you drink?') at least a couple of times before." Or, the period can be longer. A patient in brief treatment with me indicated that he was not using any substances, but he did acknowledge a somewhat strong family history of alcoholism. Two years later I received his telephone call telling me that he had a drinking problem. When we met he told me that my questions about addiction in our first meeting and the lack of judgment he felt when describing his family history made it easier for him to call.

4. *Assessment can have therapeutic benefits.* A provider may wonder whether an assessment has revealed an addiction or merely a normative behavior (see chapter 4). Given the benefits attributed to brief interventions, it is worth it to assume there is a problem and bring this concern to the patient's attention. In the case of alcohol, making this connection can provide immediate benefits; research has shown that patients will reduce or cease alcohol use simply by being made aware of the negative consequences (Poikolainen 1999). A recent study (Fleming et al. 2002) using physicians as treatment providers found that two fifteen-minute sessions and two phone calls decreased alcohol consumption of heavy drinkers by one-third (e.g., twenty-one to fourteen drinks for men and fifteen to eight drinks for women). Along with reduced drinking came a reduction in legal and negative health consequences of substance use (e.g., fewer injuries, hospitalizations, arrests, and auto accidents).

5. *Help others with addictions to get treatment.* Routine substance use assessment has an influence beyond the patient in the consulting room. Asking patients about their substance use makes them wonder about the substance use of significant others. For any given person, there is a 43 percent chance that a spouse or blood relative has an addiction issue (The Recovery Institute 1998). Even if the patient is without an addiction, the assessment can benefit both patient and therapist. The patient may refer family and friends who are struggling with addictive behaviors, or the therapist can work with the nonaddicted family member to alleviate their distress and learn ways to motivate the addicted person to get help. This in turn has larger social and economic benefits: with more people entering treatment for addiction, family life will improve and child and spousal abuse will decline along with a reduction in lost workdays and health care costs attributable to addictions (Brems and Johnson 1997).

6. *Avoid legal and ethical sanctions.* There is no evidence that screening for an addiction negatively affects treatment (e.g., premature termination).

However, not doing so leaves the therapist open to legal sanctions if an undiagnosed substance use problem has harmful consequences. Starting in the 1980s, when the strong correlation between addiction and mental health problems was highlighted, competent practitioners have been expected to include at least some exploration of substance use. Failure to do so leaves one open to charges of negligence. Psychologist and attorney Bryant Welch writes, "Being required to develop enough skill to be able to detect substance abuse really constitutes a change in the standard of practice, and practitioners who do not meet the new standard are vulnerable" (2001, 2).

7. *Enhance treatment effectiveness and avoid treatment failure.* Assessing for addiction facilitates a patient's current treatment, whether the addiction is discovered to be a part of the patient's history or is playing an influential role in the present problem. One psychotherapist I interviewed reported the following experience: "My therapy never touched on my parents' addiction. Everything was related to their character and I never said anything because, the way my parents drank, I took it as just part of my WASP family life. . . . I wonder if we prefer to see our parents as crazy and not addicted. . . . maybe, it's easier to have a crazy parent than an alcoholic one—less guilt." Recognizing the alcoholism in her own family helped her to curb her drinking, facilitated her own growth in psychotherapy, and improved her capacity to recognize addictions in patients she treated.

Without some form of addiction screening, one can never be sure whether the problem being treated is solely psychological in nature. This is because addiction and psychopathology interact in ways that cause the mood-altering effects of addictive behaviors to reduce, enhance, or mimic the symptoms of psychopathology. As a result, the wrong diagnosis is made and the wrong problem is addressed. In cases where addictive substances mimic psychological symptoms, symptoms are approached psychologically that are at least in part a result of addiction-induced biological changes. An accurate diagnosis, where the correct problem is being treated, increases the likelihood that psychotherapy is effective. This in turn avoids a common negative consequence when an addiction is unrecognized—the ultimate failure of therapy.

4

Impediments to Accurate Addiction Assessment

A striking number of people who come to psychotherapy will have some kind of addictive disorder. On average about 30 percent will qualify for a substance-related disorder. This percentage continues to grow when including process addictions and those whose substance use is considered problematic (e.g., binge drinkers). Few will enter treatment requesting help with addiction. A person who selects psychotherapy wants help for life problems that are not experienced as being related to an addictive behavior. An addiction that is not reported to the therapist is likely to go unrecognized. This occurs for a number of reasons. The typical signs of addiction are not readily apparent in those who seek mental health treatment. These patients rarely exhibit the poor health and pervasive functional impairments of those entering a detoxification or rehabilitation facility. Instead, psychotherapy patients present with psychological symptoms. People come to therapy because they are aware of being in emotional distress or having a life problem that seems unsolvable. Or if the patient is an adolescent, parents bring him or her to therapy due to declining grades and growing conflicts over a new peer group with no idea that substance use underlies their concerns.

Despite the fact that alcoholism is one of the most common psychiatric disorders, psychotherapists are not trained to link the consequences of addiction to this source. Patients, upon beginning treatment, express anxiety or feelings of sadness, difficulties concentrating, and lack of self worth. They talk about problems eating, conflicts with a boss, and a loss of sex drive. These symptoms are usually taken as evidence of depression or an anxiety disorder even though each of these feelings and behaviors can be an adverse consequence of an active addiction.

The nature of the addictive process complicates its own recognition because the consequences of addiction often mimic symptoms of psychological disorders—especially depression and anxiety. In other cases, the adverse consequences of addiction are so individualized that the connection between a presenting problem and an addictive disorder is apparent only after the addiction has ceased:

> Karen sought treatment for help with irritability. Having grown up with a mother who was unhappy and angry, Karen was very uncomfortable with how irritated she was becoming with her children. Despite inquiring about substance use in the initial session, where Karen acknowledged having no more than two glasses of wine three evenings a week, it took several months of treatment to recognize that her drinking was linked to her presenting problem. This information emerged by chance as she described her evenings. Upon arriving home from work, she spent about thirty minutes with her children; this was time she enjoyed. Once her husband arrived home, she started dinner preparations and began sipping on a glass a wine that she kept refilling until bedtime. She had assumed that the total amount of wine she consumed equaled about two glasses, but when asked by the therapist to keep careful track of the exact amount, the figure was closer to four glasses. She recognized that she was not irritable with her children before dinner; that is, before she began drinking. She agreed to stop drinking in the evenings. Only after several weeks of not drinking did she really understand how much more attuned she was to the emotional needs of those around her and, in turn, felt less irritated. Evenings with her family were more pleasurable.

Many clinical settings require that intake sessions include an inquiry into substance use. For some patients, this is a good time to ask. Some feel safer reporting the full extent of use before they get to know the therapist. For others, reporting their level of consumption at the start of treatment will not be a good indicator of the problem. In an initial interview, before a therapeutic alliance has developed, certain patients do not feel safe to report the full extent of use.

An even more likely explanation for underreporting in an intake session is illustrated in the previous example with Karen. Before being asked, a person pays only limited attention to the degree of substance use and thus the initial report is at best a good guess or estimate. Even if a patient's estimate turns out to be accurate, the psychotherapist must know how to interpret the amount reported. Individuals differ greatly in how they respond to the same amount of a substance. In the case of dually diagnosed patients, the quantity and frequency of an addictive behavior can be deceiving. This group tends to use less drugs and alcohol relative to addicted patients with no co-occurring psychopathology (Wolford et al. 1999). Even small quantities can have large effects for dually diagnosed patients (e.g., reduce medication effectiveness and exacerbate psychiatric symptoms).

WHY EDUCATION IS NOT A SOLUTION
TO UNDERDIAGNOSIS OF ADDICTIONS

Whether the initial assessment of addictive behaviors will yield accurate information or not, it is still critical that psychotherapists ask such questions. Simply asking demonstrates one's interest in the topic and can peak the patient's curiosity. Reviewed in chapter 3, assessing for addictions in psychotherapy has numerous benefits including treatment effectiveness. Given the benefits of addiction assessment, one would expect that mental health professionals would routinely screen for addiction at the start of therapy, and once treatment began, continue to listen for addiction-related problems.

Despite its importance, routine addiction assessment in health care settings is the exception rather than the rule. A recent innovative study shows that health and mental health providers rarely inquire about drinking behaviors (Weisner and Matzger 2003). Telephone interviews identified 672 individuals in the general population who, over the phone, screened positively for drinking problems. Another group of 926 people was selected based on having been admitted for alcoholism treatment. Both groups were followed for one year. At the follow-up meeting, those who had a medical or mental health visit during the previous year were asked if their drinking behavior was in any way addressed. Where only 24 percent of those making a medical visit reported in the affirmative, 65 percent of those making a mental health visit acknowledged having been asked about their drinking. Taken at face value, this latter result suggests that drinking problems are being attended to in mental health settings. However, the vast majority of this 65 percent came from the group with a history of addiction treatment (odds ratio: 4.12). The same held true for physicians where the odds ratio was 2.55 for patients with an addiction treatment history as compared to the untreated sample. The researchers account for this difference by suggesting that patients with a treatment history are more likely to self-identify as having a drinking problem and/or the provider has access to their records indicating an addiction history. Providers appear to be more comfortable asking about addictions when they know this problem has been previously identified for the patient (Weisner and Matzger 2003). In contrast, participants from the general population, who, like the typical psychotherapy patient, have never had addiction treatment, do not self-identify as addicted, and hence are rarely asked about their drinking.

Even in clinical settings, where a question or two about substance use is a mandated part of the intake, perfunctory questions do not necessarily reveal a problem to the provider. As one psychotherapist put it, "I always ask about substance abuse in my initial interview, then I file the information in the back of my mind, perhaps too far back!"

Why don't psychotherapists pay greater attention to addictions? Lack of education tends to be the primary explanation. Education about addiction in graduate schools has been spotty and many professionals do not know how to make a proper addiction assessment. The mental health field has not put a priority on addiction assessment: state licensing laws require special training in trauma or child abuse more than they require training in addiction treatment. In a random survey of 1,200 psychologists, 91 percent indicated that their clinical practices involved at least some work with substance abusers. However, the majority had no formal educational background (74 percent) or training (54 percent) in the substance abuse area (Aanavi, Taube, Ja, and Duran 1999).

Improving education will not solve the problem of missed or misdiagnosis of addictions. A 2000 study conducted under the auspices of The National Center on Addiction and Substance Abuse at Columbia (CASA) examined primary care physicians' training in the addiction field and whether this training affected their ability to recognize alcoholism. Ninety percent of physicians who graduated within the last ten years had received some education about addictions. The figure dropped slightly to 80 percent for those who graduated eleven to twenty years ago. Both figures indicate that exposure to addiction curriculum during graduate studies is far greater for physicians than psychologists. Education does have an affect on physicians' ability to recognize addiction—albeit a very limited one. Primary care physicians who had some addiction education were better able to diagnose alcoholism from a clinical vignette that contained physical signs of addiction. Of those with training, 6.7 percent suspected alcoholism in the clinical vignette, while only 1.9 percent without education was able to do so. However, the more remarkable result is how often an addiction was overlooked: 93 percent of physicians with training failed to suspect the patient's presenting problem was alcoholism.

When it comes to mental health providers, I believe that the same holds true. Educating psychotherapists about the addictive process and addiction assessment will help improve recognition—but only slightly. Apparently, there are blocks to accurate recognition of addiction that extend beyond acquiring knowledge. For psychotherapists trained in a classic psychoanalytic vein, addiction assessment is unnecessary because addictions are simply a symptom of the problem in need of treatment. As one psychoanalytically trained therapist revealed, "I feel guilty sending someone to AA; it is breaking the therapeutic frame. . . . Addiction is due to early pre-oedipal stuff and my psychoanalytic training tells me it is wrong to treat it any other way." Other impediments to addiction assessment seem to be attitudinal and emotional in nature. Turning again to the medical field, where addiction training is a routine part of the curriculum, 41 percent of physicians expressed difficulty discussing alcoholism with their patients as compared to depression where the percent expressing discomfort dropped to 18 (The National Center on Addiction and Substance Abuse at Columbia 2000). Another study found that 82 percent of physicians "avoid" or are "hesitant" to raise issues about addictions with their patients (The Recovery Institute 1998). Surprisingly, even when a drinking problem was suspected, over half the physicians reported being hesitant to ask patients directly about the problem (Thom and Tellez 1986).

To explore the source of these discomforts further, I examined the literature on attitudes toward addictions. To supplement this literature review, I interviewed mental health professionals who did not routinely assess for addiction to find out their reasons for not doing so. Out of these interviews, it emerged that some psychotherapists are more comfortable asking for a detailed sexual history than inquiring into how much drugs or alcohol a person takes each day. Others said it felt out of character ("more like a social worker" as one person put it) to do a structured assessment. Several other therapists said that it seemed "a little tricky" or "impertinent" to ask a well-dressed, articulate person who comes to treatment for help with depression about his or her drinking patterns. Why is this? The existing literature along with these interview data indicate that erroneous beliefs about who is addicted and the nature of addictions along with misrepresentations and uncertainties about how to define substance use disorders hinder the careful assessment and accurate recognition of addictive behaviors.

STEREOTYPES

Which one of the following persons is most likely to be addicted? Is it a white male in his forties in a three-piece suit carrying a brief case? Is it a twenty-five-year-old married woman who is a homemaker, exercises in the mornings, meets friends for lunch, and helps her children with homework after school? Is it a man in his thirties who is disheveled, has difficulty holding a job, and seems to have a chip on his shoulder? As reviewed in chapter 8, a diagnosis of alcohol dependence is more likely for men than for women, for whites than for nonwhites, and for single than for married persons. Addiction is more common among unemployed men (Grant 1997). Demographics such as these can easily deceive psychotherapists by creating incorrect expectations. It is critical to remember that despite these demographic distinctions, most alcoholics will have a job and a family.

In terms of professions, can a physician, lawyer, or colleague in the mental health field be addicted? Anyone would answer this question with, "Of course." And yet, reflecting on my experience and the experiences of those I interviewed, a patient's high level of functioning can interfere with an accurate assessment of addictions. As one psychotherapist articulated, professionals may be in "cultural denial" where they don't see addiction unless the person fits the larger cultural stereotype about who is most likely to be addicted.

What does the typical drug addict or alcoholic look like? Is it Dean Martin shuffling along? Is it Kurt Cobain and other members of a Seattle-based grunge band? Or is it a homeless man sleeping on a grate with an empty bottle nearby? The typical drug addict is described as disoriented, unhealthy, thin, low class, male "hippie" (Dean and Rud 1984). Some would say that this clinical picture only describes patients who are about to enter a detoxification program or a rehabilitation center. Even then, this stereotypical picture is far from a representative characterization of an individual with addiction problems. In an attempt to counter such stereotypes, Schottenfeld (1994), after an extensive review of the literature, emphasizes that substance abuse is most frequently misdiagnosed or undetected when the person is employed, married, white, insured, or a female. On a more personal note, one psychotherapist interviewee realized that "the more a patient's demographics fit my own, the harder it is for me to think that their substance use patterns are problematic."

In addition to stereotypes about who is addicted, we hold beliefs about what an addicted person acts like. It is well documented that a diagnosis of addiction is associated with negative connotations (Hanna 1991). The stereotypical alcoholic is described as "uncontrolled, negligent, insensitive, irresponsible, self-centered" (Forchuk 1984, 57). Assuming that psychotherapists prefer to treat people they find likeable, they may avoid questions that could reveal these negative characteristics in a patient. Or, more likely, psychotherapists worry that by asking about addictions a patient will feel accused or insulted. Merely asking can be interpreted by patients as implying that they embody the negative attributes of a substance abuser. In the case of primary care physicians, 25 percent indicated that they avoid discussing addiction with patients because doing so will frighten or anger the patient and the patient may seek treatment elsewhere (The National Center on Addiction and Substance Abuse at Columbia 2000). The reality is that the patient most likely to become upset is someone who is already worried that substance use is out of control. As one therapist reported, when he asked a patient, whom he knew had a history of alcoholism and was drinking again, about her drinking, "the woman said in a defensive, disgusted manner, 'Why would you ask me that? I don't use drugs.'" (Notice she said nothing about her alcohol consumption!)

The fact that clinicians are concerned about how patients will react to addiction queries has emerged in the data I have collected. One seasoned therapist admitted to worrying that patients would feel insulted if asked about substance use. "How do you tell a person they are alcoholic? Maybe I should do a family history more often. This would be an easier way to get at it—less personal." This same therapist has no problem telling patients they are depressed. Another therapist, who also acknowledged being hesitant to ask about addictions, had similar concerns about alienating patients, if drinking problems were brought to the fore, "I recall seeing a woman whose husband had just died of alcohol-related complications. She fit the WASP profile of a social drinker. She drank too much but I didn't see a way to push it. Or there is this young woman, a physician, who clearly drinks too much. I comment on it but I don't know how to present it to her. . . . She is Irish and I am wondering if I can present it to her as an Irish disease." Two other practitioners, both women, who work in clinics, where substance use assessments are mandated, acknowledged feeling anxious when asking patients how much they drank. Both were concerned that patients would feel insulted by such questions. If the patient was a male, they worried that if he were indeed alcoholic he would get angry, lose control, and become violent in the session. While research shows that substance intoxication is not associated with aggression in health care settings (Dhossche 1999), these responses made me wonder how many clinicians share similar worries but remain unaware because they are not mandated to assess for addictions.

In addition to these misrepresentations regarding who is addicted and how they behave, Schuckit (1998) outlines a set of mistaken beliefs (which he refers to as myths) about the typical outcomes of addiction to drugs and/or alcohol.

1. The average alcoholic and drug abuser lives on the streets.
   This belief is illustrated in the response of one of the therapists I interviewed. When asked to explain why she does not assess for addictions, she replied that a careful addiction assessment is unnecessary because "most of my current practice involves nice middle-class people with anxiety disorders or chronic pain, and substance use is not the presenting problem." As indicated above, the typical alcoholic is likely to be employed and have a family. He or she looks just like anyone else. In addition, it is not improbable that this therapist, who works with chronic pain patients, has a patient or two who has become addicted to their prescribed medication.
2. People with substance use problems have a terrible time quitting.
   This statement reflects the belief that treatment for addictions is not very successful. This belief arises when looking at the outcomes of abstinence-based rehabilitation centers where the "one-third rule" applies. One-third who complete treatment remain abstinent, one-third relapse and return for more treatment, and one-third go back to their addiction. Peele (1995) argues that the reason an addiction, in particular alcoholism, seems so difficult to give up is because popular twelve-step treatment approaches limit successful outcome to complete abstinence.

He argues that if the outcome was not so narrowly defined and moderate use was more often the goal, the success rates would increase, and the notion that addiction treatments are not effective would disappear. Fletcher (2001), who shares an interest in alternatives to abstinence-based treatments, discovered an array of options for resolving addiction problems. After interviewing a wide range of people about how they overcame their addictions, she concludes that some people are only successful with abstinence, while others succeed by using substances in moderation. Many needed no formal treatment. In general, her participants did not report having a terrible time changing their addictive behavior.

3. People with substance problems stay intoxicated all the time and can rarely control their substance use.

This belief, along with the former one, conveys the sense of hopelessness that often surrounds addiction treatment. However, it, too, is inaccurate; there are many patterns of problematic substance use. Binge drinking does not fit this pattern. Even the most ardent alcoholic can have some sober time during the day. A person may only drink in the evenings or on weekends and still be an alcoholic. Others will routinely be abstinent for some designated period of time that they believe demonstrates they are "in control." Others will have rules for when they can use substances or do a certain behavior: not before dinner, only at parties, not on work nights, only on weekends. Most are able to *cease* the addictive behavior for some part of a day or even months. Instead of being intoxicated all the time, it is common for people to interweave periods where use is severe with periods of no drinking or moderate use. Susan Cheever, in the autobiography of her time as an alcoholic, recalls:

> That summer I stopped drinking again. Sarah's new pediatrician suggested that I stop drinking. I didn't pause to wonder what made him suggest that. It wasn't hard to do. . . . I remember one day [later in the summer] when we were giving a dinner party and I went in the morning to buy wine at the Sakonnet Vineyards. I tasted this and that and then I walked out into the sun, just vibrating with fullness. I had started drinking and I didn't even know it. I thought of it as tasting (Cheever 1999, 158).

What makes the behavior addictive is not how often it occurs or to what extent, but the manner in which it is done. As Shaffer (1999) emphasizes, one hallmark of addiction is lack of control. The person cannot, over a prolonged period, follow their self-made rules and/or consistently limit the amount of substance use.

4. Most people with severe drug problems use drugs intravenously.

The original model of addiction, which included signs of tolerance and withdrawal, was based on use of opiates such as heroin. Since most people do not enjoy being pierced by a needle, even when in a physician's office, the image of routinely injecting oneself with a drug conveys the sense of power that a substance has over a person. Yet reliance on noninjectable drugs, such as cocaine, amphetamines, or marijuana, can be equally destructive.

In terms of addictive potential, injecting a drug is not the only means to lose control quickly over substance use. Inhaling into the lungs, like injecting, rapidly brings the chemical to the brain. Addiction is more likely when the route of administration is most efficient. That is why use of crack (a form of cocaine that is smoked) is more likely to result in addiction than powder cocaine, which is taken nasally.

5. People with substance abuse problems can't have decent moral standards.

The psychiatric condition that co-occurs most often with addictions is the antisocial or sociopathic personality (Reiger et al. 1990). However, most persons with addiction problems are not sociopathic. Many are productive and ethical members of their communities. One needs only to read the book *The Courage to Change* (Wholey 1984), which presents personal interviews with many well-known and productive persons with addiction histories (e.g., Elmore Leonard, Jean Kirkpatrick, and Gale Storm).

Patients entering psychotherapy who hold these mistaken beliefs will be unlikely to self-identify their addiction. This means that the professionals will need to recognize the problem. In order to identify addictions successfully, they will need to move beyond these stereotypic beliefs. Psychotherapists' attitudes toward addiction treatment also need to be examined in order to ensure against further impediment of assessment and recognition. If mental health care providers are like physicians, they are pessimistic about the outcome of addiction treatment. Among primary care physicians, only 3.6 percent believe alcoholism treatment is effective. The figure drops to 2.1 percent for treatment of drug abuse. These small percentages become more remarkable when compared to beliefs in the efficacy of treatment for depression (43 percent) and hypertension (86 percent) (The National Center on Addiction and Substance Abuse at Columbia 2000). One cannot dismiss the possibility that such pessimism contributes to undetected addictions. To see that a patient with whom one has established a close therapeutic alliance has an addiction brings a sense of hopelessness into the treatment. Such an unconscious pull to overlook addiction issues is further strengthened by the fact that addictions often look like depression, a disorder which psychotherapists feel competent to address.

Another treatment-related belief that can impede detection of an addiction is that addicted individuals as a group are unmotivated and noncompliant. This attitude has developed because patients often begin addiction treatment expressing a great deal of ambivalence about change (see chapter 10 on stages of change) and frequently drop out of treatment. This is not very different from other kinds of patients. Medical patients are well known to have low compliance rates when it comes to following through on a physician's recommendation (Dunbar-Jacob 1993). Similarly, as psychotherapists often discover in the course of treatment, even though a patient asks for help with a given problem, he or she often becomes extremely ambivalent about changing (i.e., status quo resistance). There is no evidence that the overt ambivalence that arises in the face of treating addictive behaviors is any more difficult to address than the covert ambivalence associated with psychological changes.

Summary

Diagnosing substance and process addictions involves more than giving a label to a problem; it entails telling patients that they have problems that society at large views in a pejorative manner. Given mental health professionals' lack of training and negative attitudes toward addictions, many professionals may not want to treat addictive disorders. Other practitioners avoid making an addiction diagnosis because it is associated with a sense of hopelessness: addictions are chronic, patients are resistant to treatment, and treatment tends to be ineffective. Still others feel that addiction treatment is outside their scope of practice: addictions must be treated within a medical setting or by someone who has a personal history of addiction. Adherence to any of these beliefs diminishes therapists' motivation to fully recognize a patient's degree of substance use—perhaps seeing it as normative rather than problematic— because it would mean losing the patient to another practitioner who is better able to provide addiction treatment. However, a referral is not necessary.

Miller and Brown (1997) and Washton (2001) have argued persuasively that addictions are behaviors that are more similar than dissimilar to the types of behaviors mental health providers already treat. There are two simple differences: (1) substance addictions involve altered states, which means that working with such patients involves greater risk for self-harm and harm to others; and (2) the patient is more likely to be overtly ambivalent about wanting help for the problem. Psychotherapists are well suited to treat addictions as long as they are willing to recognize the problem and, in the same way as the other problems they treat, learn about its unique features.

DENIAL AND UNDETECTED ADDICTIONS

Among clinicians, there is a sense of uselessness in asking about addictive behaviors because, as the literature emphasizes, those who are truly addicted are "in denial." The link between denial and addiction is so strong that some have referred to it as the "disease of denial." No doubt some patients with a history of substance dependence are quite skilled at minimizing the problem, projecting blame onto others, and, more generally, hiding or avoiding recognition of a problem. Belief in the pervasiveness of denial influences clinicians' assessment practices. Sixty-one percent of physicians report that that don't always discuss substance abuse with patients because they believe patients will lie (The National Center on Addiction and Substance Abuse at Columbia 2000).

Although denial is thought of as an intrapsychic defense, psychotherapists can unwittingly contribute to this dynamic. Part of a psychotherapist's work is to help patients express their thoughts and feelings and, in so doing, to accept the patient's report at face value. With this accepting attitude, how does one respond to a patient who gets a DUI (driving under the influence) violation? The patient laments about how unlucky he is to have been charged with this offense. He calmly explains that he rarely drinks and jokes that this DUI is like getting pregnant the first time you have sex—just plain old bad luck. Another woman explains her DUI as a result of mixing red and white wine, which is something she never did before and plans never to do again. She insists that there is no problem with how much she drinks on a regular basis. Within the empathic and supportive atmosphere of psychotherapy, it can be a challenge to deconstruct the carefully crafted alternative explanations that patients develop to conceal an addiction.

One DUI is not sufficient to diagnose a substance-abuse problem. The DSM-IV requires a person to have recurrent negative consequences of substance use. However, the lore among addiction specialists is that those who get a DUI are in fact very lucky—lucky to have *not* been caught all the other times they have been intoxicated behind the wheel. The client who gets one DUI—no matter how unfair it is said to be—should receive a more thorough assessment for alcoholism.

When a clinician wonders with a patient whether a DUI or other life difficulty is linked to problematic substance use, some of the subsequent explanations will seem reasonable. Some explanations will seem overly complicated. Other times the pieces do not quite fit together. Thus, despite an accepting therapeutic stance, on occasion, concerns will arise that a patient is minimizing or distorting the degree of substance use and its consequences. How is this to be handled? In light of traditional addiction treatments, therapists may only be familiar with confrontation as the way to address denial.

The need to confront denial arises from the assumption that it is a purely intrapsychic process that protects the person from his or her self-destructive behavior. A defense, like a wall, is best broken down and confrontation becomes the best method.

Recently the conceptualization of denial as solely an intrapsychic process has been challenged. Denial has come to be understood more broadly as both a personal and interpersonal construction (Berenson and Schrier 1991; Howard, et al. 2002). As an interpersonal process, denial becomes a way of knowing that is cocreated by the therapist and patient. To the extent that denial is conceived as a function of the therapeutic relationship, both therapist and patient have a role to play in lessening its occurrence. Understanding the interpersonal dynamics of denial illuminates how a more honest discussion of substance use can be facilitated without resorting to confrontation.

A recent qualitative study illustrates the different ways in which interpersonal relationships contribute to denial (Howard et al. 2002). Patients in an addiction treatment facility participated in focus groups where they were asked to address what denial meant to them. Their responses fell into four categories.

1. Denial as a means to avoid stigmatization.

One subset of patients voiced concern about being stigmatized because of substance use. This shame is shaped in large part by negative societal attitudes toward those who are addicted. When first facing the reality of his alcoholism, Wilbur Mills, an ex-congressman from Arkansas, explained, "my concept of an alcoholic was such that I felt lowered in my own estimation. I was the lowest thing that God let live. I was lower than a snake that crawled on its belly, because I was an alcoholic" (Wholey 1984, 55). Similar responses emerged in the focus groups where participants reported concealing their degree of substance use out of concern that they would be judged negatively (e.g., be seen as weak or defective).

Whether these face-saving maneuvers should be called denial depends on one's theoretical orientation. What this research does point out, however, is that a person may be well aware (or at least concerned) that certain behaviors are problematic or addictive but he or she will admit to the problem in some interpersonal contexts and not others. As one focus group participant reported, "Your denial runs stronger in different circles, too. There might be this family of people that I deal with where denial is going to be real strong, whereas for this friend that drank with me [it] is gonna be a lot less" (Howard et al. 2002, 375).

Concern about how one will be perceived after admitting to an addiction extends to patients' openness to reporting addictive behaviors in health care settings. In one study, 84 percent of patients in early recovery acknowledged that they had not told physicians about their addiction because they felt ashamed (The National Center on Addiction and Substance Abuse at Columbia, 2000). In the therapy setting, such face-saving maneuvers most likely occur if the patient is confronted or feels accused, or before a patient trusts that the therapist will continue to accept him or her despite the addiction.

2. The addictive behavior does not fit one's personal construction of addiction.

Patients are in no more of a privileged position than their therapists are when it comes to recognizing addiction; they, too, hold assumptions about what an addict or alcoholic is like. If their behavior does not match their beliefs, then they don't have a problem. Jersild, in *Happy Hours*, a book on women's drinking, describes Daphne's experience of her alcoholism:

> When it fleetingly occurred to her that she could have a drinking problem, she let the thought pass without investigation. After all, she never drank before four or five o'clock. . . . She didn't do all those things that alcoholics did, like keeping tiny bottles of liquor in her purse or getting up in the middle of the night to take a swig. She did take a prescribed tranquilizer at three in the morning, however. Occasionally she stopped drinking for a week—not even a wine at dinner—just to test herself and found that she could do it. She regarded this as another sign that she didn't have a problem. Alcohol was a helpful friend, an ally in her battle against depression (Jersild 2002, 54–55).

Susan Cheever (1999) makes a similar point in her autobiography. Even while attending an AA meeting with her father (John Cheever) who was in recovery, she manages to distinguish her excessive drinking from others at the meeting.

> I loved the stories I heard about hiding bottles, and about the ways people disguised their drinking while leading apparently normal lives as bankers or teachers or housewives. . . . Sometimes the stories sounded like my story, but there was always some detail that was too bizarre to fit into my life. There was always something that allowed me to keep my distance from the idea that I might be an alcoholic. I thought to be an alcoholic, a person had to be in terrible trouble. I was fine, I thought. . . . I thought that alcoholics were told again and again by their friends and doctors that they should stop drinking. No one had ever said much about my drinking (Cheever 1999, 123).

Each person seems to have some critical elements that define addiction. For some, they don't fit the stereotype of the jobless and homeless drunk or drug addict. "I thought an individual who had a problem with alcohol could not be successful, especially as a major league pitcher who could purchase anything he wanted at a very young age, as I could. I thought an alcoholic had to be lying on a street corner on skid row. That was my definition of an alcoholic" (Bob Welch cited here from Wholey 1984, 202). For others, it is that they do not have a blackout or buy drugs in the middle of night.

> I thought that everybody who drank alcohol blacked out. Anybody who drank alcohol would wake up with someone they didn't know and you know I thought that everybody did that, you know wake up on the roadside. . . . I mean it's like raisin' your first child, if you're doing something wrong, do you know it? I wasn't aware of it for a long time and when somebody started puttin' the idea to me you know that you're an alcoholic, well then I thought, well you know, I don't drink now like I did when I was younger (Howard et al. 2002, 376).

For others, addictions are hidden behind norms set by their families. Quite often patients refer to their parents' nightly ritual of two or three drinks before dinner and more later. This is normal family life that becomes part of their lives. For focus group participants, when their addictive pattern fit their family norm and no family member had been diagnosed as addicted, they seemed genuinely unaware of the seriousness of their substance use.

The literature on denial focuses solely on denial in relation to substance use. When it comes to process addictions, it is easy to see how family and larger social attitudes shape whether a person conceives of an excessive behavior as problematic. Family standards shape attitudes toward what qualifies as reasonable or moderate levels of spending, exercise, etc. A woman whose family overspent and then went to the credit union for temporary relief is unlikely to label her use of shopping to feel good about herself as an addictive behavior.

Beliefs about the kind of behaviors that qualify as an addiction not only influence whether one self-identifies a problem but also influence how significant others responds when an addiction is revealed.

> When Rose L. told her husband, his response was, "Aah, you don't drink that much." Six months later, when she tried to once again convince him, he told her that it was summer, and it made sense that she would drink at least a six pack of beer each day. Heather F. adds, "I can't tell you how

many times I worried about my drinking—to my doctor, my psychologist, even to my husband. But because I seemed like a together person, no one saw what I knew to be a serious drinking problem" (Fletcher 2001, 46).

Thinking of denial in cognitive terms, as a failure to recognize an addiction because the behavior does not fit one's personal and socially derived construction, suggests that confrontation is not necessary in order to lessen denial. In the context of psychotherapy, it would seem simple to help patients reflect on their behavior because they are not really hiding it. For this group, facilitating discussion of substance use and its consequences is beneficial. Merely speculating that some behavior is problematic, in a nonjudgmental manner, can be a sufficient catalyst for the patient to redefine the behavior as a problem.

3. Denial as a response to actual judgments and accusations received from others.

Many patients in the focus groups had been aggressively approached by family members or exposed to confrontational forms of addiction treatment. A number reported being upset after having been told by a family member or counselor that they were "in denial." They experienced this as being called a liar and became defensive.

Questions about excessive behaviors can be asked without the aggressive connotations associated with confrontation. For the most part, patients seeking health care are quite willing and open to answering questions about substance use (Vinson et al., 2004). In the process of conducting a substance use assessment, the therapist and patient, working together, might discover that the patient's problems are, in part or in whole, a consequence of an addictive behavior. A man seeking treatment for his "midlife crisis" finds out that his apathy about work and disinterest in his wife are fueled by an increasing use of marijuana and an abuse of painkillers initially prescribed for a neck injury. Connecting addictive behaviors to life problems can occur without requiring that the wall of denial be broken down.

4. Denial as a distortion of reality or truth about one's addictive behavior.

A fourth form of denial to emerge from the focus group is consistent with the traditional conceptualization of denial as a defense mechanism; the person cannot see that a certain set of behaviors is out of control and creating significant harm. This classic form of denial is poignantly portrayed in Keyes' (1998) fictional yet realistic account of addiction. Rachel, an inpatient in a traditional addiction treatment center, watches in a group session, as Neil, a fellow patient, denies that he drinks and beats his wife. Neil accuses his wife of lying. The group leader confronts

Neil with how he is acting like his father. "You drink too much, you terrorize your wife and children, and you're creating a future generation of alcoholics. . . . And Gemma, she's your eldest?—probably tries to shield Courtney's ears from the sounds of it, the way you did with your brothers and sisters." As Rachel watches Neil's continued protestation that he is not like his father, the following thought dawns on her: "There and then, for the first time in my life, I truly understood that fashionable, bandied-about overused word—Denial. It made my intestines cold with fear. Neil couldn't see it, he honestly, really couldn't see it, and it wasn't his fault" (Keyes 1998, 192–93). The humorous part of Rachel's recognition about Neil is that it will be weeks before she stops denying her own drug, alcohol, and food addictions.

Here is how Susan Cheever describes her denial:

> I had no idea that the problems I had with men, with marriage, even with my work had anything to do with drinking. I had watched my father think the same thing. . . . Even then, after all the AA meetings I had been to with my father, and after I had betrayed my husband and little girl over and over again, I still didn't see any connection between my drinking and my problems. I thought men were the problem. . . . I thought that drinking was a wonderful way I had of dealing with my problems (Cheever 1999, 158).

To understand the origins of denial better, it is helpful to consider the addicted person's perspective. "I try to remember when drinking became the focus of my life. When it evolved from a social activity to an act that defined everyday of every month. When it grew into an obsession that influenced my every move" (Moriarty 2001, 45). No one starts to use drugs, gamble, or spend money with the intent of becoming addicted. Instead, in the beginning, the behavior is associated with positive experiences (e.g., feeling relaxed, more sociable). Only over time do problems emerge—problems sleeping, faulty concentration at work, irritability around the house, difficulties remembering details. Few people are knowledgeable about the long-term psychological and health consequences of substance use even though they are living them first hand. As a result, when the excessive behavior begins to create negative consequences the behavior is rarely seen to be the cause. If any connection is made, it is not taken seriously but rather is attributed to some unique aspect of the behavior or the context in which it occurs (e.g., the particular mix of drugs, temporary extreme stress). Only after numerous occasions are adverse effects reliably connected to a given behavior pattern. Few psychotherapy patients will have such a long history. Most will be in a much earlier phase of the addictive process. Providing an opportunity to talk about substance use in a neutral manner allows patients to develop correct attributions and recognize if substance use or other potentially addictive behaviors are reliably linked to negative outcomes.

Summary

Denial in the classic psychodynamic sense is understood as an unconscious distortion of reality driven by intrapsychic needs. This model best fits a person with a long addiction history who is unable to recognize the scope of self-destruction brought on by addiction. For psychotherapy patients with co-occurring addiction issues, a reconceptualization of denial is more fitting. Denial is understood to be a complex interpersonal process influenced more by conscious cognitive variables than unconscious forces. In some cases, cultural and familial norms about substance use lead people to conclude that their use is not deviant and hence not problematic. Therapists who fail to recognize a patient's addiction because they hold the same stereotypic beliefs are not said to be in denial; they are merely mistaken and in need of education. Patients can, likewise, be mistaken and in need of education. They are in no more of a privileged position than the professionals who treat them. For these patients, questions about substance use are not likely to be met with lies or anger. Rather, through open discussion, therapists and patients discover together whether a certain pattern of behavior is problematic.

Others have reasons to avoid recognizing an addiction. The motivation is driven by a conscious wish to avoid stigmatization or other negatives outcomes should an addiction be identified (e.g., a spouse's anger, a friend's disappointment, a job loss). Understanding shame and how to manage it will be critical for a successful addiction assessment with such patients (see chapter 7).

When it comes to psychotherapy, a few patients will be in denial in the classic psychodynamic sense. Some will be in the process of worrying if their behavior is indeed a problem; they are in a state of ambivalence. The majority, however, will have yet to connect life problems to their drug and alcohol use. No matter the patient's reason for not admitting to an addiction, treatment effectiveness will, in part, depend on psychotherapists' willingness to ask the necessary questions.

DIAGNOSTIC AMBIGUITIES

What qualifies as responsible drinking? How much is too much? Is there any distinction between adolescent experimentation and a substance use problem? If one uses drugs and alcohol heavily every weekend but never uses substances during the week, does this binge method merit concern? Is it more than recreational use if an elderly woman continuously sips on a scotch every evening after dinner until bedtime? Distinguishing between recreational use, problematic use, abuse, and dependence may be one of the most difficult differential diagnostic issues.

As emphasized in chapter 1, recognizing an addiction does not depend on knowing the amount of substance use or the frequency of an addictive behavior. Rather, addiction is marked primarily by the negative consequences that result from the behavior. A diagnosis can be made relatively easily when addictive behavior has continued to the point where economic, legal, and social consequences outlined in the DSM-IV are salient—especially to significant others. The family breadwinner is no longer able to pay the mortgage due to gambling debts. A woman is arrested for her third DUI. In his autobiography, *Dry*, author Augusten Burroughs's employers require that he get inpatient treatment in order to keep his job. They have no doubt about his alcoholism; not only does he come to work late and disheveled, but they can smell the alcohol on his breath and in his perspiration. Few who choose to begin psychotherapy will be experiencing such pervasive adverse consequences.

However, the absence of apparent negative consequences does not preclude an addiction or the potential for addiction. Recognizing an addiction can be especially problematic when treating professionals, the financially successful, and individuals, with certain kinds of lifestyles (e.g., priests, entertainers) where the typical economic, legal, and work problems associated with addiction are easily masked. Up to 10 percent of physicians develop substance use problems, but these are easily hidden from colleagues because they do not use substances on workdays, they work alone, or they change work settings frequently (Cicala 2003). One white collar professional with an addiction to painkillers described the cloak of invisibility that financial resources provide, "The most invisible addict is a man in a suit and tie holding a briefcase."

The ease with which adverse consequences of addiction go undetected is illustrated in the autobiographical accounts of those recovering from alcoholism or addiction. Caroline Knapp, who wrote *Drinking: A Love Story* (1996), continued her successful journalistic career during her addiction. This does not mean that there were no negative consequences. In writing her autobiography, Knapp lets the reader see the effects her alcoholism had on her social and emotional life, but as it was happening, neither Knapp, her family, nor her therapist recognized that substance use was a concern (see chapter 12 for other examples). Dennis Wholey's (1984) interviews with well-known performers, sports figures, and political and religious figures provide further examples of people remaining quite functional while in private drinking to the point of blackouts.

Difficulty distinguishing normative from problematic use also stems from a psychotherapist's feelings about and history with addictions. Deciding whether a highly functioning patient has a drinking problem can raise questions about whether one's own substance use or that of a family member is within acceptable limits. The more a patient's excessive behavior is like one's own or that of a significant other, the greater the difficulty making this decision. While this information is not available regarding psychotherapists, addiction issues are likely to hit close to home for health care professionals; 19 percent of physicians and 38 percent of counselors indicated that someone in their immediate family was alcoholic (The Recovery Institute 1998).

How family or personal history with addictions affects a professional's ability to recognize such problems has yet to be studied. If the report of one psychologist I interviewed holds true for other professionals, then there is much to be learned. When asked why she did not routinely assess for addictions, she acknowledged that her father's alcoholism had clouded her clinical acumen. She laughed when she recalled opening her practice twenty-five years earlier and how she had not questioned herself when saying to a referral source, "No schizophrenics and no alcoholics."

Handling Diagnostic Ambiguities: Diagnosis Is Not the Primary Goal

Despite substance use being a normative behavior, it is surprising how often substance use, abuse, and dependence are written about as if they are interchangeable. While doing research for this book, I came across articles with substance abuse in the title that were really about the prevalence rates of substance use. Abuse and dependence were routinely viewed as being identical to addiction, although abuse (and even dependence) can be diagnosed based solely on negative consequences, thus omitting the element of craving and being "out of control" that characterize addiction. Failure to differentiate use, abuse, dependence, and addiction reflects the underlying dichotomous thinking that informs most substance use assessment. No substance use is good. Any substance use is bad and should be stopped (Fingarette 1988). Based on this thinking, the goal of assessment is to determine if any kind of substance-based problem exists, with the goal of treatment being the cessation of all use (i.e., abstinence).

An alternative to this dichotomous approach evolved out of the harm-reduction model. As introduced in chapter 3, substance use can be conceptualized as occurring along a continuum from nonuse to problematic use to addiction with increasingly adverse consequences, cravings, and loss of control. Assessing whether a certain behavior pattern qualifies for a DSM-IV diagnosis or reflects an addiction is not necessary for treatment to proceed. Rather, the goal of assessment is to clarify any destructive aspects of the behavior given that ameliorating these negative consequences (i.e., reducing harm) is the primary task of treatment.

Moving away from a dichotomous model of addiction circumvents the difficulty of determining if a behavior is characterized as normative or problematic. Instead of distinguishing recreational use, abuse, and dependence, a continuum model focuses attention on the problems the behavior is creating. Formal diagnosis is no longer the centerpiece of assessment; rather the goal is to determine if the extent of a behavior or substance use is in any way creating adverse effects. Identifying problematic and addictive use for those whose lifestyles easily mask negative consequences is more challenging and requires that clinicians be attuned to subtle signs of addictions (chapter 7).

Alcohol: Ground Rules for How Much Is Too Much

Although the DSM-IV relies on negative consequences in diagnosing substance-related disorders, having a standard that defines the boundary between reasonable and excessive occurrence of a behavior has clinical utility. Because it is difficult to know just how much is too much, such standards provide the clinician with a point of entry for discussing a potentially addictive behavior. When it comes to alcohol use, safe drinking limits have been set by the U.S. government.

Safe Drinking Limits

Men under 65: Two standard drinks per day

Women (all ages) and men over 65: One standard drink per day

No more than seven drinks per week.

No more than three drinks on one occasion

Standard drink: 12 oz. of 4.5 percent beer, 5 oz. of 12.9 percent wine, 1.5 oz. of 80 proof liquor

At risk or problematic drinking is defined for women as more than seven drinks per week or three drinks on one occasion. For men, at-risk drinking is fourteen drinks per week and/or more than five per day (Substance Abuse, 2002).

An article by Vinson, aptly entitled, "Alcohol is not a dichotomous variable," mirrors what has been said more generally about addiction assessment that is informed by a continuum model. The health care provider's task is not limited to deciding if a person has a substance-based diagnosis or not. Rather, the larger goal includes recognition of at-risk drinkers defined as "those drinking more than safe limits but whose problems are less severe and who are not alcohol dependent" (Vinson 1997, 147).

Knowing safe limits in no way resolves the problem of diagnostic ambiguity, but it does provide a context within which one can explore alcohol use with patients. Drinking above these government defined safe limits places a person at risk of developing alcohol-related problems. Discussing a patient's drinking behavior with reference to safe drinking standards serves an educational function and may be sufficient to prevent development of a future addiction. In this way, addiction assessment in psychotherapy can serve a preventive function.

How Master Clinicians Manage Diagnostic Ambiguities

As part of the background research for this book, I began what my students and I named the master clinician study. Eighteen clinicians who considered themselves well versed in addiction treatment were asked questions not usually addressed in the literature. One part of the interview was presented as follows: Distinguishing normal drinking from problem drinking and addiction is not always easy. Other than DSM-IV criteria, what information do you use to make these distinctions? What are some aspects of the clinical picture that help you decide that the use of drugs or alcohol is other than "normal"? Most clinicians answered the questions by providing information that helped them to distinguish normal substance use from any form of problematic use. A few, however, did discuss distinguishing abuse and dependence. While the questions focused on alcohol use, their answers have relevance for other addictive behaviors as well.

A simple way to distinguish normal and problematic use from addiction is to see what happens when the person is asked to cut back. If addicted, the person responds to this request with a lot of excuses or explanations about why the behavior is not a problem and why there is no need to change. A man may dismiss one DUI, but when he is still laughingly dismissing his third one, he is clearly avoiding addressing his alcoholism. In contrast, the problem user is willing to cut back when asked. A woman patient spoke repeatedly about her regret about having sex on the first date. It emerged that she usually drank more than usual on these dates. Upon recognition of this pattern, she willingly agreed to a trial period of five dates with no alcohol to see what would happen. Had she dismissed the apparent relationship between drinking and her promiscuous behavior or refused this trial period, then the clinician would need to wonder if her drinking was addictive.

These master clinicians listened closely to the description of substance use and its consequences in order to distinguish problematic and addictive patterns. About half of the fourteen master clinicians turned to DSM-IV criteria but indicated that some criteria were more salient than others. One clinician mirrored the DSM-IV approach, paraphrasing it as follows, "It is *not* about how much one drinks but how it affects one's life, relationships, work, and relationship with self (drink to avoid being with ones self)." Along these lines, many talked about consequences but refined their meaning.

The problem user only has problems related to the substance or behavior itself (e.g., a hangover or guilt at spending too much money). In other words, substance use has negative effects, but these have not created functional consequence. Once functional consequences occur comparable to those outlined in the DSM-IV, then addiction is likely. Instead of looking for evidence of specific adverse consequences, one clinician prefers to ask a patient: "Have you experienced any unexpected outcomes as a consequence of your alcohol use? Drug use?" For this clinician, unexpected consequences indicate that the behavior is "out of control."

The majority of master clinicians agreed that assessing whether a patient's behavior was "out of control" warranted the most attention. Here is how another therapist made that assessment: "When it comes to abuse, they talk about knowingly 'choosing' to get wasted. The dependent person may say the same, but their stories indicate that the drinking is much more compulsive with little sense of choice; in their stories things just seem to happen, out of control unpredictable things happen."

The reasons for and contexts of a behavior are another distinguishing feature for resolving diagnostic ambiguities. For example, people who drink socially have no other reason for drinking than their setting. In contrast, problem drinkers consume alcohol as a way to cope. While it is true that most people who drink will, at one time or another, drink as a means of coping, problem drinkers drink *primarily* as a way to deal with problems. Problem drinkers are distinguished from those who are addicted in the following manner: those who are addicted keep drinking after the immediate stress is gone. Similar criteria can be applied to process addictions. For example, a person may shop as a way to alleviate stress but then stop after one purchase. The buying addict continues to spend money even after the initial reduction in tension.

Abuse or dependence occurs when the behavior or substance becomes the primary way to deal with difficulty and discomfort. If this pattern emerges in the assessment, the therapist can explore how the patient reacts to the proposal that this behavior is a coping device. A patient who considers excess behavior to be a reasonable (ego-syntonic) coping mechanism is probably addicted.

Some master clinicians found that they could distinguish normal and problematic drinking by exploring the nature of the patient's relationship to the substance. Some signs of problematic use include: looking forward to a drink when arriving home or a drink becoming more important than meeting other people or doing activities. In extreme cases, the therapist may have the sense that alcohol or the addictive behavior has become the primary relationship in the patient's life. Another important sign of problematic use is when a person has difficulty interacting with others when not under the influence.

Another piece of information to consider when distinguishing normal and problematic use is how the substance affects the person—not in terms of negative consequences but rather as a source of personality change. Substance use or a behavior is a problem if the person seen in the psychotherapy office is not the person who is under the influence of an addiction. The introvert in the office becomes an extrovert when drinking. The intense worker becomes laissez faire after a weekend of gambling. Several master clinicians believed that such personality changes occur because addictive behaviors "filled in something that was missing" for these people.

One clinician I interviewed avoids the whole problem of diagnostic ambiguity in the following manner. Too often persons with addiction are coerced into treatment by professionals or family members. Instead of being identified by others, this clinician recommends that it is best if a patient self-defines the problem. This is accomplished by asking a few simple questions, such as: Have you ever thought you were an alcoholic? Have you ever worried that you exercised too much? This clinician is following a long-standing tenet of AA; people who admit to thinking they are addicted or worry that they have a problem usually are addicted.

Summary

The blurring of boundaries which occurs when trying to distinguish recreational use, problematic use, abuse, and dependence can create uneasy feelings for the professional regarding his or her degree of use as well as make diagnosing a patient more difficult. When taking an initial assessment, the discomfort of diagnostic ambiguities can be sidestepped by recognizing that the initial goal of the assessment is not to make a diagnosis but to determine if mood-altering behaviors have any significant adverse effects on the patient's life both inside and outside of treatment. If, after performing an assessment, the clinician is still left wondering whether a behavior is problematic or addictive, then he or she can turn to the criteria used by master clinicians for making such decisions. In the case of alcohol, safe drinking standards set by the U.S. government provide a valuable guideline, yet it is important to keep in mind that for many (e.g., the elderly or the physically or mentally ill) even these amounts are considered excessive (see chapter 8).

SUMMARY

Substance use and abuse is prevalent in mental health settings—depending on the patient's diagnosis, between 20 to 50 percent of those in treatment have a co-occurring addictive disorder. These figures do not include process addictions or behaviors at-risk of becoming addictive. In recognizing the scope of the problem, a seminal article in the *American Psychologist* called for psychologists to treat alcohol and drug problems (Miller and Brown 1997). To support this expansion in practice, the American Psychological Association (APA) devoted its first specialty certification to the treatment of alcohol and other psychoactive substance use disorders. Yet, long before this, psychologists and other mental health providers had been treating (not very effectively) substance abusing and dependent patients, but, more often than not, they just didn't know it! More than a mere appeal to treat addictions is needed. If addictions are to be treated effectively, psychotherapists from all backgrounds must become adept at recognizing addictions. One of the best means to this end is completing routine assessments for substance use problems with all patients. However, as I have argued above, accomplishing this goal will require more than simple educational training.

Certainly some education is needed. Providers need to be aware that the typical stereotype of a drunk or addict is drawn from a person far into the addictive process; psychotherapy patients rarely exhibit the poor health and pervasive functional impairments of those entering a hospital for detoxification. Providers also need to know about the nature of the addictive process, such as how the symptoms of addiction can mimic psychological symptoms—especially anxiety and depression—and how these can grab the psychotherapist's attention to the exclusion of addiction. Other aspects of the addictive process that impede accurate diagnosis, such as cross-tolerance, are the topic of chapter 9. In addition to education, providers need to become aware of the emotional and attitudinal blocks that get in the way of taking routine substance use assessments.

Mistaken beliefs about and discomforts with addictions impede such routine assessment. Interviews with clinicians who do not routinely assess for addiction indicate that some feel it is useless to ask about substance use because anyone with a real problem will be in denial. Reconsidering denial as an interpersonal rather than intrapsychic process lessens the sense of helplessness clinicians may feel about getting accurate information and suggests effective approaches to assessment. Other health providers worried that merely asking a patient about substance use will be met with hostile reactions. These and other beliefs about who is addicted and how an addicted individual presents for therapy hinder accurate recognition. It is important to remember that the typical alcoholic does not fit the down-and-out drunk stereotype. In fact, an alcoholic is just as likely to be married and employed. Finally, some professionals shy away from addressing addictions given the ambiguities that surround distinguishing recreational use from abuse and dependence. The more like oneself the client is, the harder it will be to make these distinctions.

5

Standardized Assessment Approaches to Substance-Related Disorders

The task of addiction assessment differs depending on the setting. Sometimes, diagnosis is the goal of assessment. Before recommending that a person enter a specialized alcohol or drug treatment center, it is necessary to know that the behavior meets the criteria for abuse or dependence. The task of assessment is different for the psychotherapist. As discussed in chapter 4, addictive behaviors can be conceptualized as occurring along a continuum from absence to addiction with varying degrees of use in between. The goal need not be to categorize the behavior as addictive but rather to detect its occurrence and assess its harmful consequences for the patient's life and psychotherapeutic treatment.

There are myriad instruments for assessing addictions, most of which rely on self-reporting. The vast majority of these are screening instruments that detect the possibility of an addiction by asking about the extent of alcohol and/or drug use and the ensuing adverse consequences. Screening is followed by further assessment, often through a clinical interview, to see if the problem merits a diagnosis. Some assessment procedures actually yield a DSM-IV diagnosis; a few involve paper and pencil measures, but most take the form of a lengthy structured interview (e.g., Structured Clinical Interview for DSM-IV: SCID). In alcohol treatment centers, it is surprising that the clinical interview remains the most frequently used means for making a final diagnosis (Myerholtz and Rosenberg 1997). Likewise, in the context of psychotherapy, once a potentially addictive behavior is detected through formal screening or a clinical interview process, a diagnosis will most likely evolve out of the ongoing clinical dialogue.

Given that the clinical interview will almost certainly remain the primary approach to assessment, one might wonder why it is important to know about standardized screening tools. The value is threefold: Knowing the content of major instruments and which ones are valid for use in mental health settings gives the clinician direction regarding what kinds of questions to ask in an interview. Secondly, upon learning about these instruments, some may want to begin to incorporate one or more of them into their practice. They are an efficient means to gathering patient information. Finally, if one plans to work with addicted populations, the ability to read relevant research and understand reports from medical and addiction treatment centers will require working familiarity with these instruments. What follows is a description of the major screening tools along with ways in which these can be incorporated into clinical practice.

TOXICOLOGY SCREENING

Toxicology screens provide an objective and reliable (but not foolproof) method for assessing substance use. Most of us are familiar with the breathalyzer, a simple and immediate means of measuring blood-alcohol level. Other toxicology screens test bodily fluids such urine, blood, and sweat for minute traces of drugs left after recent substance use. Hair samples are another source for toxicology screening that allows assessment of substance use months after the fact. Of these, urine testing is most popular because of its ease of administration and accuracy (if the sample is collected correctly).

Urine, blood, or sweat can be incorporated into the assessment process as well as the treatment. These screens are highly recommended for adolescents with suspected drug use, although cooperation is not guaranteed. The story can be quite different with adult patients where resistance to a toxicology screening can be stronger for practitioners than clients. Surprisingly often, if the therapist is comfortable making the recommendation, the patient is quite willing to go along. In fact, some adults request that the therapist implement random testing as a way to help support their motivation to change.

The Values and Limitations of Toxicology Screening

When requesting a toxicology screen, the drugs to be assessed need to be specified. Drugs to select from include amphetamines, barbiturates, cocaine, benzodiazapams, marijuana, and opioids, including methadone. For adolescents, where polysubstance use is most likely, the recommended practice is to order the whole battery of tests. Urine screens are available that assess for hallucinogens and inhalants, but these tend to be more expensive and less reliable.

Some common acronyms for the urine-based screens are: TLC, GLC, and EMIT. EMIT is often preferred because of its ability to find evidence of general drug use and still specify the substance being used with good reliability (Margolis and Zweben 1998). Other tests tend to be proficient at one or the other. Toxicology screens are not foolproof.

Screenings that rely on collection of bodily fluids to be tested in a lab lack utility when it comes to alcohol because it is quickly metabolized and cannot be measured after twelve hours. Cocaine, amphetamines, and heroin are also quickly metabolized, but trace amounts are available as long as samples are collected within twenty-four to seventy-two hours. In the case of opioids, false positives can result if the person has eaten food with poppy seeds.

Professionals in the mental health field who are not affiliated with a hospital or a large clinic will find that the greatest drawback to toxicology screening rests with the difficulty of locating someone to administer the tests. Not only must a physician authorize the lab work, but the screen also requires urine collection, ideally performed in person to ensure that the sample is being provided on the spot. The resourceful patient can come in with a urine sample from a non-drug-using acquaintance. While most centers do not allow bags or purses in the bathroom, creative addicts can find a place on their person to hide a clean sample. Any good drug-screening center, at a minimum, will test the urine sample's warmth to make sure it was just collected. However, drug users can easily get around this as well by getting a sample from a non-using friend and carefully wrapping it to ensure it stays warm (or by placing it next to a small hot pack).

Recently, test strips, (such as those manufactured by American Bio Medica), have been developed that detect traces of drugs in a urine sample. Strips are available that test up to five different drugs. This is a less expensive alternative to lab testing and can easily be used in a clinic or private practice setting. Even more efficient and practical for the independent practitioner are test strips for use with saliva.

In the case of alcohol, which must be assessed within a short time after use, the breathalyzer is available to measure blood alcohol level (BAL). BAL represents the amount of alcohol to a certain amount of blood—more specifically, it refers to numbers of milligrams of alcohol per 100 milligrams of blood. Thus, .1 means that there is 1 milligram of alcohol per 100 milligrams of blood. It is important to know that a breathalyzer usually underestimates the actual level:

.08 = Coordination is slowed and alertness lessened.

.10 = Coordination, vision, and reasoning is impaired.

.15 = Reaction time is markedly slowed, behavior is disinhibited; this is stereotypic drunk with sloppy and noisy behavior.

.30 = Increased loss of motor control, restlessness, and anxiety.
.40 = Loss of consciousness.

In the United States, the BAL used to define drunk driving once ranged from .10 to .15, although many states have lowered the legal limit in recent years to .08. The .08 level has long been the standard in Europe. A woman who has three to four standard drinks within a one to two hour period will have a BAL of .08. A man will reach this BAL if he has five to six standard size drinks in the same time period. It is unlikely that mental health professionals will use a breathalyzer as an assessment tool, although if a therapist were adamant that a patient never come to a session after drinking, he or she could keep a breathalyzer in the office.

STANDARDIZED SCREENING TOOLS

A great many instruments are available to help identify substance-based addictions. This section reviews the most commonly used instruments that balance sensitivity and specificity. Sensitivity refers to the percentage of patients with a disorder who are correctly identified by the scale. A scale with 75 percent sensitivity correctly identifies 75 out of 100 persons with the disorder. Sensitivity is balanced by a scale's specificity, which refers to its ability to correctly identify those who do *not* have a disorder. Ideally, scales have both sensitivity and specificity, although the higher the former, the lower the latter. In health care settings, the preferred screening tools are high in sensitivity, given the goal of casting a wide net in order to identify as many persons with potentially addictive behaviors as possible—even at the cost of some errors. Those so identified will receive further assessment to determine if, in fact, there is a problem.

The vast majority of substance use screening instruments was developed and validated initially in alcohol treatment or medical settings. Such testing does not guarantee their validity when administered to a mental health population. The more popular scales have been tested within mental health settings and are valid for those with concomitant psychiatric conditions., Frequently this validity research samples patients at the more severe end of the spectrum (e.g., schizophrenia, bipolar disorder), which leaves open to question the value of such scales for those with less severe disorders. Ideally, a scale that is used in mental health settings will also have been validated with a nontreatment or community-based sample that is more representative of the typical psychotherapy population.

The scales and interview formats that are most compatible with clinical practice are examined in detail in this chapter. Many of these scales move beyond dichotomous thinking (an addiction is present or absent) to assess for subclinical forms of addictive behaviors. All the screening tools presented in this chapter assess for the presence of problematic substance use; some screen for a specific substance, such as alcohol, while others just point to the likelihood that some type of substance use is problematic. A positive outcome indicates that a more thorough and ongoing evaluation is warranted. Only where noted is the outcome a DSM-IV diagnosis of abuse or dependence. While all these instruments are designed to assess for alcohol or drug use, in many cases it is a simple matter of altering the questions so that they assess for process addictions. This change in subject invalidates the instrument, but incorporation of such questions into a clinical interview yields information that can help inform the assessment of process addictions.

Self-Report Screening Instruments

The CAGE is the best known and most often used screening instrument in medical and health care settings (Mayfield, MacLeod, and Hall 1974). As the other self-report instruments described below, the clinician asks the following questions as a routine part of a clinical interview. The CAGE consists of four questions directed at the use of alcohol. All four questions can be answered within thirty seconds or incorporated into different sections of a clinical interview.

CAGE

1. Have you ever felt you should *cut down* on your drinking?
2. Have people *annoyed* you by criticizing you about your drinking?
3. Have you ever felt *guilty* about your drinking?
4. Have you ever had a drink first thing in the morning to steady your nerves or to get rid of a hangover (i.e., an *eye opener*)?

A point is scored for each affirmative reply, with a score of 2 or 3 being indicative of a substance-related disorder. However, in psychiatric populations, where even low levels of alcohol use can have adverse consequences (e.g., disrupt the effectiveness of psychotropic medications, lower compliance, exacerbate symptoms), a score of 1 merits further assessment. Given how the questions are phrased, a positive response requires further questioning to determine whether the problem is current or historical.

The T-ACE (Sokol, Martier, and Ager 1989) and TWEAK (Russell et al. 1991) were initially developed as screens for at-risk drinking during pregnancy, but they have been subsequently validated for use with diverse populations. The T-ACE is identical to the CAGE but replaces the guilt question with one that asks: How many drinks does it take for you to get high? This question assesses the presence of tolerance, which is a more reliable predictor of alcoholism than the amount consumed. An answer of five or more drinks is scored as a 2. The remaining T-ACE questions are scored in the same way as the CAGE (each "yes" reply equals 1 point). An outcome of 2 or more points is interpreted as an indication of high-risk alcohol use.

The TWEAK involves a further modification of the CAGE scale. The TWEAK is composed of five questions that address recent drinking behavior (in contrast to the CAGE, which lacks a time frame). The TWEAK questions are as follows:

TWEAK

1. How many drinks does it take before you begin to feel the first effects of alcohol? (*Tolerance* question)
2. Have close friends or relatives *worried* or complained about your drinking in the past year?
3. Do you sometimes take a drink in the morning when you first get up? (*eye opener as a way to manage withodrawal*)
4. Are there times when you drink and afterward you can't remember what you said or did? (*Amnesia* or blackouts)
5. Do you sometimes feel the need to *cut down* on your drinking?

The first question about tolerance is scored positively if a person requires three or more drinks to first feel alcohol's effects. A more conservative number is recommended for women; a response of 2 or more should be scored positively. A positive response to this query is scored as a 2. A score of 1 is given for each "yes" to the remaining questions. A total score of 2 or more is evidence of at-risk drinking for pregnant women, although with general population samples, scores of 3 or more are used (Cherpital 1997).

To address the restricted focus on alcoholism in these three scales, the CAGE-AID was developed and validated, incorporating reference to drug use into the four questions (e.g., Do you sometimes feel the need to *cut down* on your drinking and drug use? Have you ever felt *guilty* about your drinking and drug use?). The CAGE-AID is scored in the same manner as the CAGE. Another alternative for assessing drug and alcohol use is the TICS (two-item conjoint screen), a two-item screen that has been found to have good predictive ability in medical settings (Brown, Leonard, Saunders, and Papasouliotis 2001).

TICS

1. In the last year, have you ever drunk alcohol or used drugs more than you meant to?
2. Have you felt you wanted or needed to cut down on your drinking or drug use in the last year?

The TICS authors believe that a conjoint screen is better than assessing for drugs and alcohol separately. They argue that people are hesitant to admit to drug use because of the legal and/or moral ramifications. By asking about both drugs and alcohol simultaneously, a person will more readily say "yes," given that a positive response does not necessarily indicate drug use. In terms of scoring, an affirmative response to either question warrants further investigation.

A careful analysis of the CAGE, T-ACE, TWEAK, CAGE-AID, and TICS finds that their sensitivity varies depending on the population. Some are less sensitive for women; others are less sensitive for certain ethnic groups. To address culture-based variability, a new scale was developed after administering the most popular alcohol screening tools to a highly diverse population sample and analyzing the performance of individual items. The result is the Rapid Alcohol Problems Screen (RAPS). While sensitivity was slightly lower for women, especially women from minority groups, overall the RAPS was more sensitive with all groups relative to the other popular scales (Cherpital 1997). The RAPS five questions are:

RAPS

1. Do you sometimes take a drink in the morning when you first get up?
2. During the past year, has a friend or family member ever told you about things you said or did while you were drinking that you could not remember?
3. During the past year, have you had a feeling of guilt or remorse after drinking?
4. During the past year, have you failed to do what was normally expected of you because of your drinking?
5. During the past year, have you lost friends or girlfriends or boyfriends because of your drinking?

An affirmative response to any one of the five questions is indicative of a drinking problem (Cherpital 1995).

Self-Administered Instruments

For clinicians interested in self-administered self-report instruments for alcoholism, there is the MAST (Michigan Alcoholism Screening Test) and AUDIT (Alcohol Use Disorder Identification Test). These two paper-and-pencil measures can be completed relatively quickly in the office or waiting room. Within alcoholism treatment settings, the MAST (Selzer 1971) is the most commonly used screening tool (Myerholtz and Rosenberg 1997). It is composed of twenty-five yes-or-no questions that refer to common behaviors and symptoms associated with alcoholism and the subsequent functional impairments in the areas of health, work, and social life. It takes about ten minutes to complete and five minutes to score. An outcome of four to ten points is indicative of possible problematic use. Scores greater than 10 indicate alcoholism/dependence. The results provide information about lifetime usage given that the questions do not specify a time period. Shorter forms of the MAST that retain a good deal of the original test's reliability and validity are available. There is a thirteen-item Short MAST (SMAST) and ten-item Brief MAST (BMAST). The following is the SMAST along with the answers that are scored as positive responses.

SMAST

1. Do you feel you are a normal drinker? *No*
2. Do your spouse or parents worry or complain about your drinking? *Yes*
3. Do you ever feel bad about your drinking? *Yes*
4. Do friends or relatives think you are a normal drinker? *No*
5. Are you always able to stop drinking when you want to? *No*
6. Have you ever attended a meeting of Alcoholics Anonymous? *Yes*
7. Has drinking ever created problems between you and your spouse? *Yes*
8. Have you ever gotten into trouble at work because of drinking? *Yes*
9. Have you ever neglected your obligations, your family, or your work for two or more days in a row because you were drinking? *Yes*
10. Have you ever gone to anyone for help about your drinking? *Yes*
11. Have you ever been in the hospital because of drinking? *Yes*
12. Have you ever been arrested, even for a few hours, because of drinking? *Yes*
13. Have you ever been arrested for drunk driving or driving after drinking? *Yes*

Each positive response is scored as one point. A total of two points indicates a possible drinking problem, while three or more points is indicative of a probable alcohol problem. All three versions of the MAST are available to be downloaded for clinical use at www.projectcork.org/clinical_tools/index.html.

The DAST is modeled after the MAST. This self-administered, self-report scale contains twenty-eight items that yield a measure of problems related to drug use (Skinner 1982). A score of 6 or more is indicative of problematic drug use. A full version of the DAST is available at www.projectcork.org/clinical_tools/index.html.

The AUDIT (Saunders, Aasland, Babor, De La Fuente, and Grant 1993) consists of ten questions, the first three of which measure the current degree of alcohol use in order to assess if consumption is at hazardous levels. The AUDIT's seven other questions inquire about alcohol-related problems during the past year. It takes about two to three minutes to complete. Unlike most other tools, where the goal is to identify an alcohol problem either current or past, the AUDIT is designed to recognize hazardous drinking patterns that increase the risk of alcohol-related problems. A significant score indicates that alcohol problems may be present or are likely to develop. Given that psychotherapists want to identify patients who have alcohol-related problems or are at risk for developing such problems, the AUDIT is an excellent tool.

AUDIT

1. How often do you have a drink containing alcohol?
   (Never, monthly, 2–4 times a month, 2–3 times a week, 4 or more times a week)
2. On a typical day that you drink alcohol, how many drinks do you have?
   (1–2, 3–4, 5–6, 7–9, 10 or more)
3. How often do you have six or more drinks on one occasion?
   (Never, less than monthly, monthly, weekly, daily or almost daily)
4. How often during the past year have you found that you were not able to stop drinking once you started?
   (Never, less than monthly, monthly, weekly, daily or almost daily)
5. How often during the past year have you failed to do what was normally expected from you because of drinking?
   (Never, less than monthly, monthly, weekly, daily or almost daily)
6. How often during the past year have you needed a drink in the morning to get yourself going after a heavy drinking session?
   (Never, less than monthly, monthly, weekly, daily or almost daily)
7. How often during the past year have you had a feeling of guilt or remorse after drinking?
   (No; Yes, but not in the past year; Yes, during the past year)
8. How often during the past year have you been unable to remember what happened the night before because you had been drinking?
   (No; Yes, but not in the past year; Yes, during the past year)
9. Have you or someone else been injured as a result of your drinking?
   (No; Yes, but not in the last year; Yes, during the past year)
10. Has a relative or friend or doctor or other health worker been concerned about your drinking or suggested you cut down?
    (No; Yes, but not in the last year; Yes, during the past year)

Responses to questions 1–8 are scored 0–4 points. Questions 9 and 10 are scored 0, 2, or 4 points. A total score of 8 or more is interpreted as evidence of problem alcohol use for men. For women, a cutoff score of 6 is recommended, although some researchers have argued that for optimal identification a score of 4 can be used (Bradley, Boyd-Wickizer, Powell, and Burman 1998).

Most psychotherapy patients do not present the classic signs of physiological dependence (tolerance and withdrawal) such as those emphasized in the CAGE. Many others will not be using substances in ways that consistently create adverse consequences. Yet, most structured screening tools assess for signs of physiological dependence and adverse consequences. Of all the brief screens presented thus far, the AUDIT is unique given its questions on drinking patterns. In health care settings, like psychotherapy, information about drinking patterns are valuable because alcohol consumption above safe limits increases the risk of developing an alcohol problem. Thus, although the CAGE is most often recommended by medical and managed care organizations, in mental health settings, where a few extra minutes are available, the AUDIT is preferred.

With the importance of knowing the amount of alcohol consumption in mind, the Quantity/Frequency Questionnaire was developed for use in health care settings (U.S. Department of Health and Human Services 2000). It provides a slightly different set of questions to gather the same information as the initial three questions on the AUDIT.

Quantity/Frequency Questionnaire

1. On average, how many days per week do you drink alcohol?
2. On a typical day, when you drink, how many drinks do you have?
3. What is the maximum number of drinks you have had on a given occasion during the past month?

Since development of the AUDIT, binge drinking has become better recognized as a form of problematic alcohol use. This last question provides a check for binge drinking. A person may drink normally and infrequently and yet, he or she may periodically have a high number of drinks. While the AUDIT asks the frequency with which one has more than six drinks, there is evidence to suggest that amounts less than this qualify as binge drinking (see chapter 8) and thus, by not specifying quantity, the Quantity/Frequency Questionnaire is better able to recognize a binge drinking pattern.

Both the AUDIT and Quantity/Frequency Questionnaire use government standards to define low-risk and problematic drinking. Low-risk drinking (the maximum safe amount) is two standard drinks a day for men and one for women. For men, problem drinking is defined as having more than fourteen drinks per week and/or five to six drinks per day. For women, the cutoff is seven drinks per week and four drinks per day (Substance Abuse, 2002).

To the extent that one is comfortable with structured measures, the Quantity/Frequency Questionnaire (which takes less than a minute to complete) and the AUDIT (two to three minutes) provide a quick and easy way to gather information about consumption. The Quantity/Frequency Questionnaire can be either self-administered or incorporated into a clinical interview. Self-administration may be preferred. Doing so gives the patient time to reflect and think about use. It may also lead to more accurate reporting. As seen below, responding in private avoids the sense of discomfort that can be felt when having to report amount of consumption in a face-to-face situation.

VALIDITY OF SELF-REPORT MEASURES

Relative to clinical interviews, self-report measures are a standardized and potentially efficient means for gathering information. However, they are valuable only to the extent that the information provided accurately represents the problem. Questions are often raised about the validity of self-report measures. This is especially true for addiction assessment where denial is assumed to be prevalent.

Research on the validity of self-report measures shows that alcoholics can report accurately on their drinking behavior (Sobell and Sobell 1990). This finding may not generalize to the mental health setting. Most of these studies are conducted within DUI/DWI programs or alcohol treatment centers. In these settings, the person doing the responding has either self-labeled or been labeled by a professional as having a substance use problem and has answered questions about level of use before (or at least, has had time to reflect on behavior). In contrast, few psychotherapy patients will have had previous screenings and, as a consequence, the degree of substance use tends to be underestimated. Even in addiction-focused settings, participants have been observed to report higher levels of addictive behavior when interviewed a second time (Hodgins and Makarchuk 2003; Tonigan, Miller, and Brown 1997). Perhaps it is easier to access memories upon later questioning. A more likely explanation is that after having been asked about substance use, a person begins to attend more to the behavior so that what was a guess upon first inquiry becomes increasingly more reality-based with subsequent inquiries. My clinical experience is consistent with this observation. Upon entering treatment for depressive episodes, a man in his 60s reported drinking five out of seven nights with two drinks on each occasion. At his age this level of drinking was a concern, so when he returned several weeks later for a second appointment, I checked in again about his drinking. This time he reported that he was drinking daily and the previously reported two drinks an evening turned out to be more like four. If initial reports of substance use approach a problematic level, it is good practice to inquire again later.

The accuracy of self-reports also is influenced by a patient's co-occurring psychological disorders. The sensitivity of the MAST and AUDIT are lower when used with the severely mentally ill (Wolford et al. 1999). This may be due to patients' difficulty completing self-administered tools and/or their tendency to not disclose and underestimate the negative consequences of substance use.

In thinking about whether to assess for substance use during the clinical interview or through a self-administered questionnaire, psychotherapists will be interested to learn the results of a recent study examining the differential outcomes of these two formats with a community-based sample. Recall that a community-based sample best represents the population of patients who come to psychotherapy. Over 6,000 people were interviewed by telephone regarding their alcohol consumption and alcohol-related problems. An equally large sample was given a self-administered questionnaire asking for the same information. Telephone interviews yielded lower levels of reported consumption than self-administered questionnaires. The authors (Kraus and Augustin 2001) concluded that self-administered measures yield more accurate information than interview data. While this outcome would likely be replicated in psychotherapy settings, this effect may only hold true for the initial screening. In psychotherapy, addiction assessment usually occurs early in treatment before a working alliance has been established. Once established, the patient feels safer to reveal information that seems shameful. Thus, initial inquiries are likely to be more accurate if the information comes from a self-administered questionnaire. The validity of self-report measures in psychotherapy can also be compromised by a patient's lack of awareness of a behavior's addictive potential and limited reflection about the extent of the behavior and its consequences. Given these factors, the accuracy of self-reported addictive behaviors will improve over the course of several inquiries and as the therapeutic relationship develops.

SELF-ADMINISTERED SCREENS WITH LOW FACE VALIDITY

For providers who are concerned that denial or a conscious desire to fake responses will limit the accuracy of self-report measures, there are several instruments where the scale's intent is less apparent. The outcome of instruments with lower face validity is assumed to be less vulnerable to manipulation.

For many years, the MacAndrew Alcoholism Scale, now known as the MAC-R in the MMPI-2, was considered a good alcoholism screening tool that avoids the problems associated with high face validity instruments. Like the MMPI, the MAC-R does not yield a specific diagnosis but rather detects a pattern of responding characteristic of alcoholics. Outcomes of the MAC-R, along with the Alcohol Abuse Scale of the Millon Clinical Multiaxis Inventory, need to be interpreted cautiously in light of research showing low rates of success in differentiating potential alcoholics from nonalcoholics, especially in mental health populations (Carey and Teitelbaum 1996; Myerholtz and Rosenberg 1997). However, the MAC-R may still have merit within clinical settings as long as the results are interpreted more generally. Several studies conclude that when administered in a psychotherapy setting, the scale is a good indicator that the patient has a substance-based addiction which may or many not be alcoholism (Rouse, Butcher, and Miller 1999; Stein et al. 1999).

Clinicians who have access to patients' MMPI protocols have two other subscales available: the APS (Addictive Personality Scale), which is composed of personality attributes associated with development of substance-based addictions, and the AAS (Addiction Acknowledgment Scale). Scores on both the

MAC-R and APS correlate highly with psychotherapists' reports of patients' substance use problems (Rouse, Butcher, and Miller 1999). When patients being treated in outpatient clinics and independent psychotherapy practices have elevated scores on either scale, a more thorough addiction assessment is warranted.

Those interested in instruments with low face validity also have the Substance Abuse Subtle Screening Inventory (Miller 1994), now in its third revision (SASSI-3). The first section of the SASSI consists of a series of questions related to a variety of needs, interests, values, health concerns, social interactions, and emotional states. A few questions contain references to drugs or alcohol, but the instrument is considered "subtle" because as a whole the sixty-two true-or-false items do not appear to be assessing for substance use. See www.niaaa.nih.gov/publications/instable-text.htm for sample items.

The SASSI-3 has been found to reliably distinguish drug and alcohol dependent persons from those who have no substance-related problem. SASSI subscales provide additional useful information, such as a person's degree of defensiveness and degree of awareness of substance use effects. The second section consists of twenty-six items asking the usual questions regarding the frequency and amount of drug and alcohol use and the consequences. The SASSI-3 takes as little as fifteen minutes to complete and has good validity in identifying chemically dependent persons. Unlike most other scales presented here, SASSI-3 must be purchased from the developer (www.sassi.com).

The ability to consciously distort or fake responses to a screening tool is lessened when the intent of the measure is ambiguous. Hence, only a few of the sixty-two questions in the first section of the SASSI make any mention of substance use. While an improvement over instruments such as the MAST and AUDIT where the intent of the question is apparent, the SASSI is not immune to faking. DUI offenders were asked to fake their responses on this instrument, with the result that under the fake nonalcoholic condition, they did not present as chemically dependent (Meyerholtz and Rosenberg 1997). In other words, when a person knows that the SASSI assesses for addiction, they can manipulate the outcome even though the questions do not specifically mention addictive behaviors. However, in mental health settings, the SASSI is less susceptible to faking because those completing the scale will be unaware of what it is designed to measure.

OTHER SCALES FOR ASSESSING ALCOHOL AND DRUG USE

Scales are available that assess dependence on a specific drug category, such as opiates, stimulants, amphetamines, or cocaine (e.g., CAP: Cocaine Assessment Profile; see Washton, Gold, and Pottash 1985). These tools are used most often in addiction treatment centers where patient have a known history of abuse for the given substance. Compared to the general screening tools described above, the specificity of such instruments makes them less practical for the psychotherapist who is trying to determine if any drug and/or alcohol use poses problems in the patient's life.

Anyone who wants to gain familiarity with the addiction literature will need to be familiar with a number of scales that are administered primarily as part of research protocols. The ASI (Addiction Severity Index) is the most widely used instrument in addiction research (McClellan, Luborsky, Woody, and O'Brien 1980). It focuses on the following areas: alcohol and drug use, family history, psychiatric status, and functional consequences of substance use in four areas (social relationships, medical issues, employment, and legal status). The ASI is composed of 180 items that are presented as part of a structured interview, which takes thirty to forty minutes to administer and is best suited for identifying more severe forms of addiction. While a popular tool for research, the ASI will be of less value for the clinician working in an outpatient setting where drug and alcohol problems are often less severe and not the primary reason for referral.

There are a number of instruments designed to recognize dual-diagnoses and/or distinguish psychological symptoms from those that are substance induced. Their value outside the research setting is limited given that they are quite lengthy to administer (from one to four hours). For familiarity and ease when reading the research, a brief description of each follows.

Despite its name, the SADS (Schedule for Affective Disorders and Schizophrenia) is a semi-structured interview that assesses for current psychiatric symptoms, such as anxiety, depression, and psychosis, and their severity. There are a few questions about alcohol and drug use and its adverse consequences. The second section addresses the person's history of mental illness, including alcoholism. The DIS (Diagnostic Interview Schedule) assesses lifetime diagnoses of mental disorders and alcoholism. The outcome of the SCID (Structured Clinical Interview for DSM-IV) is a psychiatric diagnosis consistent with the DSM-IV. The SCID also assesses for alcoholism while the SCID-A/D has improved the reliability of the original and enhanced its sections on alcohol, drugs, and eating disorders. Finally the AUDADIS (Alcohol Use Disorders and Associated Disabilities Schedule) evaluates alcohol and drug use along with mental disorders. Unlike the others, it has been used in clinical settings. A detailed overview of these instruments, their reliability and validity, is provided by Hasin (1991).

6

Assessment of Process Addictions

Addictions can develop in the absence of psychoactive drug use. Behaviors become addictive through their self-reinforcing properties, self-medication effects, and/or by creating physiological changes similar to those that result from ongoing substance use (Goodman 1998; Orford 2002; Shaffer 1997). Theoretically, the type of behavior that has the potential to become addictive is limitless. This is because addiction has come to be defined not by the specific behavior but by how the behavior occurs. As discussed in chapter 1, the addiction construct is characterized by three attributes: the behavior occurs in an out-of-control manner, it continues despite creating negative consequences, and there is a sense of craving or need to enact the behavior. Addictive behaviors can be associated with the typical signs of physiological dependence common to alcohol or opiate addiction—tolerance and withdrawal—but signs of dependence are not required to consider the behavior addictive.

Despite the breadth of the addiction construct, the literature to date on process addictions has been restricted to a relatively small number of behaviors. Most attention has been given to gambling and binge eating. Addictive buying, exercise, work, sex, and, more recently, computer use have also been studied. As clinicians attempt to develop a shared definition of process addictions, they turn to the DSM for guidance—even though process addictions are not explicitly addressed. Some therapists model process addictions after the criteria for substance dependence, while others turn to the criteria for pathological gambling.

This chapter provides an overview of the more common process addictions and their assessment. Screening instruments are provided when available and when not, questions are suggested that can be easily incorporated into a clinical interview. Relatively little is known about individual and cultural differences in the prevalence of process addictions. Gender is most frequently mentioned.

When age differences are considered, adolescents are the group being discussed. Race and ethnic group membership is rarely mentioned in the literature on process addictions. As with substance-based addictions, individual differences based on group membership must be kept in mind during the assessment process. Doing so helps to ensure that stereotypic beliefs about who is addicted and what the addiction looks like do not cloud one's ability to recognize the problem in those who fall outside the stereotypical group.

EXERCISE

People exercise for many reasons: it makes them feel better, they want to be healthy, they want to improve their appearance, or they use it as a way to socialize. Some people run, swim, bike, or lift weights on a daily basis. Daily exercise, in itself, does not qualify as an addiction. Exercising becomes problematic when the original goals (e.g., health, weight loss) are achieved but the person continues to increase the degree of exercise, does not feel the day is complete without exercise, and insists on exercising even if there are good reasons not to (e.g., inclement weather, a major family event). Adams and Kirby (2002) describe how increasing levels of exercise can bring about biological changes that parallel those associated with substance-based addictions. For some people, frequent exercise levels must be maintained or increased in order to avoid the discomfort of withdrawal. Exercise at this intensity often creates adverse effects, especially recurrent physical injuries. When this pattern develops, exercise behavior can be considered addictive.

The criteria for exercise addiction are modeled after the DSM-IV criteria for substance dependence.

Exercise behavior is considered addictive by meeting three or more of the following criteria:

Exercise Addiction Criteria

1. *Tolerance:* which is defined as either a need for significantly increased amounts of exercise to achieve the desired effect or diminished effect with continued use of the same amount of exercise.
2. *Withdrawal:* as manifested by either withdrawal symptoms for exercise (e.g., anxiety, fatigue) or the same (or closely related) amount of exercise is taken to relieve or avoid withdrawal symptoms.
3. *Intention effects:* exercise is taken in larger amounts or over longer period than intended.
4. *Loss of control:* there is a persistent desire or unsuccessful effort to cut down or control exercise.

5. *Time:* a great deal of time is spent in activities necessary to obtain exercise (e.g., vacations are exercise related).
6. *Conflict:* important social, occupational, or recreational activities are given up or reduced because of exercise.
7. *Continuance:* exercise is continued despite knowledge of having a persistent or recurrent physical or psychological problem that is likely to have been caused or exacerbated by the exercise (e.g., continued running despite severe shin splits) (Hausenblas and Symons Downs 2002a, 113).

Hausenblas and Symons Downs (2002b) have developed a scale to screen for a current exercise addiction. The Exercise Dependence Scale contains twenty-one items where each of the seven exercise addiction criteria is measured by three questions. Respondents are asked to indicate how often, in the past three months, the various beliefs and behaviors occurred. Responses are marked on a Likert scale from 1 (never) to 6 (always).

Exercise Dependence Scale

1. I exercise to avoid feeling irritable._____
2. I exercise despite recurring physical problems._____
3. I continually increase my exercise intensity to achieve the desired effects/benefits._____
4. I am unable to reduce how long I exercise._____
5. I would rather exercise than spend time with family/friends._____
6. I spend a lot of time exercising._____
7. I exercise longer than I intend._____
8. I exercise to avoid feeling anxious._____
9. I exercise when injured._____
10. I continually increase my exercise frequency to achieve the desired effects/benefits._____
11. I am unable to reduce how often I exercise._____
12. I think about exercise when I should be concentrating on school/work._____
13. I spend most of my free time exercising._____
14. I exercise longer than I expect._____
15. I exercise to avoid feeling tense._____
16. I exercise despite persistent physical problems._____
17. I continually increase my exercise duration to achieve the desired effects/benefits._____
18. I am unable to reduce how intense I exercise._____
19. I choose to exercise so that I can get out of spending time with family/friends._____

20. A great deal of my time is spent exercising.____

21. I exercise longer than I plan._____

This scale yields seven subscores; one for each component of exercise addiction (see table 6.1).

The Exercise Dependence Scale has no single cutoff score to determine if a person is exercise dependent. Instead, each of the seven subscales is scored separately and a person is categorized as being dependent, symptomatic, or asymptomatic for each component of exercise addiction. A score of 15 or more on a subscale is indicative of dependence. Scoring as dependent (i.e., 15 or higher) on three or more subscales is evidence of exercise dependence. Scores ranging from 9 to 12 on a given subscale indicate that a person is symptomatic for the criterion; when this occurs on three or more subscales the respondent is considered to be at risk for developing exercise dependence. For a complete description of the scoring process, see www.personal.psu.edu/faculty/d/s/dsd11/EDS/EDS21Manual.pdf.

Not all of those scoring as exercise dependent on the Exercise Dependence Scale will have a primary exercise addiction. It is quite common for women who have an addictive relationship to exercise to have a co-occurring eating disorder, especially anorexia or bulimia (Bamber, Cockerill, Rodgers, and Carroll 2000). A small percentage of men who are exercise dependent also have eating disorders (O'Dea and Abraham 2002). To make a differential diagnosis it will be important to assess the purpose of the exercise. When exercise addiction is primary, the physical activity itself is emphasized (e.g., I like to be active; I just enjoy a good run). If there is evidence of disordered eating, and exercise is a means to an end (e.g., as a way to control weight), then an eating disorder is the primary diagnosis (De Coverley Veale 1987).

The Exercise Dependence Scale, by following the DSM-IV criteria for substance dependence, can serve as a model for assessing any other process addiction. With a few exceptions, simply substituting another behavior (e.g., work, have sex) for the term *exercise* provides a good picture of a patient's relationship to that behavior. I ____ to avoid feeling irritable. I ____ longer than I expect.

Table 6.1.   Subscores for Exercise Dependence Scale

Component	Item Numbers
Withdrawal Effects	1, 8, 15
Continuance	2, 9, 16
Tolerance	3, 10, 17
Lack of Control	4, 11, 18
Reduction in Other Activities	5, 12, 19
Time	6, 13, 20
Intention Effects	7, 14, 21

BUYING/SHOPPING

Instead of consuming food, drugs, or alcohol, some people are consumers of merchandise. Such people have been referred to as "shopaholics," but as consumers their behavior is more aptly described as a buying addiction. This does not rule out the possibility that some people can shop in an addictive manner without necessarily making a purchase. However, the research articles in this area focus on buying behavior more than on shopping.

Excessive buying is a process addiction more common to women. The typical compulsive buyer who seeks treatment is thirty-six years old and identifies the problem as beginning in her late teens. Items most often purchased are related to appearance, such as clothes, shoes, jewelry, and make up. Most items go unused. It is common for the buying addict to refer to finding outdated clothes in her closet with the price tags still attached (Christenson et al. 1994).

As with any behavior, defining whether it qualifies as excessive and/or problematic can be a challenge. Sometimes, the adverse effects of buying are apparent as is the case for people who purchase expensive items or shop so often that their credit card debt is far beyond their economic means. For others, the purchases made will create no hardships. Instead of debt being a clue to addiction, significant signs will be elicited by inquiring about what is purchased and what is done with the purchased items. Kohut's (1987) thoughts about the alcoholic's relationship to alcohol apply to the excessive buyer. The alcoholic cares little about whether it is good or bad liquor, just that there is liquor to be consumed. Likewise, when buying there will be the sense that what is purchased has less importance than the need to buy something. One woman I treated would buy a new handbag or pair of shoes every week only to return them the following week.

Women with buying addictions have a high incidence of anxiety, substance use, and eating disorders usually in the form of binge eating (Christenson et al. 1994). Of significance for psychotherapists is the prevalence of excessive buying in those diagnosed with a major depressive disorder (Lejoyeux, Tassain, Solomon, and Ades 1997). Thirty-eight of 119 depressed patients (or 32 percent) were identified as being addicted buyers. This group tended to be primarily women, relatively younger, and more often unmarried than depressed persons without a buying problem. Bulimia and other substance dependence disorders were also more prevalent.

In assessing for this, or any other addiction, it is worth exploring the person's experience of and motivations for the behavior. Knowing whether the behavior is ego-syntonic helps to distinguish the behavior as an addiction or a compulsion (see chapter 1). As an addiction, buying is seen as acceptable and pleasurable (although the negative consequences that ensue are a source of discomfort). Compulsions, on the other hand, are ego-dystonic; the person worries about the behavior and often struggles against doing it. One man I treated bought ties several times a week; he took little pleasure from his purchases and would obsess in the store and all the way home about whether he chose the right one. His buying was more compulsive than addictive. Another defining feature of addictive behaviors is that they often serve to manage dysphoric emotional states. Compared to normal buyers, feelings were much more salient prior to shopping, especially negative moods, for those diagnosed as having a buying addiction. Changes in mood over the course of shopping also differed. Normal buyers' feelings tended to go from positive to somewhat more negative. In contrast, the addicted group's feelings shifted from negative to more positive (Faber and Christenson 1996).

There are two measures for assessing buying addictions. The first, by Faber and O'Guinn (1992), focuses solely on buying and is administered by a clinician. The Shorter PROMIS Questionnaire (SPQ), a tool for assessing multiple addictions (see below), has a self-report scale that incorporates both shopping and buying behaviors. Each question is responded to on a six-point scale anchored by the terms "not like me" and "like me."

SPQ: Shopping Addiction Subscale

1. I have felt uncomfortable when shopping with other people because it has restricted my freedom.
2. I have particularly enjoyed buying bargains so that I often finished up with more than I need.
3. I tend to use shopping as both a comfort and a strength even when I do not need anything.
4. I have tended to go shopping just in case I might see something I want.
5. When I have been shopping with family members, friends, or other people, I have tended to disguise the full extent of my purchases.
6. I have often bought so many goods (groceries, sweets, household goods, books, etc.) that it would take a month to get through them.
7. I have preferred to keep my shopping supplies topped up in case of war or natural disaster, rather than let my stocks run low.
8. I have bought things not so much as a means of providing necessities but more as a reward that I deserve for the stress that I endure.
9. I have felt that I become a real person only when I am shopping or spending.
10. I have often gone shopping to calm my nerves.

This scale is still under development, but in initial studies, a total score of 25 had good sensitivity in identifying those in treatment for excessive buying. A score of 20 was interpreted as placing a person at risk, while scoring 30 or more identified addictive levels of buying.

GAMBLING

Gambling, one of the more common process addictions and the only one included in the DSM-IV, is on the rise. Referred to in its addictive form as pathological gambling, this increased incidence likely follows the principles of the gateway theory for substance-based addictions (see chapter 8). Gambling casinos and lotteries are no longer limited to a few states. With increased exposure comes increased access and use. While not all who gamble become addicted, with gambling available to more people, the number of those who will become addicted grows greater.

Similar to substance dependence, pathological gambling is largely defined by its negative consequences. The most salient adverse consequence is financial, but the range of effects can be broad, from a loss of lifestyle standards known only to family members to extreme debt ending in bankruptcy. Legal and employment problems are also common. Physical consequences include digestive disorders, sexual dysfunction, and circulatory problems that result for prolonged sitting (Ladd and Petry 2002).

DSM-IV Criteria for Pathological Gambling

Persistent and recurrent maladaptive gambling behavior is indicated by five (or more) of the following:

1. is preoccupied with gambling (e.g., preoccupied with reliving past gambling experiences, handicapping or planning the next venture, or thinking of ways to get money with which to gamble)
2. needs to gamble with increasing amounts of money in order to achieve the desired excitement
3. has repeated unsuccessful efforts to control, cut back, or stop gambling
4. is restless or irritable when attempting to cut down or stop gambling
5. gambles as a way of escaping from problems or of relieving a dysphoric mood (e.g., feelings of helplessness, guilt, anxiety, depression)
6. after losing money gambling, often returns another day to get even ("chasing one's losses")
7. lies to family members, therapist, or others to conceal the extent of involvement in gambling
8. has committed illegal acts such as forgery, fraud, theft, or embezzlement to finance gambling
9. has jeopardized or lost a significant relationship, job, or educational or career opportunity because of gambling

10. relies on others to provide money to relieve a desperate financial situation caused by gambling

The gambling behavior is not better accounted for by a Manic Episode (American Psychiatric Association 1994, 618).

Unlike substance-related disorders that are divided into dependence and abuse, there is only one diagnostic category for addictive gambling. Where a diagnosis of pathological gambling is made when five or more criteria are met, those meeting two to four of the criteria can be considered problem gamblers. If a patient's behavior is consistent with just one criterion, he or she can be considered to be at-risk.

The attributes of pathological gambling differ from substance dependence. Several of these differences prove to be very useful when assessing for other process addictions. Criterion one of pathological gambling indicates that the addictive quality of a behavior appears in obsessive-like ruminations and preoccupation with the behavior. Too often the presence of obsessive thought processes are used to qualify a behavior as a compulsion rather than an addiction. However, this criterion makes clear that obsessive ruminations are common to addictive behaviors as well. Criterion five makes explicit reference to the gambler's motivation to escape from or manage dysphoric mood. Knowing that a behavior occurs, primarily because of its mood-altering effects, is a risk factor in addiction. Finally, in criterion ten, lying to conceal a problem is an attribute of pathological gambling that is common to other process addictions.

The problem gambler is likely to be male (men outnumber women two to one), unemployed, and single. At least half of gamblers will have a co-occurring problem with drugs or alcohol. Women's gambling is less likely to create severe adverse financial effects; they prefer to spend money on slot machines and lottery tickets while men prefer high-stakes card games and betting on sports or animal races. While slot machines and lottery tickets may be less costly in financial terms, women who gamble are not immune to problems. Women gamblers have high rates of concomitant psychiatric disturbances (Petry 2003), making them likely candidates for psychotherapy. Like women's drinking, the course from recreational gambling to addictive levels is quite rapid, and, for this reason, early recognition in psychotherapy can prevent development of a gambling addiction.

Those working with adolescents need to be aware that the highest rate of gambling problems occurs for those ages eighteen to twenty-five with at least 6 to 8 percent of adolescents and young adults being problem gamblers. Betting on sports is their preferred gambling activity. Health and social consequences can be serious, including attempted and completed suicides, work problems, educational and family disturbances, arrests, and high rates of other addictive and psychiatric disorders (Larimer and Neighbors 2003).

Understanding the reasons for gambling can help with assessment. Men are drawn to gambling for excitement while women gamble as a way to manage stress and life dissatisfactions. Husbands have a strong effect on their wives' gambling behavior as well as alcohol use (see chapter 8). Living with a gambler or an alcoholic increases a woman's chance of becoming a problematic gambler. Thus, if a woman reports concern about her husband's gambling, it is worth looking further into her relationship to gambling. Another predictor of women's gambling is having friends who enjoy gambling (Ladd and Petry 2002). What begins as a social activity can evolve into problematic gambling.

The South Oaks Gambling Screen (SOGS) is the most commonly used gambling assessment tool. The SOGS assesses lifetime prevalence of gambling behaviors, associated problems, and the types of gambling activities the person prefers. This is a self-report measure where scores higher than 5 strongly indicate pathological gambling, while a score of 3 to 4 suggests there is a gambling problem (Lesieur and Blume 1987). A version of the SOGS that is scored online is available at www.gov.ns.ca/health/gambling/IsThereAProblem/SouthOaks/. A downloadable version with scoring procedures is available at www.dhh.state .la.us/oada/gambing-directory/gamb-screen.htm.

The SOGS was developed initially for use with persons suspected of having a diagnosable gambling problem. Because the items ask about gambling-related behaviors and their consequences, its use is most appropriate when a clinician wants to confirm a suspicion of pathological gambling. However, as discussed, psychotherapy patients often present behaviors that are at risk for becoming addictive. Recognizing the need for a screening tool to assess gambling at nonpathological levels, Lesieur and colleagues developed a shortened version of the SOGS that is effective in recognizing subclinical forms of pathological gambling (Strong, Breen, Lesieur, and Lejuez 2003).

South Oaks Gambling Screen (Short Version) for Assessing Pathological and Nonpathological Gambling Behavior

1. Did you ever gamble more than you intended to?
2. Have you ever borrowed money from someone and not paid them back as a result of your gambling?
3. Have you ever borrowed money from household money to gamble or pay gambling debts?
4. Have you ever borrowed money from banks, loan companies, or credit unions to gamble or pay gambling debts?

5. Have you ever cashed in stocks, bonds, or other securities to gamble or pay gambling debts?
6. Have you ever borrowed money on your checking account (passed bad checks) to gamble or pay gambling debts?

Each of the six items is responded to in a yes-or-no format with each "yes" receiving a score of 1. A score of 0 indicates no problem; 1 indicates a potential for problem gambling; 2 indicates problem gambling is likely; and 3 and above are taken as evidence of a significant gambling problem. Donato (2003) notes that this tool's sole emphasis on financial consequences means that it will fail to recognize problematic gamblers whose behavior primarily results in adverse personal and social consequences.

COMPUTER ADDICTION

There are many ways to use a computer—socializing, shopping, banking, gambling, stock trading, searching for information, or playing games—that can become addictive. Some prefer the term *pathological Internet use* (PIU) to computer addiction. The descriptor *pathological* reflects the fact that excessive computer involvement is modeled after pathological gambling. Computer addiction is preferred to PIU because addictive involvement with computers does not require the Internet (e.g., game playing). When it comes to computer addiction, two groups have received the most attention: college students and those who use the Internet for sexual pursuits. The latter behavior, which can culminate in a cybersex addiction, is addressed in the next section.

Labeling excessive computer use as an addiction has been met with heated opposition. Reviewing the arguments for and against the concept of computer addiction enlightens the assessment process. The major points of contention yield information that can guide a clinician in deciding whether computer use is problematic or not.

Grohol (2003), who opposes labeling computer use as addictive, acknowledges that people often use the computer excessively but rarely does such frequent and intense use develop into an addiction. He argues that a close look at people's behavior reveals that it is common for certain behaviors to occur intensely for extended periods. Teens talk on the phone or communicate by instant message for hours on end. Adults ignore family and friends while spending hours immersed in a book. Spending a lot of time on the computer is no more a sign of addiction than is talking on the phone or reading a book. This point is significant when thinking about any behavior that occurs repeatedly and in what can be described as an immoderate or overzealous manner. Skeptics of AA often remark that alcoholics who attend meetings daily have just replaced one addiction with another. But it is incorrect to equate frequent and ongoing behavior with an addiction.

What distinguishes computer use from computer addiction is a loss of control over the behavior and an onset of negative consequences. Repeated efforts to cut back on the amount of time spent on the computer fails. With more time or more money being spent on the computer, negative social consequences arise such as loss or damage to significant relationships, work performance, and financial stability. The classic signs of addiction, tolerance, and withdrawal may also be observed. Tolerance is indicated if a patient reports spending more time or money on the computer to get a similar level of pleasure. Signs of withdrawal are reflected in any uncomfortable feelings that occur when the computer is unavailable.

To better define computer addiction, Orzack has been instrumental in developing a list of criteria. Where some process addictions draw from the DSM-IV criteria for substance dependence, computer addiction, as mentioned above, is more often modeled after pathological gambling. These criteria provide clues regarding what to look for in a patient's behavior and the kinds of questions to ask (Orzack and Ross 2000, 114).

Computer Addiction Criteria

Meeting five or more of the following criteria is taken as evidence of problematic computer use:

1. Experiences pleasure, gratification, or relief while engaged in computer activities.
2. Preoccupation with computer activity, including thinking about the experience, making plans to return to the computer, surfing the web, having the newest and fastest hardware, or need to return to these activities to escape problems or relieve dysphoric mood.
3. Needing to spend more and more time or money on computer activities to change mood.
4. Failure of repeated efforts to control these activities.
5. Restlessness, irritability, or other dysphoric moods such as increase in tension when not engaged in computer activities.
6. Need to return to these activities to escape problems or relieve dysphoric mood.
7. Neglect of social, familial, educational, or work obligations.
8. Lying to family members, therapists, and others about the extent of time spent on the computer.
9. Actual or threatened loss of significant relationships, job, financial stability, or educational opportunity because of computer usage.

10. Shows physical signs, such as carpal tunnel syndrome, backaches, dry eyes, migraines, headaches, neglect of personal hygiene, or eating irregularities.
11. Changes in sleep patterns.

A second line of argument against computer addiction is that computer use, unlike many other addictive behaviors, can be inherently social seeking. Through instant messaging and chat rooms, people make friends, share common interests, and find social support. This observation is worth considering when assessing computer use or any other addiction. What is the primary motivation? Socializing? Distraction? Stress reduction? Using the computer primarily for social purposes should not be considered problematic according to Grohol (2003). However, socially motivated computer use does not preclude an addiction. The clinician will need to determine if these computer relationships in any way substitute for or alter the quality of face-to-face interactions. How important are these computer-based relationships for the patient's sense of satisfaction? This information is particularly relevant for college students. Among college students, about 8 percent use the computer in an addictive manner. Most users are technologically sophisticated males. This group tends to be lonelier than their peers. They use online gaming and chat rooms frequently. In these settings, their behavior changes; in face-to-face interactions, they are relatively shy and inhibited, but on the computer, they can become socially disinhibited (Morahan-Martin and Schumacher 2000; Nichols and Nicki 2004). In psychotherapy, failure to recognize the function computers play in these young men's lives will mask the full scope of their social anxieties.

In addition to meeting social needs, computer use can serve a number of mood-altering functions. Based on the idea that addictions can serve a self-medicating function, Orzack and Ross (2000) have found it valuable to ask computer users a question along the following lines: "What are your expectations when you turn on the computer? Are they positive or negative?" A content analysis of answers to these questions helped to distinguish those who previously had been identified as computer dependent from those who were not. As observed with substance-based addictions, dependence was more likely when computers were a means for relieving anxiety or tension.

Finally, Grohol (2003) argues that the apparent epidemic of computer addiction is likely exaggerated because computer use is phasic. Initially people are enchanted by this new way to get information and socialize. With this initial period of enchantment comes the heaviest use. Over time, people become disillusioned, cut back dramatically, followed by a return to normal use. Charlton (2002) has conducted a study to determine if attributes of computer addiction can be distinguished from the type of high engagement Grohol describes. Participants included an equal number of males and females from technical and humanistic fields of study. Their responses to several sets of questions assessing computer behavior and attitudes were factor analyzed. All the items listed below loaded heavily on what the researcher labeled as the computer addiction factor.

Computer Addiction/Engagement Questions

- I rarely think about computing when I am not using a computer. (Salience: cognitive)
- I never miss meals because of my computer activities. (Salience: behavioral)
- I often fail to get enough sleep because of my computing activities. (Salience: behavioral)
- I often experience a buzz of excitement while computing. (Euphoria)
- I tend to want to spend increasing amounts of time using computers. (Tolerance)
- When I am not using a computer, I often feel agitated. (Withdrawal)
- Arguments have sometimes arisen at home because of the time I spend on computing activities. (Conflict: interpersonal)
- My social life has sometimes suffered because of my computing activities. (Conflict: with other activities)
- Computing activities have sometimes interfered with my work. (Conflict: with other activities)
- I have made unsuccessful attempts to reduce the time I spend computing. (Relapse)

However, a number of these attributes also contributed to a separate factor that reflected computer engagement. Attributes of computer addiction shared by high computer engagement were tolerance, a sense of excitement or euphoria, and frequent thoughts about computer use. The characteristics distinguishing computer addiction from engagement included withdrawal symptoms, behavioral salience defined as involvement with the computer to the extent that self-care is neglected, and negative consequences where computer activities created arguments and/or came into conflict with other responsibilities (Charlton 2002).

Results of this study confirm that there is a great deal of overlap between computer addiction and engagement and that the two will not always be easy to distinguish. When assessing computer use and other excessive behaviors, these data provide some guidelines to help the clinician distinguish between the two. When current level of use is indicative of high engagement, the clinician will want to remain attuned to any evidence that the patient's relationship to the computer is changing. While strong engagement may be merely part of a phase, as Grohol (2003) suggests, it may also be a stage in the development of an addiction. Charlton (2002) describes this developmental sequence as follows: "one progresses through stages of high engagement at which there are no major negative consequences of over zealous computing behavior, and during which milder peripheral facets of addiction are present (tolerance, euphoria, and cognitive salience). The model would specify that these three phenomena persist when the addiction stage is reached, where the core facets of addiction become apparent: withdrawal symptoms, relapse and reinstatement, conflict, and behavioural salience"(339).

SEX AND CYBERSEX ADDICTION

The closest the DSM-IV comes to a category for excessive sexual behavior is paraphilia. Paraphilia involves sexual fantasies, urges, or behaviors directed at nonhuman objects, children, or nonconsenting persons and may involve suffering or humiliation of oneself or partner. Sexual offenses against children and sadistic sexual practices with a nonconsenting adult are two common examples. Like a sexual addiction, paraphilic behaviors continue despite significant adverse consequences. But there are differences.

The most significant difference is that paraphilias represent a circumscribed set of behaviors. Goodman (2001) contrasts this with addiction where "a pattern of sexual behavior is designated sexual addiction, not on the basis of what the behavior is, but on the basis of how the behavior relates to and affects a person's life" (204). While paraphilias are not the same as sexual addiction, it is possible for paraphilic behaviors to occur in an addictive manner (Goodman 1998). Take for example a man whose daily masturbation involves women's underwear. Repeated attempts to cut back or stop have failed and he no longer has sexual relations with his wife. Most sexual addictions are nonparaphilic in nature. Here, socially acceptable sexual behaviors occur in an addictive manner (e.g., gratification of sexual urges impedes work performance and is done indiscriminately, raising the risk of HIV).

Collecting prevalence data for sexual addictions is challenging. It is difficult to imagine getting accurate information about sexual activity through the kind of household interview surveys used to gather data on the prevalence of substance use. Instead, collecting demographic data on sexual addictions involves seeking out participants who meet a predefined set of criteria. Using this method, Kafka and Prentky (Goodman 1998) advertised for persons interested in evaluation and treatment of sexual addictions. The typical respondent was male, thirty-four years old, white, and from a Catholic background.

He had graduated from college, married, and was earning a middle-class income. Among this group, sexual addictions had a common developmental course. The behavior began sometime in adolescence or early adulthood and peaked in frequency during the respondent's late twenties and thirties.

To assess for sexually addictive behavior, whether the form is paraphilic or not, there is the Sexual Compulsivity Scale (Kalichman et al. 1994; Kalichman and Rompa 2001). Each item is responded to on a four-point rating scale anchored by the phrases "not at all like me" to "very much like me."

Sexual Compulsivity Scale (SCS)

1. My sexual appetite has gotten in the way of my relationships.
2. My sexual thoughts and behaviors are causing problems in my life.
3. My desires to have sex have disrupted my daily life.
4. I sometimes fail to meet my commitments and responsibilities because of my sexual behaviors.
5. I sometimes get so horny I could lose control.
6. I find myself thinking about sex while at work.
7. I feel that my sexual thoughts and feelings are stronger than I am.
8. I have to struggle to control my sexual thoughts and behavior.
9. I think about sex more than I would like to.
10. It has been difficult for me to find sex partners who desire having sex as much as I want to.

The SCS has no established norms for defining sexually addictive behavior. Most studies using this instrument have been correlational in nature. In a large-scale study of online sexual behavior, the mean score for men was 17.79, and for women it was 16.59. Respondents with scores of 23.78 and 29.93 (representing one to two standard deviations above the mean) were considered moderately sexually addicted, while those above 29.93 were considered sexually addicted (Cooper, Scherer, Boies, and Gordon 1999).

When assessing for a sexual addictions, it will be important to rule out any organic etiology. Given that sexual addictions tend to have a characteristic course of development, with the behavior appearing initially in the late teens and increasing in frequency over a period of years, a sudden increase in sexual thoughts and activities along with any other signs of organicity casts doubt on whether the excessive behavior truly represents a sexual addiction (Goodman 1998).

With growth of the Internet has come a special form of sexual addiction known as cybersex addiction. In this addiction, a person spends extensive time on the Internet pursuing sexual materials. Not all sexual use of the Internet is addictive. Most persons who use the Internet for sexual purposes do so less than one hour per week. These so-called recreational users have few or no negative consequences and are able to limit their time online.

In a study of cybersex addiction, over 9,000 participants answered an online survey that assessed Internet use and involved completing the SCS (Cooper, Delmonico, and Burg 2000; Cooper, Scherer, Boies, and Gordon 1999). Participants were divided into four groups: noncompulsives (scoring below one standard deviation above the mean), moderately sexually compulsive/addicted (between one and two standard deviations above the mean), sexually compulsive/addicted (two standard deviations or more above the mean), and cybersex compulsive/addicted (sexual compulsives who spent eleven hours or more per week online seeking sexual pursuits). Cybersex addicts (like sexual addicts) were predominantly male. However, some interesting demographic differences were observed as a function of gender. Where women composed about 12 percent of the sexually compulsive group, the figure jumped to 21 percent for the cybersex addicts. Of the participants who self-identified as gay/lesbian or bisexual, 6 percent and 9 percent respectively scored as sexually compulsive while the figures increased to 16 percent and 21 percent in the cybersex addiction group. Among men, those in the cybersex-addicted group were more likely to be single or dating than married. Chat rooms were by far the most frequently used source of sexual encounters for women. For men, chat rooms and specific sites on the Web were equally preferred for sexual pursuits.

While assessing addictions can be associated with uncomfortable feelings, these are compounded when assessing for sexually addictive behavior, especially cybersex activities. Therapists will need to examine their attitudes about sexual activities outside committed relationships and how these beliefs apply to online behavior. Is a sexual liaison on the Internet the same as having an affair? Cooper (Cooper, Scherer, Boies, and Gordon 1999) considers online sexual activities to be a potentially adaptive way of facilitating sexual exploration and socializing.

Assessment of a cybersex addiction includes gathering information about time online and the nature of the online activity (e.g., chat rooms, downloading pictures) as well as information about the goal of the behavior (e.g., a sense of excitement or adventure, arousal with or without sexual release). It is important to remember not to equate lengthy periods of time online with addiction. As Grohol (2003) has argued for computer addictions, time involved may be phasic, with extended time online merely a function of an initial period of high engagement.

A thorough assessment will incorporate questions designed to elicit evidence of tolerance and withdrawal and any negative impact on current functioning (e.g., work performance declines due to ruminations about the last online encounter. Motivation for seeking online sexual encounters also needs to be examined along with any resulting changes in mood. Are online sexual activities a way to handle disappointments in current relationships or a way to dissolve lonely feelings? Has one felt more lonely or depressed since becoming involved online? Have significant interpersonal relationships changed? Have sexual relations with a significant other been altered?

If a cybersex addiction is diagnosed and treatment is being considered, it will be important to distinguish between two types (Cooper, Delmonico and Burg 2000). One group is composed of individuals whose sex addiction is primary; they are prone to sexually addictive behavior independent of the Internet. For this group, the Internet merely serves as one forum for excessive sexual behavior. This is illustrated in the case of a homosexual man I was treating for a sexual addiction that involved picking men up at clubs. After several months of therapy, he reported a marked improvement in his behavior. In a subsequent session, it came to light that he had begun spending hours online. He did not connect his declining club attendance with the many hours now spent online in chat rooms seeking out men. Those whose sexual addiction is primary need treatment for this addiction separate from their Internet involvement.

The other group with a cybersex addiction is composed of computer users who have had no history of sexual addiction and would not have developed one if sexual material were not so readily available on the Internet. For this group, the nature of sex on the Internet—which is anonymous, easily accessible, and affordable—creates the circumstances for the development of a cybersex addiction (Cooper, Delmonico, and Burg 2000). Psychotherapy has a potentially significant role to play for patients whose cybersex is primary. Clinicians can prevent development of an addiction. Similar to brief interventions with problem drinkers, simply recognizing the at-risk behavior can be sufficient to reduce the behavior and its negative consequences.

Couples and family therapists need to be attuned to the possibility that computer or cybersex addictions are complicating the presenting problem, especially if treatment is sought for a poor sexual relationship. Complaints of being uninterested in the partner or a loss of sexual drive can mask ongoing sexual activity through the computer (Schneider 2000). In assessing for a cybersex addiction, the therapist can ask the couple if there are large chunks of time unaccounted for by the spouse and if there have been any changes in the amount of time the family or partners spend together. A common scenario parallels what happens with the alcoholic spouse who stays up to drink after the partner goes to bed. In this situation, the spouse uses this time to find sexual gratification online.

ASSESSMENT OF MULTIPLE ADDICTIVE BEHAVIORS

Polysubstance abuse is the norm. A person who abuses alcohol is likely to use drugs and the person who abuses drugs is likely to use alcohol in an excessive manner. Research also indicates that those who are involved with substances are prone to develop process addictions (Greenberg, Lewis, and Dodd 1999). Substance and process addictions can occur simultaneously or sequentially. When entering addiction treatment, patients often present with a single primary addiction while a secondary addiction goes unreported (Christo et al. 2003). In other instances, as one addictive behavior declines, a once moderate behavior becomes excessive. In light of the co-occurrence of different forms of addictive behaviors, the Shorter PROMIS questionnaire (SPQ) was developed to assess multiple addictive behaviors (Christo et al. 2003).

The SPQ is extensive in scope assessing for sixteen different types of substance-based and process addictions. The sixteen scales assess addictive use of alcohol, nicotine, recreational drugs, prescription drugs, sex, gambling and risk taking, caffeine, food bingeing, food starvation, exercise, shopping, working, involvement in dominant relationships or submissive relationships, and compulsive helping where the respondent's role is either dominant or submissive. Each of the sixteen SPQ subscales contain ten items that are responded to on a six-point scale from 0 to 5, with 0 indicating "not like me" and 5 meaning "like me." Some sample questions from process addictions not covered previously appear below:

Compulsive Helping Dominant:
- I have often stayed up half the night having helpful conversations.
- I have found life rather empty when someone for whom I was caring gets better and I have felt resentful at times when I am no longer needed.

Compulsive Helping Submissive:
- I have tended to remain loyal and faithful regardless of what I may endure in close relationships.
- I have often helped someone close to me more than I intended to.

Relationship Dominant:
- I have preferred to have power and influence in all my relationships rather than allow myself to be vulnerable.
- In a new relationship, I have felt uncomfortable until I hold the most powerful position.

Relationship Submissive:
- I have tended to think that a close friendship is when someone else really looks after me.
- I have tended to get irritable and impatient when people look after themselves rather than me.

Work:
- I have found that once I start work in any day I find it difficult to get "out of the swing of it" and relax.
- I have taken on a piece of work that I actively disliked not so much out of necessity but more simply to keep myself occupied.

The SPQ is still under development and not all scales have been fully validated. The scales that have been found to have good reliability and validity assess for alcohol, recreational drugs, prescription drugs, gambling, and problematic relationships with food (bingeing and starving). All scales have strong face validity, which means that a patient can fake their responses in a way that minimizes their problem. For this reason, several positive responses indicate that further inquiry is necessary.

A recent study of the SPQ described its value as follows:

A detailed assessment procedure covering a broad range of potentially problematic areas will have implications in terms of treatment. If a treatment is aimed at a single presenting problem behaviour then it may fail to be effective as one that addresses all problem areas. Treatment may decrease an individual's engagement in their presenting problem area, but may be followed by an increase in associated behaviours that may facilitate relapse (Donovan 1988). Therefore, it is useful for all potentially addictive tendencies to be identified at treatment entry, whereupon they can be addressed as part of the treatment process (Christo et al. 2003, 236).

SUMMARY

The value of the SPQ rests with its scope; it helps the clinician recognize if a mix of substance and process addictions are complicating the patient's life. However, there are times when a more focused screening for a single addiction is desirable. A clinician may have a hunch regarding the presence of a particular addiction and may want to use a specific screening tool, like those presented above, as a way to get a better sense of the intensity of the problem or as a means to invite the patient to speak more about the behavior. When it comes to structured screening tools for process addictions, there is no equivalent to the SASSI; all have high face validity.

As an alternative to self-report instruments, a clinician may prefer to alter questions from the substance-based assessment tools and incorporate these questions into a clinical interview or therapy session: Have people annoyed you or criticized you about the way you spend money? Have you felt you wanted or needed to cut down on your use of the Internet in the last year? How often have you found it difficult to stop exercising once you started? Although such modifications invalidate the screening tool, the answers still provide useful clinical information. More on interview-based approaches to addiction assessment appears in the next chapter.

7

Interview-Based Approaches to Assessment

The goal of intake sessions in alcohol treatment settings is to confirm a diagnosis of substance dependence or abuse. In contrast, when psychotherapists conduct an intake, they are casting a broader net. Not only are they interested in knowing if there is an addiction, but they are also speculating about whether a behavior is creating adverse consequence and if it goes unmoderated, whether an addiction will develop. How this information is gathered depends greatly on the treatment provider's style.

Unless mandated, most psychotherapists, like those in private practice settings, will not do a formal screening for addiction. For these providers such information will emerge out of the clinical dialogue. Some will take questions from structured screening tools and ask directly about potentially addictive behaviors. Others will ask questions about lifestyle and social relationships to reveal an addiction. Still others will ask no questions until the patient's report suggests that an addictive behavior is likely.

Even if an addiction is determined to be absent upon intake, during treatment a clinician should remain attentive for signs of addiction because once moderate behavior can become excessive. Knowing how addictions present in psychotherapy is necessary for the clinician who lets evidence of addictive behavior emerge out of the clinical dialogue. For alcoholism, one might listen for evidence of a hangover, regular drinking, or drinking more than intended. A gambler may complain about how much money has been lost. While some patients will make direct reference to the problematic behavior and its effects, most psychotherapy patients will mention psychological and interpersonal consequences of excessive behaviors (e.g., depression, arguments) that are not recognized to result from addictive behavior. Thus, clinicians must rely on less obvious signs available in a patient's history, lifestyle, and behavior in therapy. If successful assessment of addition is dependent on such clues, it is imperative that the treatment provider knows what to look for and what to listen to.

SUBTLE SIGNS OF ADDICTION

Repeatedly, treatment providers—even those familiar with addictions—can recall a time when they wished they had not taken a patient's casual reference to substance use at face value. One therapist recalled a young man with a sexual addiction who openly discussed his sexual activities in therapy. In the process of explaining the previous week's sexual experiences, the patient would occasionally mention that he had smoked marijuana. The psychotherapist made no further inquiry. When, later in treatment, a referral was made to a psychopharmacologist who did conduct a thorough substance use assessment, this man's degree of marijuana use was found to be consistent with a diagnosis of abuse. Thus, any time a patient makes an explicit reference to substance use or a behavior that is potentially addictive, especially if he or she has a current addiction or history of addiction, the topic merits further exploration by simply asking the person to say more about that behavior.

From my own lengthy history of believing (albeit, mistakenly) that I had never worked with an addicted person, I became curious about whether there were clues to addiction of which I was unaware. I was unsure how to begin this search now that I understood that the typical alcoholic has a job and family and that patients entering psychotherapy are unlikely to show the impaired functioning and pervasive health problems more common to those entering a detoxification or rehabilitation program. In order to find out if there were any nonobvious clues to addiction, I began a research project on what came to be called subtle signs of addiction. Mental health practitioners who self-identified as having expertise in addiction assessment were interviewed regarding what they looked for in a person's behavior—either as reported outside of treatment or in therapy—which for them would indicate there may be an addiction. What follows is a summary of what these eighteen master clinicians considered subtle signs of addiction. While their responses focused on alcohol and drug problems, many of these subtle signs can be clues to revealing process addictions.

These providers were well versed in co-occurring disorders, and thus for them subtle signs included a patient's report of depressed feelings, generalized anxiety, or low motivation, all of which can be symptoms of active substance use or withdrawal. Where most psychotherapists hear these types of symptoms and lean toward a diagnosis of depression or anxiety, these master clinicians routinely wondered if the symptoms were tied to addiction rather than psychopathology. The connection between substance use and psychological symptoms and how to make a differential diagnosis is addressed in chapter 9.

Lifestyle was another source of subtle signs. These clinicians took notice of any activity, whether related to hobby or career, in which the focus was on appearance—especially weight—as a clue to listen more closely or probe directly about addiction. Bodybuilders or gym fanatics, besides being addicted to exercise, may be abusing steroids. Dancers or runners may use cocaine to enhance energy and weight loss. At the other end of the spectrum, providers also noticed if a person neglected appearance or appeared unkempt—this stood out if appearance was incongruent with what would be expected in light of the patient's line of work or financial means. How a person has fun was another important source of information:

- Does the person who regularly mentions ending the day by meeting friends at a bar have a drinking problem?
- If the patient acknowledges a close connection between drinking and socializing, one can probe for any negative consequences of this connection, e.g., when drinking, have you ever done something at a party you regretted?

A history of poor impulse control has been linked to addictions, so it is not surprising that master clinicians were attuned to how patients handle their impulses. Is the person volatile (e.g., quick to express anger or prone to angry outbursts)? Other signs included evidence of promiscuity and an unstable social life, which was evidenced by multiple relationships where instant gratification takes precedence over meaningful relationships. Or, just the opposite may occur and impulses and feelings are minimized. A female patient reports that terrible things happen to her, but attempts to better understand the events do not engage her interest or her answers are vague and uninformative. In such cases, these master clinicians would be concerned if an addiction was the root of the problem and if attempts to explore it went nowhere because the patient's addiction clouded her memory, she wished to hide the addiction, or had not yet recognized that the bad things that kept happening were linked to addictive behaviors.

The nature of relationships was mentioned most often as a significant source of subtle signs of addiction. Flores (2001) has argued that attachment issues underlie all addictive disorders. Healthy interpersonal relationships are a sign that addictions are less likely, while a lack of such relationships points to a greater chance of an addiction. Two noteworthy relationship patterns mentioned by the master clinicians were: (1) patients are socially isolated or routinely complain about a lack of friends but remain unmotivated to do anything to change the situation, and (2) patients have many friends but relationships are short lived or don't seem to develop. One provider recounted the following as an example: "I worked with a lesbian who wouldn't stay over at the other woman's house; it turns out she needed to get home to drink instead of staying connected. There are people who say they don't connect with their mate, people who hope dates or evenings end so substance use can start. Of course, no one explains it like this; I pick it up through the relationship patterns and then ask questions."

Other aspects of relationships that serve as a sign of addiction include a patient who mentions having arguments with significant others following an off-handed reference to drinking and active socializing that involves casual but frequent mention of drugs or alcohol. In the case of adolescents, a change in peer group or a declining interest in family, hobbies, or sports is considered noteworthy.

While a lack of relationships or a lack of intimacy in relationships is a clue, it is important to remember that most addicted individuals will be married and have a family. For those who are married, a spouse's addiction becomes a sign. As discussed in chapter 8, the quantity of alcohol a woman consumes is greatly influenced by her spouse where as for men, peer relationships are a better predictor of drinking patterns. One psychotherapist recalled overlooking the addiction of a patient whose spouse was alcoholic. "I recall seeing a woman whose husband had just died of alcohol-related complications. She fit the WASP profile of a social drinker. There was no clue that she had a drinking problem. Then one session she told me she thought she needed to go to AA."

Work life and money also contain potential clues to addiction. Does the person report hating Mondays? One psychotherapist reported the following incident: "I worked with one guy and it was almost a year before his alcoholism came out. We were working together on early trauma issues and I totally missed how he was using alcohol to cope. It eventually came out because he mentioned having trouble getting a good day's work in on Mondays more than once." Another pattern to be on the look out for is periodic and unexplained disruptions in work performance. No matter what job the person has, the boss and/or coworkers always seem to be a source of difficulty. Frequent absences from work due to vague physical complaints involving headaches and upset stomach are also noteworthy. Unexplained financial problems also require further probing. The person who earns plenty of money but never seems to have enough may have a shopping addiction or a problem with drugs or gambling.

Descriptions of drinking behavior were something master clinicians listened to closely. Casual mention of "downing" a six-pack or getting "plastered" as if this is the way all people socialize was one sign that further questioning was needed. For these master clinicians, any time a patient mentioned that a behavior was excessive, such as getting drunk, spending more than planned, or exercising to the point of injury, they would explore the topic further. Other providers reported that any time substance use was mentioned (and not necessarily excessive use), they took this as an opportunity to inquire further about the frequency and quantity of consumption and its consequences.

Master clinicians routinely reported not only listening carefully when the topic of substance use comes up, but looking closely at the patient as well. There can be an increased level of excitement or enthusiasm when talking about a substance. Evans (1998) refers to a different set of behavioral signs: "Clients with SUD's have developed conditioned responses elicited by talking about substances, thinking about substances, seeing substances, and seeing paraphernalia for using substances. Involuntary behavioral manifestations that can help the counselor determine what line of questioning to pursue are often demonstrated in the interview. An example of this might occur with a client who uses substances intravenously (IV) but is not revealing this in the interview. The counselor can often elicit behavioral changes in the client that suggest use by discussing the act of IV drug use. These behavioral changes might include agitations, fidgeting, flushing of the face, and loss of eye contact while listening to the discussion" (Evans 1998, 330).

When substance use is mentioned in the session, master clinicians are sensitive to any changes in demeanor that could be indicative of defensiveness. On the one hand, a patient may overtly or nonverbally convey surprise that the clinician is interested in knowing more about this kind of behavior. Other signs of defensiveness include a brief acknowledgment of substance use followed by a change of topic or the sudden appearance of a joking attitude whenever substance use is mentioned. Or, a patient who usually provides quite detailed descriptions of his or her experiences becomes vague and circumspect when the topic of drug or alcohol use comes up.

Another common sign that a patient has an undisclosed concern about a behavior is revealed when a patient attempts to justify drug use without ever being asked to do so.

> In relating the happenings of the previous weekend, Sally, a college student, mentioned in passing a Friday night of binge drinking with her girlfriends. This was followed by a spontaneous comment meant to reassure the therapist (and probably herself): "There's nothing to worry about; it's just a girl's night on the town. The guys do it all the time."

Or a patient may mention drinking or some other potentially addictive behavior but make sure to emphasize the uniqueness of it: I *only* drank last night, it was *just* four glasses of wine, I *never* got drunk like that before; Yes, I ran longer than expected but it was *only* twelve miles. Rationalization and minimization are common ways of responding for patients who consciously or unconsciously worry about whether a behavior is excessive.

Defensiveness also appears in the form of unsolicited comments regarding what did *not* happen after substance use. "My wife and I didn't get into a fight." "I didn't miss work." " I didn't spend too much money." "My knee is really hurting, but I am sure it's not due to that long run." Here it is useful for therapists to be aware of their own feelings. Any time a patient reacts as if the therapist had responded in a challenging manner, when the therapist has said nothing or merely asked a question, it is worth wondering if this defensiveness is driven by the patient's discomfort about the behavior in question.

The range of subtle signs extends beyond what is happening in the session to include certain types of historical information. A history of trauma is highly correlated with current substance abuse. Likewise, as is well known, a family history of addictive behavior is associated with an increased incidence of addiction. Most of this research has been conducted with alcoholics: a person whose closest relative is an alcoholic is three to four times more likely to have an alcohol-related disorder than those whose closest relative is not an alcoholic. Familial alcoholism is an even stronger predictor if it is on the father's side (Foroud and Li 1999; Margolis and Zweben 1998). When asking about the family history, it important to know that research shows that having a family history of one addiction, such as alcoholism, increases the likelihood of developing any type of addictive disorder, not just alcoholism (Goodman 1998).

Any sense of a chaotic early family life, even if the patient reports no addiction history, may be a sign of a hidden addiction within the family of origin. Failure to identify an addiction in one's family can occur because the family member's behavior does not fit the stereotype of addiction. One young man whose early home life was characterized by mess, disorder, and frequent moves never realized that his father was an alcoholic until he began therapy. He knew his father drank, but he had never considered him an alcoholic because, as a quiet drinker, he did not fit the son's stereotype of a loud and angry drunk. Failure to identify an addiction in one's family also can contribute to a failure to recognize addiction in oneself. Another man I worked with recalled how his father, on the way home from work, would call from the train station to tell him to make sure a six-pack of beer was getting cold in the refrigerator. As an adult, this man never considered that his father might have had a drinking problem. Not surprisingly, when this patient drank, it was never less than a six-pack. He thought nothing of drinking this amount because, in his familial way of categorizing things, a six-pack was "just a beer." As a result, he never connected his failure to follow through on household chores—a constant complaint made by his wife—to his drinking.

During an addiction assessment, it is routine to ask about family history. Usually this is done by simply asking, " Is there any alcoholism or addiction in your family?" To many patients this question is asking, "Did anyone ever diagnose or treat a family member for addiction?" More significant information concerns the patient's experience of a family member's drinking or potentially addictive behavior. Such questions focus on how the patient or other's in the immediate environment experienced or reacted to specific behaviors. The following are some examples of questions that assess for a parent's history of addiction:

- Did you ever think that your parent drank too much? Spent too much money?
- What kind of affect did your parent's drinking have on you?
- Was anyone in your family affected by your parent's drinking? Spending too much money?

A patient's open acknowledgement of a personal history of addiction does not preclude the need to assess for addictions in the current treatment. Addictive behaviors tend to co-vary. There is good evidence that as a person stops or lessens one addictive behavior, another behavior, which had been moderate, becomes excessive. As drinking declines, shopping increases along with credit card debt (see the discussion of polyaddictions in chapter 9). A person with a history of an addiction who is currently using another substance, even at a moderate level, is at risk for relapse. For example, those in recovery from cocaine abuse have been known to return to this drug after beginning to drink alcohol (Smith 1986). Another common pattern is for individuals to shift from one addiction to another. Thus, whenever a patient reports an addiction history, it is important to assess whether current substance use or a potentially addictive behavior is increasing in frequency.

The various physical consequences that result from addiction can serve as a subtle sign. While ideally these consequences will be recognized by a physician, the patient may not have had a recent check-up or, as is common, physicians, like psychotherapists, too often misattribute the physical consequences of addiction to some other illness (The National Center on Addiction and Substance Abuse at Columbia University 2000). Alcohol-induced stomach problems are simply treated with antacids after a few questions about diet. Consequently, it is important that psychotherapists are aware of the more common physical consequences of addiction. With alcoholism, upset stomachs and ulcers are common. Sleep problems are also worth noting. Drugs and alcohol disrupt the quality of sleep so that a person complains of fatigue or of never feeling rested despite getting a good night's sleep. Gamblers often have leg problems from prolonged sitting.

Difficulty getting a clear picture of the problem or making progress in therapy can be a subtle sign. When reports of depression, anxiety, and/or a variety of physical ailments (especially head and stomach problems) have no explanation, the psychotherapist should be alert to the possibility that there is an addiction. Similarly, the therapist should become curious when a new patient enters treatment expressing a strong desire to change, to make things different in his or her life, and yet there is little or no progress. What appears to be a resistance to change can be the result of an unrecognized addiction.

Summary

Psychotherapy patients are unlikely to enter treatment reporting an addiction or recognizing that behaviors at risk of becoming addictive are creating the problems that bring them to treatment. In other cases, an addiction may develop over the course of treatment as a patient uses a substance or excessive behavior to avoid or manage feelings that are surfacing during treatment. For these reasons, it is important that psychotherapists remain attuned to subtle signs of addiction throughout therapy. No one sign is indicative of a problem. Sleep disturbances, lowered moods, or fights with a spouse have many different origins. However, as subtle signs begin to accumulate, it is imperative that the psychotherapist explores the possibility of an addiction through questions in a session or by using a screening instrument.

SUBTLE INTERVIEWING TECHNIQUES

Some psychotherapists will be uncomfortable asking directly about addictive behaviors out of concern that the patient will experience such questioning as a criticism or insult. One participant, in the study presented earlier on why psychotherapists do not assess for addictions, reported that when she began working with a divorced woman whose ex-husband had been an alcoholic, she wondered if the patient had an alcohol problem too. The therapist was hesitant to ask directly about the quantity and frequency of alcohol consumption because of the woman's venomous degradation of her drunken ex-spouse. The therapist feared that the patient would interpret such questions as implying that she was a drunk as well. While this imagined outcome most likely reflects the therapist's discomfort about assessing for an addiction, there are a number of less transparent questions that elicit information about addictive behaviors. Some possible questions that help uncover substance or process addictions are:

- What do you do after work?
- What do you do for pleasure?
- How do you have a good time?
- Have you ever behaved in a way that was not consistent with your value system?
- Has there ever been a time that you did something that you regretted later?
- Are there certain days/times when you find it hard to follow through on your responsibilities?
- How often have you failed to do what is expected of you?
- How do you relax? How do you cope with stress?
- Follow a patient's reference to a trauma or stressful situation with the question: How do you cope or deal with that situation?

Asking questions that expose the motivations or reasons for a behavior are very revealing when it comes to identifying an addiction or at risk behaviors. Most people who use substances do so in order to be sociable, conform to group norms, or, on occasion, as a way to relax. However, research repeatedly shows that those who routinely drink or use drugs in order to avoid feelings such as anxiety, depression, stress, or fear are more likely to develop an addiction (Cooper, Frone, Russell, and Mudar 1995; Fouquereau et al. 2003). The significance of motivation for predicting substance abuse and dependence has been addressed by Boys and Marsden (2003). These researchers assessed whether adverse consequences, negative effects, or the function of substance use best predicted patterns of use among younger users. Across five different substances, intensity of use was best predicted by the participants' perception that substance use served to relieve negative mood states.

Behaviors that serve the function of eliminating, avoiding, or moderating negative affective states also have greater potential to become addictive. Excessive buying behavior has been shown to be a way of alleviating depression and other distressing affects. The moods of addictive shoppers are more likely to change from negative to positive after shopping while normal shoppers show the opposite pattern (Faber and Christenson 1996). Likewise, those who indicated that the computer was a means for relieving anxiety or tension were more likely to be dependent than those who reported more neutral or less affective reasons for computer use (Orzack and Ross 2000).

Based on the idea that an addiction serves a self-medicating or mood-altering function, one can ask some of the questions listed above that elicit information about how the patient copes with stress and other specific emotional states. Or one can ask directly about how the patient feels after the behavior. How do you feel after three drinks? After buying those new clothes?

Research shows that expected outcomes may be as strong a predictor of addictive behaviors as actual outcomes (Jones, Corbin, and Fromme 2001). Adolescents who expect alcohol consumption to be a positive experience are more likely to become drinkers. Thus, if the therapist suspects a behavior may be problematic, he or she can ask the patient, "What do you expect will happen after you _____?" where the blank is filled in with a specific behavior (i.e., drink, shop, gamble). What outcomes do you expect from exercising? From smoking marijuana? Even if a current behavior is nonproblematic, if the patient expects it to moderate mood states and/or artificially enhance positive outcomes, then the therapist should remain attentive to any increase in that behavior's occurrence.

Another indirect method for bringing the topic of addictions into therapy is to show interest when a patient refers to the substance use or addiction of a significant other (Evans 1998). The patient can be asked to describe this person's use with the questioning designed to elicit as much detail as possible. If the patient shows any significant emotional or behavioral changes during this discussion, then the therapist can speculate about these changes and what they mean to the patient. Even if the patient does not have overt reactions, the therapist's neutral and even-handed inquiry about another person's addictive behavior will help the patient to feel more confidence and less shame about discussing his or her use.

Patients' knowledge about their addictive behavior can differ dramatically for those seeking addiction treatment as compared to psychotherapy. Most persons who enter treatment for an addiction have been struggling for years with the impact of their excessive behavior. This is less likely to be the case for patients coming for psychotherapy. Quite often, I find that psychotherapy patients have not thought much about their excessive behavior and whether it is problematic. Continued questioning can help the therapist and patient decide together if there is a potential problem. If a behavior seems to be occurring in an excessive manner, there is one follow-up question I have found very useful: *How much enjoyment or pleasure do you get from the substance or behavior?*

The value of this question is illustrated in the case of a man who recently came to see me for problems achieving his professional goals. In the process of talking about his home life, he let it be known that he had trouble sleeping and would stay up late, after his wife went to bed, "having some beer." When asked how much beer, he guessed that he consumed between four and eight beers on most occasions. He expressed surprise at how he responded when asked, "How much do you enjoy drinking alone like this?" Before being asked this question, he had not realized how long it had been since he enjoyed drinking. Until that moment, he held on to memories of hanging out with the guys in college and enjoying the special comradery that came with having a few beers. This realization led to further explorations into his desire to drink and his increasing lack of control over alcohol. For others, I have found that this question stays with them and they will come back later to report how they no longer enjoy the substance or behavior and are conflicted about continuing its use.

This was the case for a middle-aged man who dealt with feelings of loneliness by going shopping and spending money. While he had sufficient money to spend, he found himself with lots of shirts and shoes that he never wore. When first asked if he enjoyed shopping, he readily replied in the affirmative. But the question stayed with him and he began to recognize that he usually went shopping when his wife was away on business; being in the company of sales people, who were helping him, temporarily relieved him of feeling alone. While he enjoyed shopping for this reason, he realized he did not enjoy buying. He bought to relieve the guilt he felt for taking up the sales person's time. These reflections provided the opportunity to discuss alternative means to manage these different feelings.

If information from the clinical interview suggests that substance use is occurring in a problematic or addictive manner, then a more thorough and systematic assessment is warranted. The MAST, AUDIT, or SASSI-3 can be administered or if one wishes, further information can be gathered in the therapy through the use of more direct questioning and Shea's validity techniques (1999) described below. A thorough inquiry will collect information about frequency, quantity, and maximum amount consumed on any one occasion. Other information that will be relevant in treatment planning includes the context of use (alone, with friends, at home, in a bar), the experience of use (is it always pleasurable?), and its consequences (e.g., legal, health, social, or work-related problems). Chapter 10 provides a more elaborate description of the assessment process.

FACE-VALID APPROACHES TO INTERVIEWING

It is easy to modify questions from the CAGE, TICS, or other screening tools and incorporate these into a clinical interview. In order to do this, clinicians need to be familiar with these screening tools so that questions can be modified and asked at the appropriate moment. In the process of describing his experiences on a blind date, a patient reports drinking more than usual. In addition to exploring the feelings behind his excess drinking on this occasion, a therapist can ask a number of other questions that draw from screening tools: Have you ever felt bad about your drinking? Has your drinking ever created a problem in a relationship? For process addictions, one only needs to change the behavior. A woman reports a weekend of long-distance biking that has left her legs so sore that she is finding it hard to walk. Some questions that help determine if this is part of an exercise addiction would be: Do you ever find that once you start biking that it is hard to stop? Recently, have you failed to do what was expected of you because you were biking long distance? Do you ever feel like you should cut down on your exercising?

If a patient is talking about a party from the previous weekend where he woke up with a hangover, a question from the TICS can be used: Are there other times that you have used more drugs and/or alcohol than you meant to? Have you ever felt guilt or remorse after drinking? Or one can ask directly about degree of use. A women reports being upset about a fight she had with her husband on the way home from a long dinner with friends. This may be a pattern—fights on the way home after socializing. Inquiring about the degree of alcohol consumption is warranted. As most know, it is not recommended to ask a yes-or-no question such as "Did you drink that night?" Given that some use is normative, instead ask, "How much did you drink over dinner?" or simply state, "Tell me about your drinking that night."

Most psychotherapists working in clinic settings are required to ask about substance use, but regretfully they do so in a perfunctory manner without following up on an answer such as, "Oh, just a couple of drinks on the weekend." Clinical wisdom recommends that one never stop the inquiry at this point. A couple of drinks regularly on a weekend may hide a binge drinker. Binge drinking is defined as at least five drinks for men and four for women on a single occasion within a two-week period (see the section on late adolescence in chapter 8). The meaning of "a drink" can vary greatly. For one patient, his reference to a beer was actually a six-pack. A glass of wine can be in a juice glass or a jelly jar. It is even worth asking what defines "a weekend." For some, weekends start on Thursday evening and don't end until Monday. The importance of doing a careful inquiry is reflected in one physician's experience with a patient who unexpectedly began to seizure postoperatively. The chart dutifully noted that the patient had two alcoholic drinks a day. However, a follow-up with family members revealed that these two daily drinks were glasses of vodka sipped from a beer stein. Given that alcohol dependence is associated with life-threatening withdrawal symptoms, any suspicion of abuse or dependence must be followed by an assessment of the frequency, amount, and, especially important, the length of time between drinking episodes. A patient who can go twenty-four hours or more without a drink is unlikely to experience severe withdrawal.

The AUDIT and Quantity/Frequency Questionnaire follow the practices of a good substance use assessment by inquiring about both quantity (usual and maximum) and frequency. However, it is important to remember that the quantity consumed is more revealing than the frequency of use. This is because frequency of substance use is greatly influenced by social factors. The college student who belongs to a fraternity or the businessman whose job involves taking clients to dinner has many opportunities to drink. But how much is consumed on any given occasion is more individually determined. The college student who drinks each weekend to the point of passing out is more likely to have a binge drinking problem than one who drinks every weekend but rarely exceeds two or three drinks. Likewise, the businessman who has two or three martinis over dinner is a very different kind of drinker from the man who sips on one. Even if the response to "How much do you drink?" is "I don't," a more thorough inquiry is warranted. Given that alcohol consumption is a normative behavior in this society, a patient's reference to not drinking should be followed by a brief investigation into why. The patient perhaps has had a personal history with alcoholism, there is involvement with some substance or behavior other than alcohol, or a family member or significant other is struggling with addiction.

VALIDITY TECHNIQUES

Whether the focus is on substance-based or process addictions, the previous subtle and direct clinical interview questions help to establish the possibility that a behavior pattern fits the characteristics of an addiction or is at risk of becoming addictive. To further identify and clarify the scope of a problem, other questions need to be asked. To this end, validity techniques are an effective means of yielding extensive information that, with one exception, requires a minimal amount of direct questioning.

Hidden addictions are not the only type of problem that adversely impacts a patient's well-being and treatment outcome. Suicidal ideation, criminal behavior, or a history of sexual abuse, like addictions, are sensitive topics that patients do not report on readily. If acknowledged, descriptions of these concerns are often lacking in detail and accuracy. Recognizing that certain topics are challenging for patients to fully discuss, Shawn Christopher Shea (1999, chapter 5) developed what he refers to as validity techniques. These six general interviewing principles are designed to elicit accurate and detailed clinical data while circumventing discomfort: (1) gentle assumptions, (2) denial of the specific, (3) shame attenuation, (4) normalization, (5) behavioral incident questions, and (6) symptom amplification. Used as needed, validity techniques help the therapist and patient develop a comprehensive picture of the problem.

Gentle assumptions are already a component of a good addiction assessment interview. With gentle assumptions, the psychotherapist begins with the supposition that the problematic behavior is occurring and then asks a question reflecting this theory. Given that alcohol is a socially normative behavior, unless otherwise informed, a clinician assumes the patient does drink. Instead of wondering, "Do you drink?" the patient is asked, "How much do you drink?" Whether the behavior is normative or not, questions informed by gentle assumptions are asked in a way that conveys that a positive reply is expected and acceptable. Thus, after a patient mentions having smoked marijuana over the weekend, the therapist can ask in a matter-of-fact tone, "What other street drugs have you used?" A patient who angrily reports an arrest for driving under the influence of alcohol (DUI) can be asked, "How many other times have the police stopped you after you were drinking?" Chapter 4 explained why psychotherapists avoid asking about addictive behavior out of concern that a patient will feel criticized by a question that implies an addiction. Shea (1999) suggests that if a therapist has such concerns, then a phrase such as "if at all" can be added to make the assumption even more gentle. "How much time do you spend looking at pornography on the Internet, if at all?" "How much money have you lost gambling, if you gamble at all?"

Another technique for facilitating discussion of sensitive topics is denial of the specific. Denial of the specific is a variant of gentle assumption questions. Shea (1999) argues that it is easier to deny a behavior when it is described in a generic rather than a specific manner. One only needs to recall President Clinton's denial of having had sex with Monica Lewinsky to see the value of asking more specific questions. With denial of the specific, when a patient responds with a "no" to the question "Do you use any street drugs?" then the therapist begins to inquire about specific substances (e.g., Have you tried heroin? Have you snorted cocaine?). It is not significant whether the initial "no" reflects the truth, is a function denial, or the patient's interpretation of the question (in this case, what defines a "street drug") because in the end the technique circumvents the problem no matter its origin. Another occasion when denial of the specific is useful occurs when a patient acknowledges a close connection between drinking and socializing and the clinician wants to probe for any negative consequences. A generic question, such as those asked on screening instruments (e.g., Have you ever had any adverse effects from your drinking?), may yield less information than questions that include reference to a specific context or consequence. "When drinking at last Saturday's party, did you ever say something or do something you later regretted?" "Have you ever had sex when drinking and later wished you had not?" "Last night, when you used the computer, did you do so for a longer time than intended?" There is one caveat when using gentle assumptions and denial of the specific: the therapist must be familiar with the topic. For example, asking an adolescent about specific drugs without knowing the current street names for the different drugs will tarnish the interview (see appendix A).

As previously discussed, the defense mechanism of denial, when not a function of unconscious processes, can be a conscious attempt to manage shame (chapter 4). The third validity technique is designed to attenuate shame. In this method, questions are asked in a way that does not leave a patient feeling guilty or like a bad person when answering in the affirmative. Successful use of shame attenuation requires that the therapist understand or empathize with the patient's source of discomfort and then ask questions in a nonaccusatory manner. When a man enters therapy reporting extreme anxiety over financial pressures, yet his lifestyle should be easily covered by his income, a therapist may suspect there is an addiction. By using a shame attenuation technique, the therapist begins by letting the patient know that he or she empathizes with this man's wish to be a good provider for his family and the importance he places on providing financial security. Within this accepting context the therapist then asks, "Given the financial stress you are under, I wouldn't be surprised if it is hard to relax. How often have you taken a drink to manage these feelings?" Note that this example includes a gentle assumption (i.e., there is an addictive behavior), but this gentle assumption is preceded by a few sentences conveying the therapist's understanding of the motivations for the problematic behavior without condoning the behavior itself.

A fourth validity technique is called normalization. Where shame attenuation focuses on the patient's experience, normalization places the patient's experience in the context of how other people behave or feel. Normalization works because it too lessens feelings of shame surrounding a particular behavior, thus making denial or distortion less necessary. In this technique, the therapist introduces a question by first indicating that others have shared the patient's feelings and/or behavior. Shea (1999) provides several examples of normalization statements which begin with phrases such as, "Sometimes when people are . . . " "A fair number of my patients have told me . . . " "Clients often tell me that sometimes . . . " One complete example: "Sometimes when people are under a lot of stress, they just can't seem to find a way to relax, so they decide to have a drink but end up drinking more than they intended. Has that ever happened to you?"

These four validity techniques help the patient feel safe to reveal sensitive material. The other two validity techniques are directed at obtaining a better sense of the problem's scope.

There is more room for patients' personal needs and interpretations to intervene when they are asked about beliefs and opinions as opposed to a description of what happened in a certain situation. The validity technique known as behavioral incident questions involves asking for identifiable behaviors or thoughts at a specified time and in a defined context. Shea (1999) delineates two forms of behavioral incident questions. The first asks directly and in a nonevaluative manner about the details of a specific behavior. If the clinician has gleaned from the session that alcohol was involved in an incident the patient reports, then he or she begins to ask for details. "How many beers did you have before you and your wife got into that fight?" Asking about facts is very different from asking for an opinion: "Do you think that beer contributed to the fight?" Suspecting an exercise addiction is creating frequent injuries, a psychotherapist would not ask, "Do you think your exercise is the cause?" Rather, a therapist might simply ask for some descriptive information, "How many miles had you run on the day you noticed this injury?"

The second type of behavioral incident inquiry involves continuous questioning about exact events in order to reveal as much information as possible. "Where is your computer? What happened when you first logged on? What happened next? How did you find that pornographic site?" Again it is better to ask about facts than opinions. Instead of asking, "Did you plan to buy cocaine Wednesday evening from X?" one's inquiry would contain a series of specific questions: "Where did you meet X? How did you know X was there?

Where were you and what were you feeling when you made the phone call?" Asking for specifics makes the incident more alive, brings back more of the details of what happened and cuts through the distortions of more general recall. As Shea (1999) notes, the drawback of behavioral incident questions is that they are time consuming.

Symptoms amplification is another validity technique for acquiring accurate information about a behavior and its frequency. In this practice, the clinician sets a level of behavior that will be in excess of the patient's actual behavior. As a result, the patient's response minimizes the therapist's suggestion. "How much do you drink in a night—a six-pack, two six-packs, a case?" "When you go shopping, how often do you spend more than two thousand dollars in a day?" The patient may reply, "I never spend that much, more like five hundred to a thousand." The success of this technique depends on the therapists having some sense of the scope of the patient's excesses. Also, as with gentle assumptions, the therapist needs to have some knowledge about how drugs are used and how much is considered a lot. Asking a patient, "So, you did a pound of cocaine last night?" will be met with disbelief.

SUMMARY

There are many approaches to addiction assessment from which to choose. Some psychotherapists will routinely assess for addictions. A few may use toxicology screens, but more often assessment will involve self-administered instruments and/or questions that are incorporated into the clinical session. Two of the more valuable pieces of information concern the degree of pleasure currently being derived from the behavior and the motivation or reasons for the behavior. Other psychotherapists prefer to ask questions about leisure time and coping mechanisms that, while not asking directly about an addictive behavior, can be equally informative. Finally, others will ask no questions at all until there is evidence that some behavior may be occurring excessively. The problem here is that a patient consciously or unconsciously may make no mention of addiction-related behaviors. In such cases, the addiction is likely to go unrecognized unless the clinician is aware of the subtle signs that emerge in the clinical dialogue.

8

Addiction Assessment with Diverse Populations

Who is more likely to become addicted? Men or women? The elderly or adolescents? African Americans, Caucasians, or Hispanics? The answers depend on which addiction you have in mind.

Alcohol is the most commonly used, socially accepted substance to which one can become addicted. Among all addictions, psychotherapists are most likely to treat patients who have problems related to alcohol consumption. For this reason, this chapter reviews the literature on the impact of gender, age, and race on assessment of alcohol use. Implications of diversity for assessing other types of substance-based addictions are discussed more briefly. What little is known about individual differences in process addictions was addressed in chapter 6.

Gender, age, and race all have a role to play in who is most likely to develop an addiction and how symptoms of alcohol and drug addictions are manifest in psychotherapy. The significance of group membership for the assessment process is reflected in the burgeoning number of studies that examine how the sensitivity of alcohol screening instruments varies as a function of group membership. In light of these differences, assessment tools designed for specific populations have been developed. These screening instruments will be discussed along with strategies for making a clinical interview assessment more effective for patients from each group.

GENDER DIFFERENCES

Common across all age groups and nationalities, more men than women experience problems related to alcohol consumption. Recent statistics indicate that the gap may be closing in the United States where adolescent girls' experimentation with alcohol is equal to boys'. However, so far, this effect has not been translated into a greater incidence of abuse and dependence for women. In the general population of the United States, which includes college age and young adults, men remain two to three times more likely to be diagnosed with alcoholism (Wilsnack, Vogeltanz, Wilsnack, and Harris 2000). When it comes to drug use, women also make up a smaller percentage.

Health care providers' diagnostic practices may contribute to this gender bias. Among physicians, only 6 percent recognized alcohol abuse in a clinical vignette, but recognition rates varied greatly by gender. When the hypothetical patient was male, alcoholism was recognized by 8.2 percent of the physicians, and when the hypothetic patient was female, only 1.6 percent recognized alcoholism (The National Center on Addiction and Substance Abuse at Columbia University 2000). Similarly, medical and mental health providers inquire about drinking behavior significantly less often with their woman patients (Weisner and Matzger 2003). Pediatricians who work with teenagers have a much better rate of recognition (59 percent), but there is still a gender gap. When the hypothetical patient was a boy, substance use was recognized by 64 percent of the physicians compared to 51 percent when a girl (The National Center on Addiction and Substance Abuse at Columbia University 2000).

Given that women's substance addictions are often overlooked, gender differences in prevalence rates are likely overestimated. There are a number of factors that contribute to the underdiagnosis of alcoholism in women. The negative consequences of substance use, which form the primary basis for making a diagnosis, are more consistent with male experience. Women are less likely than men to experience adverse legal and financial consequences associated with substance abuse. In the case of alcohol, men encounter the legal system when arrested for a DUI. Women have fewer DUIs because they are less likely to drink and drive. They often drink at home alone or, if socializing as a married couple, the man is more commonly behind the wheel. Another reason the gender gap is overestimated is because the prevalence data come from the census at addiction treatment centers where fewer women seek treatment; they compose only about one quarter of the population. Instead of going to alcohol treatment centers, women with drinking problems are more likely to use other health care services—especially mental health services (Wasilow-Mueller and Erickson 2001).

Understanding the reasons why women are more likely to seek treatment in mental health settings provides information that can facilitate more effective assessment. First, relative to men, women suffer more often from co-morbid addiction and mental illness, especially depression. This difference does not simply mirror women's greater incidence of depression in the general population. While male alcoholics are as likely to be diagnosed with depression as men who are not alcoholic, the rate of depression is higher for women who are alcoholic than those who are not (Hesselbrock and Hesselbrock 1997). The connection between depression and substance use also differs for men and women. Women's depression and anxiety are more likely to precede alcohol dependence, while men's depression develops after the addiction. Further evidence for a close link between depression and alcoholism in women is indicated by the high incidence of women who, well into sobriety, continue to experience symptoms of depression. What this means for women is that their depression and anxiety symptoms will be more longstanding and have greater salience than their more recent drinking behavior. From this vantage point, it makes sense to seek help at a mental health care setting. In contrast, for men, psychological symptoms are more often secondary to the addiction.

Another reason woman with addictions seek out mental health treatment is that they fail to attribute their distress to addiction. Clinicians who treat women are in danger of making the same mistake. As noted, women's symptoms do not fit the typical pattern of adverse legal, monetary, and social problems more common among men and more consistent with the image of an alcoholic. Not surprisingly, negative consequences for women are frequently interpersonal in nature involving conflicts with family and friends. Adverse effects on health, both physical and emotional, also are prevalent (Wilke 1994). As little as two drinks a day increases the risk of an early death, liver disease, and breast cancer (Bradley et al. 1998). As a result, assessment tools that focus on behavioral consequences or define safe drinking based on male norms will underestimate the severity of a woman's problem or miss the problem altogether.

Clinicians who prefer to gather information about addictions from the clinical dialogue can miss signs of alcoholism in their female patients if they are not attuned to the gender differences in alcohol-related symptoms. Milly's presentation in psychotherapy provides a good example of how easy it is to miss alcohol problems.

Milly, a casually dressed twenty-seven year old came to therapy reporting problems sleeping and feeling rested. She had a poor appetite and generally felt she was having a hard time coping. Her husband, concerned about these changes and upset by her angry outbursts, had strongly encouraged her to get some help. He was currently being treated in an outpatient alcohol rehabilitation program after being arrested for his second DUI. They had two children, ages two and four. Milly did not work outside the home, but she kept busy tending to their household. She was feeling more stressed since her husband began treatment. Where he once helped her in the evenings, now that he attended his treatment program every night, she complained bitterly of having little time for herself or her friends.

Milly's presenting problem contains a number of classic signs of depression, and it would seem a simple matter to accept this as the central issue to work on in therapy. However, her symptoms, most of which can be a consequence of substance use (her difficulty coping, her problems sleeping, and her husband's drinking history [see below]) suggest that her substance use should be assessed.

I began by asking questions about her husband's recent changes. Did she previously drink with him? She did. What was it like to have a husband who no longer drinks? She acknowledged missing their time together but was adamant about not missing the ensuing fights. Her main complaints since he stopped drinking were that he was busy evenings and they had little time for each other. When I asked how she coped with the extra stress she was under, Milly became rather vague and provided no specific ways in which she relaxed other than to say that it helped to get together with friends, although she emphasized that there were few opportunities to do so. When asked what she missed about her get together with friends, she hesitated but then revealed that one of the pleasures was having a drink in the afternoon. When asked how much she was currently drinking, she acknowledged keeping a few small bottles of vodka hidden in her purse, which she drank as way to relax while the children took a nap or to help her sleep at night.

Another gender difference to keep in mind is that the quantity of liquor that qualifies as low-risk drinking differs for men and women. For women, low-risk drinking is defined as one drink per day, no more than two drinks on any one occasion, and no more than seven drinks a week. Women's lower ratio of water to blood is one explanation for this difference. Given that alcohol is water soluble, a woman will have a higher blood alcohol level (BAL) than a man after consuming the same amount. A dangerous BAL will thus be reached more quickly (Becker and Walton-Moss 2001).

The incidence of alcoholism is highest for thirty-five to forty-nine-year-old women (Becker and Walton-Moss 2001), although drinking levels should always be assessed for pregnant patients or patients who express plans to become pregnant. Early detection at any age is especially important for female patients. While women start drinking later in life than men, the progression from drinking regularly without a problem to being substance dependent occurs at an accelerated rate. Early detection and intervention can derail this process.

In terms of subtle signs of addiction, there are two that, if present in a woman's life, indicate a direct screening for addictions is warranted. The first is a history of childhood sexual abuse. Seventy percent of women being treated for an addiction have this history. In mental health settings, among women diagnosed with PTSD, 30 percent to 40 percent have a coexisting addiction problem (Brems and Johnson 1997; Wasilow-Mueller and Erickson 2001).

A second subtle clue is the substance use of a patient's partner. Milly's marriage to an alcoholic is not that unusual for a woman with her own alcohol use problems. Alcoholics are likely to be married to other alcoholics. In some cases, the relationship is a function of two people with similar drinking patterns getting married. In other cases, this effect is due to one partner's drinking pattern influencing the other partner. Marriage has a more profound effect on women's drinking than on men's. In marriage, a wife's alcohol consumption mimics her husband's, but a wife's consumption level does not influence her husband's (Leonard and Mudar 2003). Thus, the clinician should take note when a female patient reports excessive substance use by her significant other. Her own drinking may already be excessive or the assessment process may serve a preventive role by making her less susceptible to her spouse's drinking pattern. Exploration of a couple's alcohol consumption is especially important for recently married women who plan to have children. Although current drinking may be minimal, a gradual increase in drinking can pose a danger to the fetus by the time she becomes pregnant. For men, friendship, not marriage, can be a subtle sign of addiction. Because male friends and acquaintances influence men's drinking patterns (Leonard and Mudar 2003), clinicians should consider asking about a male patient's substance use when he reports frequent socializing where heavy drinking plays a central role.

Among one group of male alcoholics, there is a high genetic loading for alcoholism: these men usually have alcoholic fathers, began drinking at a young age, and exhibited antisocial behavior in adolescence. They drink for alcohol's mood altering and stimulating effects. Cloninger (1987) refers to this group as Type 2 alcoholics. Type 1 alcoholics are equally common among men and women. Their alcoholism is less severe with a later onset and better prognosis. Type 1 alcoholics are more likely to drink as a way of coping rather than for its mood altering effects.

The attributes of Type 1 and Type 2 alcoholics have been shown to generalize to drug users. Evolving out of Cloninger's work, Babor (Babor et al. 1992) has used statistical means to develop a typology that describes two distinct patterns of substance use. Type A individuals, like Cloninger's Type 1, have a later onset of abuse, fewer negative consequences, and a better prognosis. Environmental factors are of greater etiological significance than genetics in the development of Type A addictions. Type B individuals are similar to Cloninger's Type 2 alcoholics; they have an earlier onset of addiction-related problems, poorer prognosis, and a history of familial addiction, which is most apparent on the paternal side. Men are equally as likely to belong to Type A or B, while women are more common to the Type A group.

While the consistency with which substance abusers can be classified into one of these two typologies has been called into question (Sannibale and Hall 1998), the attributes belonging to each typology remain informative risk factors. When a patient's behavior or history fits any of the criteria of Cloninger's Type 2 or Barbor's Type B (i.e., familial substance use problems, male gender, early onset of problem drinking, and antisocial attributes), the clinician should directly explore the patient's relationship to addictive substances. Doing so is crucial for this group given that early intervention can prevent development of more severe forms of addiction and thus improve the prognosis.

Gender-Based Assessment Practices

Diagnostic criteria for substance-related disorders contain a gender bias. Screening instruments have incorporated this bias in two ways: (1) the negative consequences that define abuse and dependence are more descriptive for men than women, and (2) scales that assess for quantity of alcohol consumption (e.g., AUDIT) have not always taken into account women's lower response threshold to alcohol. Thus, it is not surprising to find that most scales are more accurate in recognizing problematic substance use in men than in women (Cherpital 1997).

In an extensive review of research on the sensitivity and specificity of alcohol screening questionnaires, Bradley et al. (1998) observed that when using traditional cutoff scores, the CAGE, AUDIT, and TWEAK are better at identifying abuse and dependence in black women than in white women. They concluded that, for optimal identification of alcohol problems for all women, cutoff scores need to be modified. They recommend that "reasonable cutoff points are 2 or more for the TWEAK questionnaire, 4 points or more for the AUDIT questionnaire, and 1 point or more for the CAGE questionnaire"(Bradley et al. 1998, 170).

As an alternative to modifying cutoff scores, a screening tool was developed that takes into account the fact that women's alcoholism is strongly affected by relationships, and that negative consequences are more likely to occur in their interpersonal world. The 5 P's Scale for Women's Alcohol Problems is a modification of the 4 P's that was originally developed for use with pregnant women (Center for Substance Abuse Treatment 2004; Washington State Department of Health 2002).

1. Do your *parents* have a problem with alcohol?
2. Have you had a *partner* who had a problem with alcohol?
3. Do you have *peers* (friends) who have problems with alcohol?
4. Have you used alcohol in the *past?*
5. Has anyone ever told you that you had a *problem* with alcohol?

Positive responses to three or more items are indicative of an alcohol problem. The 4 P's version omits questions 3 and 5 and includes a question that asks directly about pregnancy and alcohol use: Have you ever used drugs or alcohol during this *pregnancy?* In the 4 P's version, any positive response requires further assessment.

When assessing for alcoholism, the clinician needs to take into account the markedly distinct social norms surrounding what defines acceptable drinking behavior for men and women. Men go out and drink together; drinking and getting drunk is something men can do without necessarily meeting social disapproval. In contrast, a woman can drink moderately in social situations, but once substance use exceeds moderation and appears out of control, her behavior is met with intense social disapproval. This means that compared to a man, a woman is prone to feel greater shame about substance use problems.

Feelings of shame can contribute to a woman not acknowledging an addiction to herself or others. When conducting an addiction assessment, the clinician will want to intervene in a manner that ensures that shame is not accentuated. Shame attenuation and normalization techniques discussed in chapter 7 are useful in this context. Normalization, as an interview technique, can counteract the negative norms associated with a woman's drinking by placing it in the context of how other's feel and behave. Through normalization, the therapist lets a patient know that she is not alone by incorporating a phrase such as "A number of women patients have told me." With shame attenuation, the interviewer conveys empathy for the patient's intentions and needs while not condoning the behavior. For example, if a patient drinks in order to cope, the clinician would empathize with her feeling overwhelmed with all her responsibilities and desire to take a break and leave all tension behind. These reflections could be followed by an intervention that combines normalization with a gentle assumption. "When a woman in your situation finally gets a break, it is not unusual to find herself drinking more than expected (normalization). When did this happen to you (gentle assumption)?"

ADDICTION ASSESSMENT AT DIFFERENT LIFE STAGES

Adolescence

Alcohol, cigarettes, and marijuana are the substances most often used by adolescents. The frequency of use is high; among twelfth graders, 50 percent have used alcohol, 33 percent have consumed alcohol to the point of being drunk, and 23 percent have smoked marijuana in the past month (Johnston, O'Malley, and Bachman 2003). Most adolescents who experiment with drugs and alcohol will not develop a substance use disorder; ultimately 6 to 13 percent will.

Relative to adult populations, health care providers seem to be more attuned to an adolescent's addictive or at-risk behaviors. Where only 6 percent of physicians recognized signs of alcohol abuse in a vignette describing an adult patient, 59 percent of pediatricians saw substance abuse as a potential diagnosis when

Chapter 8

the patient in the vignette was a teenager. Signs of substance abuse included red eyes, frequent sore throats and runny noses, headaches, fatigue, loss of appetite, loss of interest in school, and worsening relationships with parents (The National Center on Addiction and Substance Abuse at Columbia University 2000). While over half the physicians correctly attributed these signs to alcohol abuse, 40 percent did not. Even if mental health care providers are similarly attuned to substance use in their adolescent patients, this leaves a dangerously high percentage of patients whose addiction will not be recognized.

Assessment of addictions can be more challenging with adolescents than adults. Few middle and high school students volunteer information about their use of drugs and alcohol. Upon direct questioning, an adolescent may divulge drinking some alcohol, trying a bit of marijuana, or smoking a few cigarettes. Some would argue that any substance use by this age group is abuse, especially if it involves an illegal substance such as marijuana. The DSM-IV does not take this position; adolescent substance use is evaluated on the same criteria as adult use. However, when treating adolescents, a provider will want to address substance use before it becomes sufficiently problematic as to meet diagnostic criteria. How is substance use most effectively approached with an adolescent who drinks a beer or two with friends and takes a few puffs of marijuana now and then when it is offered? What distinguishes normative experimentation from problematic use? If use is normative now, what determines if it will become problematic?

The ambiguity around distinguishing normal from problematic use, which complicates adult addiction assessment (chapter 6), is even more apparent with an adolescent population. The topic can be further clouded by a psychotherapist having gone through his or her own adolescent experimentation with drugs and alcohol without experiencing any long-term consequences. Other therapists will struggle with competently discussing their patients' experimentation when, in their own homes, they have been ineffective in handling their children's explorations with drugs and alcohol.

Recognizing these potential sources of countertransference feelings should help clinicians from underreacting (or overreacting) to an adolescent patient's substance use. At a minimum, psychotherapists should understand that what was age appropriate in the past carries far more dangers with it today. The range of drugs has expanded and is available to patients at a younger age (e.g., see below regarding the proliferation of heroin use in suburban settings). Negative consequences of substance use are expanding and becoming more harmful (e.g., unprotected sex while intoxicated and use of needles that spread HIV).

Increased accessibility, especially to "harder" substances, greatly enhances the chance of developing a substance addiction. Where the course from regular use to full dependence takes two to seven years for an adult, the course is condensed for adolescents. The route to full dependence can occur in as little as twelve to eighteen months. Separate from the possible long-term consequences, the psychotherapist will want to attend to any immediate dangers linked to current substance use, such as accidents, risky behavior, and violence. In light of harmful consequence and the speed with which an addiction can develop, all substance use by an adolescent should be discussed in therapy. Early and accurate detection can prevent immediate problems and/or circumvent a full-fledged addiction from developing.

While therapists can feel uncertain about how best to approach adolescent drug use, an adolescent patient will have no such doubt. From an adolescent's viewpoint, drug use is normal; they drink and use drugs for social reasons— their friends do it. Simply asking about what substances are taken and in what quantity can be enough for the young patient to suspect that the therapist is a critical and moralizing figure. Any suspected criticism may be dismissed with remarks such as, "A lot of kids drink when we go out. Is being sociable a problem?" Given that adolescence is a time of life when adult authority is suspect, a psychotherapist who responds to such comments by teaching about the dangers of substances will be ignored (wisely, DARE and other prevention programs designed to educate students about drugs begin in the earlier grades).

Although grade school prevention programs have exposed most adolescents to the risks associated with drugs and alcohol, they do not necessarily link these risks to their current behavior. In one study, nine out of ten sixteen- to nineteen-year-olds, who were classified on the AUDIT as hazardous drinkers, did not recognize the hazardous consequences of their drinking (Miles, Winstock, and Strang 2001). Instead of teaching about the general consequences of drug use, the psychotherapist's assessment will be more effective if the process facilitates the creation of memories that link an adolescent's substance use to its current consequences. This process begins with an open discussion of the adolescent's experience on drugs. For the patient who is hesitant to acknowledge personal use, a good first step is to talk about what happens when friends use substances. If the patient does not spontaneously begin to link substance use to adverse effects, then the therapist can gently begin to make these connections. In this way, the adolescent patient begins to link the abstract notions of risk that were learned in school to the actual effects of his or her current intake of alcohol and drugs.

Some typical substance induced problems for this age group include acting out of character; reckless behavior, such as driving under the influence or unprotected sex; carelessness leading to physical injuries; and acting in a way that is later regretted, such as regrets about one's sexual behavior and unsuccessful attempts to avoid peer pressure. For the adolescent who insists that using substances is equivalent to being social, substance use outside a social context (e.g., when home alone) is a significant warning sign that merits further discussion. By the time experimentation turns into abuse, adverse consequences, if not apparent to oneself, will be apparent to others. Parents will bring their child for treatment expressing concerns about declining school performance, changes in peer relationships (e.g., friends no longer visit the home or the new peer group is suspected of using drugs), large periods of time that are unaccounted for, or increased conflicts at home that can involve physical acting out. Less apparent to parents are changes in health (e.g., coughs, reports of flu-like symptoms, and an increased susceptibility to illness). Parents may or may not be aware that their concerns are a consequence of substance abuse.

An adult who fails to recognize that adverse effects are signs of addiction is said to be in denial. It is a mistake to interpret the adolescent's apparent lack of concern as denial. Unlike adults, an adolescent's rapid course from experimentation to addiction and relatively brief history of substance use makes it more difficult to recognize that adverse consequences are reliably connected to the addictive behavior. Further contributing to the adolescent's insistence that adults are overreacting is that he or she has not had a protracted history of unsuccessful attempts to stop the behavior.

The following example illustrates how to help prevent development of an addiction by fostering a connection between substance use and its consequences.

On Saturdays, Jason, a fourteen-year-old awkward adolescent boy goes to the park to hang out with his guy friends. One Saturday a group of girls joins them. They banter and Jason notices that the other boys seem to get along easily with the girls while he struggles to find something to say. The same thing happens the next two Saturdays and, on the fourth week, one of the older girls brings marijuana. She lights a joint, gives it to her two girl friends, and then offers it to the boys. Each one takes a few puffs, including Jason. He is both scared and excited, and, perhaps for this reason or because the marijuana is having some effect, he speaks to the girl standing next to him. He even makes a joke that the group laughs at. These weekly Saturday afternoon "chance" meetings in the park continue, as does the marijuana smoking. Jason likes smoking marijuana because, in his mind, it allows him to be more outgoing. By the seventh week of this routine, Jason is feeling totally comfortable and makes what he believes to be a funny comment about one of the girls. Only later is he overcome with embarrassment when he realizes that he has hurt her feelings and angered her friends.

If Jason had spoken about these experiences during an intake or in therapy, there would have been ample opportunities to address his shyness and the subsequent marijuana use that he used to cope with it. The therapist could have helped Jason to reinterpret his growing comfort with this crowd, to see it as following from familiarity and his increased participation in the group and not just from smoking marijuana. While these discussions might not have circumvented the embarrassing moment, once it happened the therapist could have helped Jason explore whether the loss of control that resulted from smoking marijuana outweighed the benefits of feeling more relaxed.

Experimentation with alcohol or marijuana among adolescents takes on a larger meaning in light of the gateway theory of addiction development. Simply put, prior drug use predicts future drug use. According to this model (Kandel 1982), use of a readily available substance like alcohol provides a gateway to using illegal and/or more physically addictive substances. Adolescents try what is available. Usually, this means alcohol and cigarettes, although recently marijuana has become one of the first drugs of experimentation. Once high school and college students drink or smoke, they are more likely to be exposed to peers who do the same. Exposure to peers then provides further opportunities to accept the offer to use.

The gateway theory provides one explanation of why women are less likely to be diagnosed with alcoholism than men. At one time it was assumed that women were simply less prone to developing addictions. A recent study suggests that gender differences have less to do with addiction tendencies and more to do with early exposure to substances. Adolescent boys are exposed to drugs and alcohol more than girls are. With exposure comes access, and with access comes the opportunity to develop problematic use. By controlling for differential rates in early exposure, the gender difference disappears. Once girls accept the offer to use drugs, they are as likely as boys to become dependent (Hansen 2000).

Most adolescent experimentation with drugs goes no further. But for some, experimentation becomes the gateway for using other illegal drugs and physically addictive substances, such as crack or heroin. Children ages twelve to seventeen who smoke, drink, or use marijuana are up to 266 times more likely to use cocaine later (The National Center on Addiction and Substance Abuse at Columbia University 1994). Where experimentation seems to be largely a function of social factors and peer group, the transition to abuse and dependence is greatly influenced by genetics, family environment, and psychological factors.

When following up on an adolescent's reported experimentation with substances, it is useful to remember the characteristics of adolescents who are most likely to become addicted. They start drinking early, between ages fourteen and twenty. In their recovery stories, the authors frequently refer to starting to drink during this period. Such was the case for Pete Hamill (1994) who grew up with a frequently unemployed father and a mother who struggled to keep the family together. Just as he entered his teens, he began sneaking beers while his alcoholic father got drunk with friends in the living room. Autobiographies about addiction (chapter 12) illustrate what research documents is the role of genetics and family environment. Parental addiction is a significant risk factor as is a family environment where a parent, usually the father, is diagnosed with an antisocial personality disorder (Cadoret, Troughton, O'Gorman, and Heywood 1995).

Psychological characteristics predictive of a future addiction have been isolated in studies of adults with addictions and longitudinal studies that examine how experimental use becomes an addiction. The common factors in this research are affiliation with peers who use substances, low religious participation, and/or low levels of conventionality. Low educational achievement and expectations are also common (Wills, McNamara, Vaccaro, and Hirky 1996). Sensation seeking and difficulties with affect regulation, especially with aggression, have been identified as risk factors. Not surprisingly, adolescents whose substance use is most likely to escalated have been experiencing greater life stress and have less adaptive modes of coping. Additional signs of inadequate coping (other than substance use) include anger, helplessness, or loafing (Weinberg, Rahdert, Colliver, and Glantz 1998).

Of course, no one risk factor dependably predicts if an adolescent's experimentation will become abuse or dependence. As with an adult patient, when confronted with an adolescent who denies substance use, confidence in one's clinical judgment can be shaken. When faced with uncertainty, keeping the previous risk factors in mind can support one's confidence in following through on an ongoing assessment for addiction problems. Even if the adolescent is just experimenting, modifying the previous risk factors in psychotherapy (e.g., by improving coping skills or clarifying personal standards) can help ensure that experimentation does not develop into abuse.

Assessment Practices for Adolescents

A psychotherapist can be placed in an ethical quandary if he or she knows that an adolescent patient is using or abusing substances. Is this information confidential? Do parents need to be notified that a child may be in danger? Those who regularly treat adolescents are familiar with these dilemmas. Before doing an addiction assessment, a decision must be made regarding the confidentiality of that information. At a minimum, a therapist must know the state laws regarding the age of consent. A more proactive stance involves discussing the laws and issues around confidentiality with the parents and adolescent before a formal assessment is made. The psychotherapist can acknowledge that he or she does not know if such information will be revealed, but that before assessment and treatment can begin, a policy must be in place. There can be an open discussion of the pros and cons of keeping the outcome of sessions private. Privacy allows the child to feel more trusting about revealing problems, but this also means that the parents must be willing to relinquish that knowledge. Ideally, whatever is agreed upon is signed off on by all parties.

Scales designed for adults can be used with adolescents as long as it is recognized that there are questions that do not necessarily reflect an adolescent's experiences, for example: Have you had trouble at work due to your drinking? Have you ever had a drink first thing in the morning to steady your nerves, known as an eye opener? Have you attended an AA meeting? For this reason, scales designed for adult populations require lower cutoff scores when used with adolescents. Research (Knight, Sherritt, Harris, Gates, and Chang 2003) indicates the following optimal cutoff points: AUDIT (2 or more points where the adult norms range from 4 to 8) and CAGE (1 or more points where the adult cutoff is 2 or more). The TWEAK has been found to perform well with a cutoff of 2 points (Chung et al. 2000).

A number of scales have been designed specifically for an adolescent population. The PEI (Personal Experience Inventory), a scale similar to the MAST but modified for adolescents, assesses problematic substance use including drugs and alcohol (Winters 1992). The ASMA (Assessment of Substance Misuse in Adolescents), a recently developed, brief, six-item scale, assesses for drugs only (Willner 2000). The ASMA has been validated on a community sample, thus making it an appropriate screen for use in a general psychotherapy practice. It also is quite valuable in a psychotherapy setting because scores are designed to distinguish at-risk drug use (i.e., it could become a problem), and problematic use.

Each ASMA questions has a three-response format: "I don't use drugs" (scored as 0), "no" (scored as 1), and "yes" (scored as 2).

ASMA (Assessment of Substance Misuse in Adolescents)

1. If you use drugs, do you have a favorite drug you use?
2. If you use drugs, do you ever do so alone?
3. Do you use drugs because you're bored, lonely, or anxious?
4. If you use drugs, do you think a lot about drugs and drug use?
5. Do you plan your day to make sure you can use drugs?
6. Do you need to use more and more drugs to get high?
7. Do you feel irritable or anxious if you don't use drugs?
8. Do you miss your favorite drug if you don't use if for a while?

An adolescent who scores greater than 8 points but less than 12 is considered to be at risk for developing a drug use problem. A score greater than 12 suggests that use is already problematic. While the scale's name implies that it assesses for any substance misuse, the questions' wording focuses solely on drugs alone. Thus, when using this scale, it will be important to determine if an adolescent considers alcohol a drug and if so, to provide instructions that limit the scope of the term "drugs" to substances other than alcohol.

The POSIT (Problem-Oriented Screening Instrument for Teenagers) is another screening tool that can be administered in a mental health care setting (McLaney, DelBoca, and Babor 1994). One scale measures substance use, including drugs and alcohol, while the other nine scales gather information about various aspects of the adolescent's life that are relevant for treatment, including delinquent behavior, social skills, recreational activities, educational status, aggressive behavior, and family relations. The POSIT, with 139 items, is self-administered, but because it takes twenty to thirty minutes to complete, it may not be useful in all clinical settings.

Usually, scales developed for adolescent populations assess current problematic use and call the clinician's attention to potential risk factors. This is true for the CRAFFT (Knight et al. 1999), which was designed initially for use by pediatric physicians. Based on adolescent patients receiving routine medical care, the CRAFFT's six questions assess for both drug and alcohol use. Thus, in many settings, the CRAFFT will be of more value than the ASMA (because of its sole focus on drugs). Any of these questions are easily incorporated into a clinical interview.

CRAFFT

1. Have you ever ridden in a *car* driven by someone (including yourself) who was high or had been using alcohol or drugs?
2. Do you ever use alcohol or drugs to *relax*, feel better about yourself, or fit in?
3. Do you ever use alcohol or drugs while you are by yourself (*alone*)?
4. Do you ever *forget* things you did while using alcohol or drugs?
5. Do your family or *friends* tell you that you should cut down on your drinking or drug use?
6. Have you ever gotten into *trouble* while you were using alcohol or drugs?

(The name of this instrument—CRAFTT—is created by combining the italicized word in each question).

Each question is responded to with a "yes" (scored as 1) or "no" (scored as 0).

Affirmative responses to any of the first three questions suggest that substance use could be problematic. Responding "yes" to any of the remaining three CRAFFT questions strongly suggests that substance use is already problematic because either physiological consequences are occurring or substance-related problems have significant effects (e.g., are noticed by others). Each positive response to these three items should be explored further. Two or more affirmative responses to the six CRAFFT questions are taken as evidence of problematic use.

The first three questions on the CRAFFT are valuable because they high-light critical risk factors and point out the kind of information clinicians, who prefer not to administer screening tools, can listen for in an interview.

1. Have you ever ridden in a *car* driven by someone (including yourself) who was high or had been using alcohol or drugs? This is not only an important question for assessment but has ethical implications as well. This question is asked out of concern for the patient's ultimate well-being. Once it is determined that a patient is driving under the influence or with others who are, a plan for an alternative means of transportation needs to be developed (e.g., calling a friend who is not at the party, ar-ranging for a parent pickup).
2. Do you ever use alcohol or drugs to *relax*, feel better about yourself, or fit in? Most adolescent experimentation is driven by peer pressure; ado-lescents drink and use drugs to fit in or be "normal." This question helps the clinician to determine if substances are also being used for their ef-fect. The clinician will want to keep in mind the additional list of effects presented in the ASMA: Do you use drugs because you're bored, lonely, or anxious? Another way to ask more generally about the reasons for substance use is by posing the following question: "Is the effect of the substance more important to you than the adventure of use?" (Swadi 1997). A "yes" response can be followed up by questions regarding the desired effects and the contexts in which these mood-altering effects are most likely to be sought.
3. Do you ever use alcohol or drugs while you are by yourself (*alone*)? An adolescent who uses drugs outside the context of his or her peer group is certainly not using drugs in a normative fashion. A "yes" answer sug-gests a more serious problem is developing.

The more valuable adolescent screening tools serve two functions: to screen for and to educate about addictions. Both the ASMA and CRAFFT can fulfill these functions. The ASMA focuses on potential negative consequences of drug use. Because adolescents do not readily connect their experience with substances to their risks, this screening tool provides a way to give feedback about the current effects of drug use and those that may develop. Each ques-tion on the CRAFFT, as illustrated above, can become a means for further ex-ploring the adolescent's substance use behavior and associated risks.

The face-valid screening tools just described will not yield accurate infor-mation for the adolescent who is not interested in letting his or her substance use be known. For this group, the SASSI-3, the low face-valid scale, dis-cussed in chapter 5, has a version especially designed for adolescents. Ques-tions on the SASSI have no explicit connection to substance use, thus making it difficult to fake responses. The adolescent version of the SASSI has good validity when it comes to identifying substance use problems.

As a complement or alternative to structured screens, additional questions can be asked by a therapist. These questions are derived from an understanding of the factors that contribute to adolescent use. The gateway model emphasizes that early access greatly increases the chance of addiction. Given that access plays such a critical role, a good question to ask is: *What kinds of drugs are available these days?*

This question lowers defensiveness because it is not directed at the patient's own drug use. The answers provide information about how accessible drugs are, how much the young patient knows, and it opens up the topic of substance use for discussion in therapy. Any acknowledgment of use needs to be followed up with an interest in what drugs are being taken. Polysubstance use is the norm among adolescents given that whatever substance is used depends on availability. A group of teens drank alcohol last Saturday because a friend was able to steal some liquor from home, and they smoked because another adolescent had a pack of cigarettes; this Saturday, they smoked cigarettes and drank cough syrup because another friend said this was a good way to get high.

In addition to accessibility of drugs and alcohol, clinicians will want to explore an adolescent's beliefs about the positive effects of substances and their prevalence among peers. Because the belief that substances have positive effects increases the likelihood of experimentation, a patient can be asked the following question: *What is it like/what would it be like to drink alcohol or use _____ (name of a specific drug)?*

It can also be productive to ask questions that reveal an adolescent's beliefs about the degree of use among peers. Social norms research (Reis and Riley 2000) shows that within a school's culture, substance use increases as a function of the belief that drug and alcohol use is widespread (whether true or not). One can ask: *How often are kids drinking alcohol at your school? How many kids were smoking marijuana at that party on Saturday?* In line with Shea's validity techniques (chapter 7), the more specific the question, the better the information received.

Sometimes the only way to know if an adolescent is using substances is to perform urine testing or another toxicology screening (see chapter 5). If a therapist chooses to take this path, "urines," as they are called, should be presented as a routine part of the assessment process and not as an indication of the therapist's mistrust of the client. Some argue that toxicology screening should only occur if a patient willingly complies with the request. Coerced or involuntary drug screens do nothing to deter use and may damage the therapeutic relationship that ultimately is more effective in addressing addiction issues. Deciding against toxicology screenings can be difficult because parents often want random screenings to ensure their child is no longer exposed to harm. When the parents' wishes contradict those of the adolescent patient, it is helpful if the psychotherapist does not take on the role of overseeing the toxicology screens. Instead, the provider can support the parents in taking responsibility for the drug testing either by using over-the-counter drug testing packages or through the help of a family physician.

When alcohol use is suspected (it need not be at problematic levels), a therapist can offer the patient a BAC Zone™ (www.baczone.biz). This small card is easy to carry and, based on gender and weight, it provides a way to calculate BAL by the number of drinks and time of consumption. These cards have been used as part of a harm-reduction strategy on college campuses to decrease the likelihood that dangerous levels of drinking occur, especially driving while intoxicated (Sivestri, Pollaci, and Genco 2003). With these cards, adolescents have a way to determine if they have had too much liquor to drive.

Moving from screening to formal diagnosis poses further challenges. It is important to know that the substance use of a chemically dependent adolescent differs from that of a substance dependent adult. An adolescent who shows signs of dependence will drink lower quantities of alcohol and less frequently than an alcohol dependent adult. Adolescents diagnosed with alcohol dependence do not drink every day but, on average, every other day (Hasin et al. 2003). Also, some of the DSM-IV diagnostic criteria are difficult to apply to adolescents. For example, one criterion refers to using more of a substance than intended. This can be difficult to determine with adolescents because they do not know if they drank more than they intended to given that they had no amount in mind in the first place.

Late Adolescence and Early Adulthood: Binge Drinking

Twenty- to thirty-five-year-olds consume the most alcohol, although alcohol is not the only substance they consume. "Club drugs," such as OxyContin, LSD, and MDMA or Ecstasy, are a few of the more popular drugs used in party or club settings. Raves, popular with homosexual men, are a place where drugs use is associated with unsafe sex.

When asked about substance use, patients in this age group respond quite differently from adolescents. Living away from home and developing their own lifestyles, these young adults are prone to speak freely about their social activities and unselfconsciously report on the drugs and alcohol they consume. In talking about the previous weekend, one of my patients, a single man just out of college and in his first job, reported meeting friends for drinks on a Saturday evening. They left the bar for a dance club where he took two Valiums. He arrived home in the early morning hours only to awaken late the next day to join some friends to drink beer and watch sports all afternoon. It can take time to assess if this pattern of use is having adverse effects, especially if the patient appears to be functioning adequately in school or at work.

Binge drinking is a special form of alcohol consumption most common to this age group. *Bingeing* on alcohol, as the term implies, involves heavy consumption of alcohol in a short period. What qualifies as a large amount? Initially defined as five drinks in a row, Wechsler and Nelson (2001) strongly argue that gender specific amounts are necessary given woman's metabolism rate results in alcohol accumulating far faster in the blood. Their gender-specific definition of binge drinking is: five drinks in a row for a man and four in a row for a woman where this level of consumption has occurred at least once in the previous two weeks. Drinking in this manner three or more times in a two-week period is identified as frequent binge drinking.

Definitions of Binge Drinking

Drinking according to the following pattern at least once in the previous two weeks

Men: Five standard drinks in a row

Woman: Four standard drinks in a row

Frequent binge drinking

Drinking in a binge manner three or more times in the previous two-week period

Students on college campuses recognize binge drinking as a problem, but their definition of a bingeing involves drinking more alcohol than the limits set by professionals. College-age men define binge drinking as six or more drinks in a row, while women define it as five drinks (Wechsler and Kuo 2000). While on average men binge drink more often than women, women are potentially in greater danger because they are less likely to recognize it as a problem. Among frequent binge drinkers, only 8 percent of women (as opposed to 22 percent of men) considered this drinking pattern worthy of concern (Wechsler et al. 1995). These more liberal definitions of bingeing and frequent failure to see it as problematic means that young women, as well as men, will not accurately assess their degree of impairment. This is especially true for the adolescent who has limited experience with alcohol. One can wonder how many alcohol-related traffic fatalities are a result of an adolescent or young adult, who does not usually drink excessively, drinking in a binge manner. Interweaving accurate information about what defines binge drinking into the assessment process can help the patient begin to redefine his or her drinking behavior and the associated risks.

While the binge drinking literature focuses on the college-age population, this drinking pattern is not age specific. In one sample of highly educated employees, 29 percent reported binge drinking in the previous three months (Matano et al. 2003). Before becoming aware of how frequently addiction issues complicate psychotherapy, I worked with a man in his mid-thirties who turned out to be a binge drinker. Kevin, a frustrated musician, had become a successful promoter of classical music performers. He came to therapy due to depressed feelings that appeared shortly after his wife completed her MBA and began a financially lucrative job. We were making some progress on his presenting problem when he came into a session angry with himself for having missed a significant business meeting. When asked what happened, he reported that he had overslept due to drinking the previous evening. Further questioning revealed that after his wife went to sleep, he had taken a bottle of vodka to his study and drank it until he fell asleep. He repeated this pattern one or two times a week. The next day he would sleep in late, wake up, and exercise away his hangover. In between binges, he drank normally (a glass of wine with dinner).

This patient did not enter psychotherapy expressing concern about his bingeing, but once it became a topic for therapy, he admitted that the real reason he sought treatment was out of concern that his drinking might be getting out of control. This is a common occurrence; a patient comes to treatment asking for help with "psychotherapeutic issues" while both hoping and fearing that the psychotherapist will recognize a substance-related problem. For this patient, once his binge drinking was addressed in treatment, we were much better able to address the negative feelings about his marriage that had precipitated his depressive episode.

Assessment Practices for Binge Drinking

The Quantity/Frequency Questionnaire (see chapter 5) is a good tool for determining if drinking fits a binge pattern because it asks questions about frequency of drinking, usual quantities, and the maximum amount consumed on a single occasion. When the maximum is five drinks for men or four for women, follow-up questions are asked about how often this maximum amount is consumed to see if the person is a frequent binge drinker. A clinician will be better able to assess binge drinking if he or she is aware of some disputes concerning how to define and recognize this pattern of alcohol use.

The first area of dispute concerns how binge drinking is measured. Wechsler and colleagues define bingeing in terms of quantity of alcohol consumed within a certain period. Although Wechsler's quantities are gender specific, defining any form of problem drinking in terms of quantity is prone to inaccuracies because alcohol's effects vary depending on a number of factors, including body weight, time since the last meal, and the interval between drinks. The second dispute challenges the need to distinguish binge drinking from other forms of alcohol consumption. There is no unique DSM-IV diagnostic category for binge drinking; it is subsumed under alcohol abuse or dependence. For this reason, some clinicians have suggested that the concept of "binge drinking" be abandoned. A third source of dispute concerns whether the term *binge* is too confusing. Reference to a *binge* is often misinterpreted as equivalent to a bender, where a person drinks excessively and continuously for days at a time. To clarify the difference, some journals prefer the phrase *heavy episodic drinking*. College students as well as professionals have questioned the clarity of the term *binge* and the benefits of defining problem drinking by quantity rather than impairment. In order to avoid alienating patients in this age group, clinicians are advised to focus on negative consequences without necessarily emphasizing amount consumed within a given time (DeJong 2001).

Binge drinking is most common among white males and college-age populations. Recognizing its negative consequences is complicated by the fact that between binges this group functions well and drinks moderately or not at all. The following list of common adverse effects of bingeing can prove useful during the screening process: missing classes, falling behind in schoolwork, acting in a regretful way, forgetting what happened, arguing with friends, engaging in unplanned sex, and driving after drinking. Forty to sixty percent of binge drinkers report these alcohol-related problems. Twenty percent of frequent binge drinkers report additional effects including the occurrence of property damage, personal injury, and unprotected sex while intoxicated. Clinicians should be aware that students who binge less frequently still have similar negative effects but at a lower frequency (Wechsler and Nelson 2001).

While substance use is acknowledged more readily by young adults than by younger adolescents, gathering information about the negative effects of substances requires active questioning either in the clinical interview or through use of a screening instrument. For this purpose, screening instruments designed for adults or adolescents can be administered with the choice depending on the patient's developmental level. These tools must be used with caution, however. The negative consequences of binge drinking are not identified consistently by typical screening tools. One study of the CAGE's and AUDIT's ability to identify problematic binge drinking in an employed and educated sample found that while the CAGE performed best, overall both instruments had low sensitivities (Matano et al. 2003). Thus, clinicians will want to use standard instruments in an exploratory manner, combining them with interview questions in order to clarify the negative consequences of binge drinking.

Older Adults

The overall quantity of alcohol a person consumes declines with age. Although the older adult, variously defined as over sixty or sixty-five, drinks less, this reduced quantity is offset by the fact that as one ages, it takes less alcohol to become intoxicated. Consumption levels that qualify as normal drinking in midlife are indicative of a problem if over age sixty-five. The safe drinking level for older men and women is defined as one standard drink (.5 ounces alcohol) per day (Menninger 2002). Even this may be dangerous depending on a patient's medical condition, current prescription medications, and use of over-the-counter medications that contain alcohol.

The incidence of heavy drinking is relatively small in the older adult population. Only 7 percent of men and 2 percent of women are considered heavy users. However, the figure increases to a high of 24 percent for older adults with co-occurring medical and psychiatric conditions (Menninger 2002). The true prevalence of substance-based problems are likely underestimated for this group because the typical negative social, occupational, and legal consequences of addiction are not necessarily consistent with an older adult's life style. For example, one DSM-IV criteria for substance abuse is spending a lot of time in substance use-related activities. Given that low consumption can have large consequences, adverse effects can occur without requiring much time or effort. Other criteria also are less relevant. A retired person does not risk being fired from a job due to substance use. The older person, who is more likely to live alone, does not have a spouse with whom to argue. Fights may occur with extended family members who, while aware of the drinking, are hesitant to define it as a problem. Drinking can even be condoned as adaptive. "Mother has some right to relief." "Dad's drinking doesn't bother anyone; it's the only pleasure he has left."

Failure to recognize an addiction in an isolated older adult is illustrated with the case of a seventy-five-year-old woman suffering from increasing levels of hip pain. She was initially prescribed a short-term course of OxyContin, an opioid pain reliever, often used for cancer and other chronic pain. Painkillers are the drugs most likely to be misused by the elderly. Her pain did not fully abate and a variety of other unspecified pains appeared. Her physician supported her use of daily OxyContin for over a year, as did her family who were relieved when the medication finally brought some relief and an end to frequent calls asking for help they could not provide because they lived in a distant city. Only when this woman moved to a supported-care environment—where her daily functioning was of concern to a larger community—did the new physicians express serious concern that her cognitive decline was a function of her addiction to pain killers.

When treating older adults in psychotherapy, it will be necessary to inquire about negative consequences that are less visible. Such adverse consequences are often related to the direct physiological effects of alcohol. Alcohol facilitates bone loss, a major concern for women, and hastens age-related decrease in muscle mass. These physical changes, combined with alcohol's numbing effect, lead to increased accidents around the home and falls that result in more severe injuries. Other consequences include periods of time that cannot be accounted for, sleep disturbances, and physical complaints such as digestive problems or ulcers. Complaints that a medication has lost its effectiveness merit follow-up, given that alcohol use is contraindicated for many medications because alcohol counteracts the desired effects.

Mental health providers may expect a patient's physician to notice these signs of addiction, but this cannot be counted on. A man who initially came with his wife for couple's therapy continued to see me in individual treatment in order to address his wife's concern that he was depressed. This seventy-year-old man had been drinking above the normal limits for about twelve years with no days off. His physician has yet to question him about his substance use.

As with younger woman, physicians frequently miss alcoholism in their older women patients. When physicians were asked to diagnose an older woman whose presenting concerns contained classic signs of alcoholism (e.g., irritability, weight loss, loss of energy), less than 1 percent considered a diagnosis of alcoholism (The National Center on Addiction and Substance Abuse at Columbia University 1998). Signs of alcoholism often merge with other health-related problems that catch the physician's attention. When alcoholism is misdiagnosed as depression or anxiety, there is the risk that a physician will prescribe medications that interact negatively with alcohol and exacerbate the symptoms the medication is intended to treat.

Unlike other age groups, alcohol is not the most commonly misused substance among older adults. Older adults are more likely to abuse prescription drugs, and this is true for older women more than for men (The National Center on Addiction and Substance Abuse at Columbia University 1998). Abuse of medication includes taking more of the medication than prescribed and/or using alcohol or other substances along with the medication when the interaction of the two is known to be dangerous. Health care providers can contribute to inappropriate use. Adults over age fifty-nine receive an average of nineteen prescriptions a year with about five medications being taken at any one time (The National Center on Addiction and Substance Abuse at Columbia University 1998). An aging adult sees numerous physicians, each of whom is unaware of the patient's full range of medications due either to an inadequate assessment or to the patient's inability to recall them all. Prescribing more medication without ensuring that the current list of medications is accurate is one way that physicians and nurses become unwilling accomplices in medication abuse.

Assessment Practices for Older Adults

When choosing a screening tool for older adults, the AUDIT has been found to outperform the CAGE in mental health settings (Philpot et al. 2003). Several questionnaires have also been developed uniquely for older adults. There is a geriatric version of the MAST, known as the MAST-G (Blow et al. 1992). Items unique to the geriatric version, which can be incorporated into a clinical interview, include: *Does alcohol make you sleepy so that you often fall asleep in your chair? Did you ever increase your drinking after experiencing a loss in your life? After drinking, have you ever noticed an increase in your heart rate or a beating in your chest?* With twenty-three items, it is quick and simple to administer. Five or more affirmative responses require further investigation. Like the MAST, questions on the MAST-G are in the form of "did you ever," and thus, it is necessary to clarify if alcohol problems are current. Like any good screening tool, administration of the MAST-G can become a starting point for a discussion of substance use, including but not limited to alcohol.

The ARPS (Alcohol Related Problems Survey), which takes twelve minutes to complete, and its short version, ShARPs, which takes less than five minutes to complete, are new self-administered instruments designed specifically for older adults (Moore, Beck, and Babor 2002). Like other screening tools, these two assess quantity and frequency of alcohol use and resulting adverse consequences (e.g., memory problems, difficulty sleeping, depression, stomach disorders, bumping into things). In light of its use with an older population, questions are included that inquire about adverse health consequences where alcohol consumption is causing or worsening medical or psychiatric symptoms. Other questions assess whether alcohol intake is adversely affecting prescribed medications by diminishing their effectiveness or creating problematic interaction effects.

One of the ARPS's major contributions is a section where patients specify the types of medications they are taking (see below). This checklist serves as a memory aid, which makes it less likely that some medications will be omitted. Based on responses to the ARPS, patients are divided into three categories: (1) the harmful drinker who has adverse effects due to alcohol use alone, (2) the hazardous drinker who has or is at risk of developing adverse effects due to current medical and psychiatric conditions, and (3) the nonhazardous drinker and abstainer. Both versions of the ARP are copyrighted by Dr. Arlene Fink who will provide a copy of a self-administered version or access to a computer-administered and scored version by e-mailing her at afink@mednet.ucla.edu.

The emphasis on alcoholism screening in an older population is misleading given that misuse of prescription drugs is a more common problem. However, because there is no formal screening tool used solely for this purpose, a psychotherapist must be willing to gather information on current medications.

The two most problematic drug groups are benzodiazepines and analgesics/ painkillers, whether prescribed or purchased over the counter. Some adverse consequences of inappropriate use include drowsiness, memory loss, confusion, and accidents, especially falls. The ARPS's section on medication is provided below to help with gathering information on specific medications and drugs that a patient is currently taking.

1. How many different medications do you use at least once a week? Count all medications, even if you get them without a doctor's prescription. (Do not count eye drops, vitamins, minerals, ointments.)
2. Do you now take two or more regular or extra strength (325 mg or more) aspirin every day or almost every day?
3. Do you now take any of these medications at least *once a week*?
   a. Sedatives or sleeping medicines such as Valium, Dalmane, Librium, Xanax, Ambien, Ativan, Halcion, chloral hydrate
   b. Tranquilizers such as Thorazine, Mellaril, Haldol
   c. Narcotic medications such as Darvon, Demerol, codeine, morphine, Percocet, Vicodin
4. Do you now take any of these medications every day or almost every day?
   a. Ulcer and stomach medicines such as Zantac, Tagamet, Prilosec, Pepcid
   b. Arthritis and pain medicines such as Motrin (*Ibuprofen*), Voltaren, Clinoril, Naprosyn, Tylenol, Advil
   c. Tolinase, Diabinese, or Orinase
   d. Other blood pressure medicines such as Cardizem, Vasotec, Lotensin, atenolol, Cozaar, Norvasc, water pills
   e. Nitrates such as Isordil, Nitropatch
   f. Other medicines for the heart such as digoxin, Lasix
   g. Coumadin (warfarin)
   h. Seizure medicines such as Tegretol, Dilantin, or phenobarbital
   i. Depression medicines such as Elavil *(amitriptyline),* Pamelor *(nortriptyline),* Paxil, Prozac, Zoloft
   j. Prescription antihistamines such as Claritin, Zyrtec, Allegra
   k. Tylenol PM, Benadryl, Chlortrimeton or other nonprescription antihistamines

(This material is copyrighted by and provided courtesy of Dr. Arlene Fink.)

Addiction assessment with older adults also needs to include the natural history of substance-related disorders. Older adults with substance use problems fall into one of two groups. There are those whose current use is merely a reflection of an ongoing problem. Substance related disorders began earlier in life and have been treated on and off or gone untreated. A second, late on-set group has used substances reasonably throughout life and first developed a problem after age sixty (e.g., upon retirement or death of a spouse). This latter group is very amenable to treatment (Menninger 2002).

No matter the patient's age, the assessment process can serve a very important educational function. This is true even for older adults, many of whom are unaware that changes in metabolism affect their response to alcohol and that what was a reasonable amount to drink at age forty or fifty is now too much. They are also naïve about the adverse physical effects of alcohol that occur with aging. Sometimes excess alcohol consumption is alleviated by simply informing a patient about recommended drinking levels (i.e., no more than one standard drink per day). This occurred when an eighty-year-old woman was referred to me by a psychiatrist who had prescribed a trial of antidepressants. She complained that the medication was making her dizzy, especially in the evenings. As it turned out, she drank a glass of wine with dinner, but it was a large glass, closer to 8 oz. rather than the recommended 5 oz. She greatly appreciated understanding that the wine was interacting with the medication and agreed to stop drinking while on the medication.

RACIAL AND ECONOMIC FACTORS

Beliefs about who is most likely to become addicted to specific substances can hinder a psychotherapist from assessing for addictions or accurately interpreting typical signs of problematic use (chapter 4). Stereotypes about drug addiction are perhaps strongest around racial and economic differences. A quick overview of the research literature on addiction reveals that frequently, participants come from minority populations or have limited financial means, for example, unwed pregnant teens, adolescent runaways, the homeless. Such studies foster the impression that substance addiction is necessarily more prevalent and problematic among the less affluent and non-Caucasian groups. This impression is not supported by epidemiological data. When it comes to alcohol dependence, Caucasians outnumber non-Caucasians. For drug dependence, the figures are equal for both groups.

Stereotypes concerning greater substance use in minority populations appear to influence mental health providers' inquiries about drinking. Nonwhites visiting a mental health provider are more likely to be asked about their drinking than whites, this is especially true for Hispanics (Weisner and Matzger 2003). Surely these stereotypes are in effect when physicians request that pregnant minority women be tested for substance use more frequently than Caucasian women even though drinking rates are higher among Caucasian women

(Goldberg 1995). This practice among physicians should serve as a reminder to psychotherapists to not overlook the possibility of problematic substance use in their white patients—especially those who are pregnant.

Racial and ethnic patterns of substance use are beginning to shift. Historically, alcohol disorders have been highest among young Caucasian males. While still true, recent data show an increase in alcohol abuse among African Americans and Hispanics, with the rate for Hispanics equaling or slightly greater than Caucasian males. Blacks remain less likely to be alcohol dependent, with numbers declining further when controlling for higher education levels and economic status. Native Americans and Eskimos are the only two minority groups with an overall incidence of alcohol and drug dependence that is higher than Caucasians. Historically, Asian Americans have had a low prevalence of alcoholism. This was attributed to a genetic response some Asians have to alcohol that involves a noticeable flush to the face. However, despite this unpleasant reaction, alcoholism among Asian Americans living in North America is on the upswing, especially for Japanese, Koreans, and Pacific Islanders, including Native Hawaiians (Substance Abuse and Mental Health Services Administration 2003).

Racial and ethnic differences in substance use need to be refined in order to convey the demographic picture more accurately. Wallace describes what has been called the "'two worlds' of minority alcohol use" (1999, 1124). One world is composed of a relatively large number of persons who abstain or drink lightly. Forty-three percent of African Americans and 35 percent of Hispanics report not using alcohol in the past year, as compared to 32 percent of whites. The other world is composed of heavy alcohol drinkers (five or more drinks, one or more times per week). Here the difference is most striking among men: 23 percent of Hispanic and 15 percent of African American males drink at this level compared to 12 percent of whites. Thus, while overall fewer blacks and Hispanics drink alcohol, the clinician needs to know that of those who drink, a larger percentage do so excessively. With higher consumption comes an increase in alcohol-related problems. Interestingly, blacks and Hispanic show more severe social and physical consequences at lower levels of consumption relative to whites. However, these differences are not necessarily a function of racial or ethnic factors. The increased severity of adverse effects holds most strongly for those living in poorer and less organized communities where the effects of alcohol interact with pre-existing levels of poor nutrition, housing conditions, and health.

Economic conditions are inextricably mixed in with stereotypes about race and substance use. Those who are poor or disadvantaged show the highest rates of addiction. Education level is negatively correlated with substance dependence, as is annual income. Those with less than a high school education are about one and a half times more likely to develop a substance-based addiction.

Current employment status is the strongest economic predictor. Unemployed persons are two to three times more likely to be substance dependent. Among the employed, substance use is greatest among young male workers with low education and low paying positions. Illicit drug use is highest in the transportation and relocation fields, while heavy alcohol consumption is highest in construction (Substance Abuse and Mental Health Services Administration 2003).

Not only must economic and educational factors be considered in any discussion of the relationship between race and addiction but an individual's level of acculturation also plays a significant role. As members of a racial or ethnic group become acculturated (i.e., take on the values of the larger society), the average liquor consumption increases. Maintaining one's racial or ethnic identity through a strong connection to traditional cultural norms and values is associated with a lower frequency of substance use problems (Herd and Grube 1996).

Although less education and fewer financial resources are associated with a greater incidence of addiction, the treatment provider should not forget that professionals at higher income levels still use substances and develop addictions. Many are impaired professionals—psychologists and physicians form a large group. Current prevalence rates likely underestimate the incidence of addiction for those in higher socioeconomic brackets because life circumstances make it easy to hide addiction's consequences. For example, a psychotherapist in private practice interacts with patients all day and not colleagues. While a patient may suspect a problem, he or she will not able to confer with the provider's other patients and will be very hesitant to make a report that cannot be substantiated by others. In light of limited research on addiction in employed professionals, Matano et al. (2002) studied the pattern of substance use and abuse in this group. Thirteen percent consumed three or more drinks daily, 15 percent were binge drinkers, and 11 percent used illicit drugs, with marijuana and cocaine being most common. Depending on the assessment tool, 12 to 23 percent qualified as alcohol dependent, although only 1 percent had sought treatment for alcoholism.

Even the face of heroin has changed. The image of the typical drug addict is a heroin user, a youngish, economically disadvantaged, disheveled man on a street corner with bruises and needle puncture marks along his arm. Less than ten years ago, those seeking treatment for opioid dependence fit this picture. But today the image has changed. Heroin has become a drug common to suburban settings, among white, affluent adolescents. Part of the reason for this shift is that purer forms of heroin are entering the country, which, when snorted, produce a high similar to the injected form. The most recent demographics also show a radically different gender pattern: women entering treatment outnumber men two to one. This may be due to heroin being used among adolescent girls to lose weight or stay slim (Rosenker 2002). Reflecting this demographic shift, Ann Marlowe, a Wall Street analyst who became a writer and music critic, published a memoir about her years of using heroin entitled *How to Stop Time: Heroin from A to Z* (1999). While heroin users are thought not to consult psychotherapists, this new group may well be psychotherapy patients.

Racial, Ethnic, and Economic-Based Assessment Practices

As Wallace (1999) has observed, other than the previously noted differences in demographics, research is lacking in understanding the unique determinants and features of addictions as a function of racial and ethnic differences. Not surprisingly, to date no screening tools have been designed for use with distinct ethnic and racial groups.

There is some evidence to show that responses to the more popular screening tools do vary somewhat with race. These effects are due primarily to specific items. Relative to Caucasians, African Americans are more likely to indicate a need to cut down on drinking, but they are less likely to positively endorse items related to AA attendance (Cherpitel and Clark 1995). Responding to these variations in response as a function of race, Cherpitel (1997) was instrumental in developing the RAPS (described in chapter 5), which has been shown to have the best sensitivity and specificity for African American and Hispanic populations.

In terms of economics, one side of the spectrum involves recognizing addiction among fellow professionals. Addressing a colleague's addiction is an event ripe with conflict. Even when the addiction is apparent, the thought that one's actions might ruin a colleague's career can take precedence over the knowledge that not reporting the problem represents unethical behavior. While one's initial preference will be to approach a colleague privately, Cicala (2003) discourages this action because it most likely will be met with anger, disbelief, and possible further self-harm on the colleague's part. Instead, the information should be presented to the appropriate authority (e.g., dean of the department, head of an institution's impaired professional or personnel committee, or, if in private practice, the state professional organization). There are major advantages to approaching these peer review groups rather than trying to handle the matter on one's own. Once the peer review process begins, the "resulting investigation is usually completely confidential and, in most cases, is protected from any outside legal discovery process under peer review laws. If, however, the problem is not reported until legal issues or questions of competence are raised, the right of the physician to confidentiality may be lost and the problem becomes a matter of public record" (Cicala 2003, 43). Confirmation of a problem is usually followed by an intervention and an offer of treatment.

SUMMARY

This chapter has looked at some of the ways group membership affects the ease of recognizing substance-based addictions and the accuracy of screening tools. The sources of individual differences that were examined—gender, age, race, economic factors—were each shown to make a unique contribution to keeping addictions hidden. Shame is most salient for women who, as a result, may not disclose addiction to themselves or others. Adolescents' addiction may be mislabeled as normal peer group experimentation. An older adult may miss addiction because he or she does not recognize that the amount of alcohol consumed five or ten years ago without consequence is now harmful. The increased effect of alcohol can be in response to a medical condition, medication, or age-related changes in metabolism.

The contribution that race and economics make to unrecognized addictions primarily rests with providers' beliefs about who is most likely to be addicted and what an addiction looks like. To the extent that addictions manifest differently as a function of group membership and this presentation does not fit the clinician's stereotype, the addiction will remain hidden.

One way to counteract such stereotypes is to be familiar with the demographics of addiction. Thus, this chapter discussed, in some detail, how the prevalence of drug and alcohol addiction varies as a function of racial and economic factors.

Compared to process addictions (chapter 6) much more is known about how individual differences can mask substance-based addictions and make assessment less reliable. Diversity as a function of gender, age, race, and economic factors was emphasized. These few grouping are far from inclusive. Much more work is needed in order to understand how the signs and symptoms of addiction are affected by the four variables discussed in this chapter as well as factors that were not emphasized such as level of acculturation, education, or sexual preference. More research into the demographics of addiction and how addiction symptoms differ as a function of group membership will help shape the development of more sensitive screening tools and effective clinical interviewing strategies.

9

The Nature of Addiction:
A Further Source of Camouflage

No substance or behavior is inherently addictive. Even heroin, the drug most often associated with physiological dependence, has been used in moderate amounts for extended periods of time (Shewan, Dalgarno, Marshall, and Lowe 1998). The addictive potential of a drug or behavior arises out of a complex interaction of biological, personal, and environmental factors.

Likewise, addictions are not inherently difficult to recognize once one understands the various forms of camouflage—of which there are many. Earlier chapters considered psychotherapists' and patients' contributions to making addictions difficult to recognize. Psychotherapists' limited education and inaccurate impressions about addicted individuals and their treatment leave many unprepared to identify such problems in their patients. This is further complicated if the provider or the provider's family have undiagnosed addictions; to remain hidden from oneself, the addiction must remain unrecognized in others. There are also misconceptions about who is most likely to be addicted and how an addicted individual seeking psychotherapy behaves. Few patients in psychotherapy present with the pervasive functional impairments typically seen in addiction treatment settings. Those whose addictions are most often missed are employed, married, white, insured, and female (Schottenfeld 1994). Recently, old age has been added to this list (Weisner and Matzger 2003).

On the patient's side, failure to self-identify an addiction is complicated by the same stereotypic misconceptions held by therapists as well as familial and cultural variations in what qualifies as addictive behavior. In addition, addictions are not acknowledged to another because of the shame this would bring. These cognitive and interpersonal reasons for not self-identifying an addiction are often taken as evidence of denial. These forms of denial need to be distinguished from classic denial, which involves an unconsciously motivated distortion of the reality of one's addictive behavior and its negative consequences.

Even when clinicians are not hindered by stereotypes and are comfortable assessing and working in this area, addictions continue to be overlooked because of the other ways in which an addiction can be camouflaged. The nature of the addictive process itself can serve to mask its presence—both to the person who is addicted and to the mental health provider. In such cases, the diagnosis of addiction is missed all together or there is a misdiagnosis where the symptoms of addiction are interpreted as evidence of some other problem—usually depression or anxiety.

CROSS TOLERANCE, POLYSUBSTANCE USE, AND CROSS ADDICTIONS

When listening to a patient or actively assessing for substance use, what can be concluded from the following report made by a male patient during a first session, "I don't drink much—never more than two glasses of wine, two or maybe, three times a week"? Further inquiry into the amount reveals that he drinks wine by the glass with each drink being equivalent to about five ounces (i.e., one standard drink), and he is in good physical condition with no known medical condition that alcohol consumption could complicate. In terms of standards defining nonhazardous drinking, this overall amount sounds reasonable, nothing more than social drinking. But this conclusion could be an error without knowing the person's involvement with other potentially addictive substances or behaviors. There are three reasons for this: (1) cross tolerance, (2) polysubstance use, and (3) cross addictions.

Cross Tolerance

Cross tolerance is one way in which apparently moderate use masks an addiction. Cross tolerance occurs when a person uses two or more drugs from within the same class of drugs (see appendix). While each substance is used in a reasonable manner, drugs in the same class work in a biologically similar manner. The effects of consuming one substance along with another from the same group are cumulative. Cross-tolerance is observed most often with substances belonging to the class of depressants: alcohol, barbiturates, benzodiazepines (Valium), and other sedatives. A person may report taking no more than a couple of drinks and half of a five milligram Valium on a daily basis. Each drug alone may not be harmful, but because they are within the same class, combining their separate sedating effects sufficiently alters consciousness resulting in judgment and reaction times that are impaired. When looking for evidence of cross tolerance, it is important to remember to ask about prescription and over-the-counter medications that contain alcohol and/or have sedating effects. Among the elderly, combining such medications with alcohol increases the risk of injury and impaired judgment.

Substance users who are unaware of cross-tolerance effects are at greater risk for accidental overdose as evidenced by how often news reports of drug-related deaths involve substances with depressant effects. Overdose is more common with this class of substances because of their long half-life (the time it takes for the drug to reach half potency). With a long half-life, toxic levels begin to accumulate even if drinks and pills are taken at different times.

For process addictions, there is no term equivalent to cross tolerance, although something similar can happen if a series of comparable behaviors are combined. An example of cross-tolerance with a process addiction might include a combination of different forms of exercise. A person whose exercise has only involved running long distances might add daily weightlifting and yoga. No single activity is excessive, but taken together this kind of commitment to exercise can create harmful consequences, such as a neglect of daily responsibilities and a sense of craving or a need for the activities. In the case of gambling, a person who does not overspend on scratch cards may also be playing poker and slot machines during the week with the overall effect of negative financial consequences. Thus, as with substance-based addictions, as psychotherapists assess for process addictions, they need to be attuned to the many forms a behavior can take in order to determine whether comparable behaviors—each of which is unremarkable—are working together to create negative consequences.

Polysubstance Use and Dependence

Polysubstance use is another way in which apparently moderate consumption serves to mask addiction. For those who use drugs and alcohol in a problematic manner, polysubstance use is the norm. The majority of drug users report drinking liquor and the majority of those with alcohol problems take drugs. Frequently, both drug and alcohol consumption qualifies for a diagnosis. For example, more than half of those in treatment for alcohol dependence also are dependent on at least one drug (Staines et al. 2001).

There are several reasons why substance use so often involves an assortment of different substances. Polysubstance use is one way to avoid becoming dependent on any one substance. As a person senses that he or she is losing control or beginning to crave one substance, he or she switches to another substance. More often, the availability of a given drug, especially illegal ones, fluctuates thus leading to the use of whatever drug is accessible. While a specific substance is preferred, ultimately which one is used depends on its availability. In other cases, a person forgoes the preferred drug, even when available, because the current social group is involved with a different drug. The gateway theory of adolescent substance abuse illustrates the role of availability in creating polysubstance use. In high schools, alcohol is most readily available and it, along with cigarettes, usually is the first drug of experimentation. When marijuana comes along, the student starts smoking it while continuing to drink when alcohol is available.

Another reason that polysubstance use is prevalent is because one drug is being used to counteract the effects of another. This occurs most frequently in drugs with depressant qualities (e.g., alcohol) that are taken to alleviate the jittery effects of a stimulant such as cocaine. Or stimulants are used to counteract the drowsy feelings that come with depressants or over-the-counter medications (e.g., pain pills, antihistamines). Opioids are taken to alleviate paranoid and aggressive feelings resulting from protracted cocaine abuse. For most substance users, drug and alcohol use merges together and different substances are taken simultaneously or one right after the other. Less than 10 percent of users report alternating between drugs and alcohol, in which case, drugs and alcohol are used on separate and distinct occasions (Staines et al. 2001).

As with cross-tolerance, polysubstance use is dangerous because it greatly increases the chance of an overdose. Carrie Fisher, in *Postcards from the Edge*, a semi-autobiographical reflection on her drug dependence, aptly conveys the danger of polysubstance use. Upon her admission into a hospital following an accidental overdose, she recalls the following: "One of the therapists came in to admit me and asked how long I'd been a drug addict. I said that I didn't think I was a drug addict because I didn't take any one drug. 'Then you're a *drugs addict*,' she said. She asked if I had deliberately tried to kill myself. . . . [I]t wasn't like I'd planned it. I'm not suicidal. My behavior may be, but I'm certainly not" (Fisher 1987, 10).

Polysubstance use not only increases the negative effects of substance use but it can also become an impediment to successful treatment. The therapist needs to think carefully about how to handle the outcome of an addiction assessment that indicates a patient is dependent on one substance while using others in an intermittent and reasonable manner. One substance often becomes a stimulus for using another. If treatment involves stopping only the primary substance, these other drugs can trigger a relapse through their association with the primary drug. A young man in treatment for a marijuana addiction had a history, albeit infrequently, of taking a Valium or two while high. After a month of successful abstinence from smoking marijuana, a friend offered him a Valium. Before the evening was over, he was smoking again. Another common scenario with polysubstance users is that, as the preferred substance declines in use, the quantity increases for other substances. There are many stories of alcoholics who have successfully become abstinent through AA followed by a dramatic increase in their smoking and caffeine consumption.

Polysubstance dependence is probably one of the less well-known substance-related diagnoses in the DSM-IV. This diagnostic category reveals that negative consequences can occur when a variety of substances are each being taken moderately. A diagnosis of polysubstance dependence is made when multiple substances (other than nicotine and caffeine) are being used but where no single substance meets diagnostic criteria for dependence. In the DSM-IV, this diagnosis can only be considered if a person is using at least three substances; the ICD-10 requires only two. Polysubstance dependence is diagnosed if the combination of multiple drugs creates consequences that fit three or more of the criteria for substance dependence outlined in chapter 4 (Schuckit et al. 2001). For example, there is evidence of tolerance for marijuana, failed attempts to cut back on alcohol, and a great deal of time is spent acquiring cocaine.

In terms of demographics, the clinician will want to know that, compared to persons who are dependent on a single substance, individuals diagnosed as polysubstance dependent tend to be the kind of patients for whom addiction is overlooked. Those meeting the diagnostic criteria for polysubstance dependence have fewer substance-related problems (e.g., health consequences), are often female, and, independent of gender, have a more stable lifestyle as evidenced by higher levels of education, marriage, and employment (Schuckit et al. 2001).

Typically polysubstance abuse or dependence involves alcohol and a number of illegal drugs. The clinician should consider polysubstance problems where alcohol and/or illegal drugs are combined with use (often misuse) of prescription and/or over-the-counter medications and household chemical products. Vicodan, OxyContin, and Valium are a few of the more commonly misused prescription drugs, while cough syrups are the over-the-counter medication most likely to be abused. Products, especially those that can be inhaled, are a source of concern when treating adolescents. Sources of readily available inhalants include airplane glue, hairspray, paint thinner, and fingernail polish remover. A person using a little of this and that, here and there, may not be addicted to any one substance, yet taken together, the combination of substances interferes with normal functioning.

Cross Addictions

The combining of addictive behaviors is not limited to substances. Substances can be combined with a process addiction or several process addictions can coexist. When potentially addictive behaviors interact with each or with substance use to create an addiction, the outcome is referred to as cross addiction, overlapping addictions, or polyaddictions. Just as people have a tendency to become involved with multiple substances, several researchers have documented that a person who uses substances addictively is prone to behave excessively in relation to sex, work, gambling, eating, shopping, exercise, and playing video games (Christo et al. 2003; Greenberg, Lewis, and Dodd 1999). Sometimes two process addictions co-occur without substance involvement. Among one group of sex addicts, 32 percent had an eating disorder, 13 percent could be considered addicted to buying, and 5 percent had a problem with gambling (Schneider and Schneider 1991, cited here from Goodman 1998). Other research demonstrates an increased incidence of bulimia among those with a buying addiction (Faber et al. 1995).

The possible permutations of substance and process addictions are numerous. In one pattern, substance use and a behavior occur both excessively and independently, where each qualifies as addictive. Certain pairings of substance and process addictions are more common than others—drinking and gambling are a good example. Pathological gamblers have seven times the rate of alcoholism compared to nonpathological gamblers with 30 to 50 percent of gamblers being alcohol dependent (Petry 2002). Other common co-occurring substance and process addictions are drinking and shopping, abuse of steroids and exercise, cocaine and eating disorders, and cocaine and pornography. When cocaine abuse co-occurs with an eating disorder, cocaine is usually being taken as a means to control weight.

Another pattern of cross addiction involves substance use that facilitates the occurrence of a behavior that, over time, becomes addictive. Early recognition of this co-occurrence can prevent the behavior from developing into an addiction. This did not happen for Daron, who came to treatment with a drinking problem and an addiction to Internet pornography.

> Daron would end his day by drinking beer. By the time he was on his second beer, his wife and kids were usually in bed. He would then get on the computer to check stock quotes and, later in the evening, he would search the Web on a topic of recent interest at work. Sometimes he ended the evening at a pornographic site. For a long time he did this once or, twice a month. After one prolonged stressful period at work, he discovered that he was drinking close to a six-pack nightly as he stayed up later and later visiting pornographic sites. The result was that he rarely went to bed with his wife, their sex life declined, and he was often too tired to function effectively at work the next day.

Daron had no history of a sexual addiction and attributed his cybersex addiction to the availability and easy access of pornography on the Internet and the disinhibition he felt after drinking alcohol. For Daron substance use and excessive behavior occur simultaneously. Another common pattern of cross addictions involves a sequential shifting from one addiction to another.

Susan was about eight months into recovery from drug addiction when she started using overeating to regulate uncomfortable feelings. She became concerned about her excess weight and a plan was developed to exercise and eat more moderately. After a few false starts, she successfully lost the excess weight and was able to keep it off. During this time, she developed a romantic relationship that lasted for over a year. Shortly after the break up, she began to mention clothes shopping on Saturdays. She bought an expensive jacket at an upscale department store and then went to a more reasonably priced department store and bought more clothes. The therapist made little note of these comments; Susan had just found a well-paying job and the therapist knew she had not purchased new clothes for quite some time.

Given Susan's history of overeating after ceasing drug use, followed by what might have been an addictive relationship, a therapist attuned to the possibility of cross addiction would have taken note of Susan's off-handed comments regarding shopping on a regular basis. Why was Susan conveying this information to the therapist? Over the course of the next three months, Susan developed a large credit card debt. With experience using therapy to address her addictions, Susan brought her money concerns into treatment. Given that Susan was being responsible with money in all other areas, the problem was identified as a buying addiction that was, in part, a response to feelings of being deprived since the loss of her romantic relationship. As Susan put it, "I don't have drugs anymore; there is no food, so now I have shopping."

Polysubstance and cross addictions are difficult to recognize because the quantity used of a single substance or the occurrence of a behavior is not creating negative consequences. However, when all substance use is taken into account or substance use co-occurs with a potentially addictive behavior, negative outcomes ensue. Another way in which addictions can be camouflaged, and hence go unrecognized, is a result of the negative consequences created by addictive behaviors.

SUBSTANCE EFFECTS MIMICKING PSYCHOLOGICAL SYMPTOMS

Patients begin treatment by sharing the problems and experiences that led them to make an appointment. They feel depressed, sluggish, disoriented, jittery, anxious, preoccupied, and/or tired. All these experiences are induced by excessive behaviors, active substance use, or withdrawal. The new psychotherapy patient may not recognize that presenting problems are connected to addictive behavior, not because they are in denial but because the psychological consequences and physical discomforts are separated in time from the behavior or are not connected consistently with its occurrence. Cocaine use is not always associated with paranoid thoughts. Fear of social situations arises only intermittently after smoking marijuana. A man who has sworn off gambling would never think to report that his low mood and difficulty concentrating reflect withdrawal symptoms. Similarly, a person who drinks to get relief from insomnia may not know that alcohol exacerbates sleep problems. The therapist, like the patient, is unlikely to consider that the presenting problem is connected to an addictive behavior. Instead, having only the patient's self-report, the therapist will probably make a misdiagnosis and link what is heard to common forms of psychopathology, especially depression and anxiety. This type of misdiagnosis is common. In fact, distinguishing substance-induced states from psychiatric conditions remains one of the most challenging forms of differential diagnosis (Myrick and Brady 2003).

An awareness of how the consequences of substance use and withdrawal mimic psychological symptoms is critical to revealing a hidden addiction. In the case of substances, each grouping is associated with a different set of psychological sequelae. Symptoms that mimic psychological problems occur at all phases of substance use: in the acute or active phase (when the person is under the influence of the substance), with prolonged or chronic use, and as a result of withdrawal. The DSM-IV has a large section on substance-induced disorders (291.x) that includes alterations in mood, thought, memory, sleep, and sexual functioning.

A description of the psychological changes induced by different classes of drugs follows. Not all categories of drugs and effects are covered. The focus is on substance-induced psychological changes that potentially camouflage an addiction by mimicking psychological symptoms.

Alcohol and Sedatives: Ongoing use of substances that depress nervous system functioning, such as alcohol or sedatives (e.g., Valium, Xanax), can lead to memory lapses that, in extreme cases, become blackouts. Chronic use is associated with sleep problems, sadness, anxiety, irritability, and difficulty concentrating. A twenty-five-year-old recently married woman enters psychotherapy reporting a lack of energy, difficulty getting to work on time, lack of confidence on the job due to increasing mistakes, and her husband's annoyance at her general lack of response to him. This presentation sounds like an adjustment reaction or depression until she complains about her husband, "He doesn't want me to have any free time, he even gets on my case for meeting my girlfriends for some drinks." In light of her symptoms, this statement should serve as a clue to the clinician to inquire about her drinking. For others with chronic use of depressants, anxiety will be salient and expressed in the form of nervousness or worry that is mistaken for a generalized anxiety disorder. The symptoms of alcoholism can also be mistakenly attributed to borderline personality disorder. The symptoms they share are poor anger control, unstable interpersonal relationships, suicidal or dramatic behavior, and identity disturbances (Lilenfeld and Kaye 1996).

As has been emphasized, psychotherapy patients do not necessarily connect psychological symptoms, such as anxiety and depression, to their substance use. This failure to connect is very common when the substance is alcohol or a sedative. In the acute phase, alcohol and sedatives are effective in reducing negative affective states. For this reason, people often turn to this group of drugs as a way to alleviate stress, worry, or dysphoria. After months of use, the person does not think to connect the return of dsyphoric or anxious feelings to the drug that in his or her mind has been effective in reducing such feelings.

Stimulants: In the acute phase, cocaine and stimulants, such as amphetamines (e.g., Ritalin), are associated with restlessness, mood swings, and, in more chronic phases, paranoia. Cocaine, in the initial response, acts like an aphrodisiac. In a clinical setting, a sexually active male may come in complaining of sudden sexual difficulties. Initially, cocaine helps to facilitate arousal, but with chronic use comes the inability to orgasm. More common are men whose cocaine use is associated with fantasy and masturbation. Sixty percent of men with cocaine addiction also report sexual addictions, such as excessive use of pornography (Washton 1989).

Cocaine is popular as an appetite suppressant among those with eating disorders or those whose appearance is a major component of self-esteem. Withdrawal symptoms following cessation of regular stimulant use mimic depression. Symptoms include lowered energy, poor concentration, and a general withdrawal from life where there is less pleasure and interest in daily activities. This withdrawal phase can last eighteen weeks or longer so it is quite possible that a psychotherapist could see a patient who appears to be suffering from a major depressive episode but the symptom picture is actually a reflection of ongoing withdrawal from stimulants.

Caffeine is the most widely used psychoactive substance, but it is not considered to be a diagnosable addiction. As a result, its role in a client's presentation is often overlooked. Caffeine's acute effects include anxiety, sleep disturbances, mood change, and cardiovascular complaints (palpitations) that can be misinterpreted as symptomatic of panic attacks. Withdrawal from caffeine is associated with headaches and irritation.

Cannabis: Marijuana is the most frequently used illicit drug. With chronic use an amotivational syndrome arises which involves low energy, blunted affect, apathy, and sexual dysfunction. A patient may not connect these psychological changes to the effects of marijuana given that THC is stored in body fat and released up to several days later; by the time symptoms emerge, many other events, besides using marijuana, have occurred. Further complicating recognition is the fact that symptoms develop gradually over time

(Schuckit 1998). When marijuana-induced psychological changes are not attributed to drug use, they can be experienced as a sense of depression that warrants psychotherapy. When presented with symptoms of an amotivational syndrome, the psychotherapist who has not completed a substance-use assessment is likely to interpret them as evidence of depression. A client with marijuana-induced amotivational syndrome may also appear in a psychotherapy office with difficulty discussing feelings that the therapist mistakenly attributes to either depression or alexithymia.

Opioids: Opioids, such as heroin, are no longer a class of drugs associated with urban and/or poor areas. Heroin has become popular among young affluent suburbanites. Instead of injecting heroin, with its risk of transmitting HIV, this group prefers to snort the drug. In its acute phase, heroin creates euphoric feelings that can be accompanied by lethargy. Heroin-induced psychological changes are unlikely to bring a person to psychotherapy. The feelings are short lived and reliably linked to the drug. Flulike withdrawal symptoms (achy joints, runny noise), are more likely to lead to a medical visit than a psychotherapist's office. The only heroin users who may attribute emotional discomfort to psychological causes is the intermittent heroin user (e.g., so-called weekend warrior) who, upon stopping use altogether, becomes generally more anxious over the course of several weeks. Given that previous vacations from heroin have not been associated with anxiety, this type of heroin user make seek psychotherapy to address the problem. These anxious feelings, when presented in psychotherapy, can be mistaken for a generalized anxiety disorder (Myrick and Brady 2003).

Hallucinogens: Hallucinogens vary in popularity. While LSD, popular in the 1960s and early 1970s, is still being manufactured illegally, newer drugs, such as Ecstasy or MDMA have replaced it in popularity. Hallucinogens create breaks from reality and are most commonly associated with hallucinations. If disturbing, these hallucinations may lead a user to seek help, but this will usually be through an emergency room. Appropriately trained medical professionals will not mistake these hallucinations as evidence of a psychotic episode given that drug-induced hallucinations are distinct from those associated with a psychotic condition. Drug-induced hallucinations are usually visual and tactile without delusions, while those associated with psychosis are auditory and can be accompanied by delusions (Johnson, Heriza, and St. Dennis 1999). Individuals with a history of taking hallucinogens are more likely to seek psychotherapy to address problems that arise as a consequence of drug use (for example, flashbacks).

Process addictions: Process addictions can be hidden behind what appears to be routine psychological symptomatology. Gambling is associated with sleep disturbances, stomachaches, and depression. Sexual and cybersex addictions present in psychotherapy as problems in interpersonal relationships and/or declining sexual interest in a significant other. Computer addiction, especially in adolescents, can be misdiagnosed as an adjustment disorder where limited socializing has been replaced by gaming or other online activities. Withdrawal from any process addiction can produce symptoms of depression or anxiety.

Protracted withdrawal. In addition to short-term withdrawal effects, the diagnosis of an addiction can be missed or misdiagnosed due to a protracted withdrawal syndrome. Many people stop substance use without formal treatment (Fletcher 2001) and a short time later come to psychotherapy to address other problems in their lives. If not asked about their history of drug use (some popular screening tools address current use only), patients may discuss existing issues in solely psychological terms because they have stopped substance use and significant withdrawal symptoms have ceased or never occurred. From the ex-drug users' perspective, the absence of withdrawal symptoms is evidence that the physiological effects of drug use have passed and that drugs are no longer a relevant issue. However, withdrawal symptoms can extend much longer than expected. Schuckit (1998) indicates that, "bothersome symptoms remain for several months. These tend to be quite subtle and thus are sometimes ignored. One important symptom is a feeling of 'unease' because the heart and breathing rates are not responding adequately to changes in the environment. Other common symptoms of protracted withdrawal syndrome, seen with depressants, stimulants, and opiates, are feelings of nervousness and problems sleeping" (58–59).

Differential Diagnosis

The relationship between addictions and psychological symptoms is complex and takes a number of different forms. Psychological symptoms that are solely addiction-induced abate when substance use ceases. More commonly, a psychological disorder and an addiction represent two co-occurring problems that may or may not share a common underlying etiology. When the two co-occur, the addiction (in its active or withdrawal phase) creates symptoms that either: (1) exacerbate pre-existing psychological problems or (2) mask the severity of psychological symptoms (e.g., through a substance's self-medicating effect). Understanding which relationship holds for a given patient has treatment implications.

Once a therapist begins to wonder whether psychological symptoms are the outcome of substance use, excessive behavior, or part of a withdrawal response, how is a differential diagnosis made? The simplest and most direct method to determine which is primary is to have the patient experience a prolonged period without the substance or behavior. In the DSM-IV, at least four to six weeks of abstinence is recommended. This is a conservative amount of time in light of Schukit's (1998) prolonged withdrawal syndrome. A protracted history of severe cocaine use that is contributing to depression or anxiety can require at least three months of abstinence (Brems and Johnson 1997). Johnson, Heriza, and St. Dennis (1999) conclude that periods longer than six weeks are warranted with up to eighteen or more weeks recommended in the case of stimulant cessation.

Whenever a patient agrees to stop substance use, the therapist needs to be attuned to the possibility that ongoing psychological distress is a function of a protracted withdrawal syndrome. In such a case, the patient benefits greatly by having the therapist label it as such and provide reassurance that the discomfort will decrease with continuing abstinence. Not doing so increases the risk of relapse. Schuckit (1998) argues that a patient may subconsciously link the sense of unease to their history of substance use and thus chose to alleviate the ongoing discomfort by returning to active use.

Other than waiting to see what happens once the addiction stops, questions about the course and nature of psychological symptoms help to disentangle the complex relationship between addictions and psychological disorders. Some questions that contribute to making a differential diagnosis are:

- Did the psychological symptoms of concern precede the use of substances?
- What is the patient's impression of the relationship between psychological discomfort and substance use?
- What is the relationship between the intensity of psychological symptoms and the amount of substance being used?
- Have previous psychological treatments while using substances been helpful to alleviate these psychological problems?
- What is the personal and family history of psychological and addictive disorders? (Miele, Trautman, and Hasin 1996)

If there is no family history of addiction and psychological symptoms vary as a function of substance use, then it can appear that psychological symptoms are addiction-induced. However, this conclusion may be incorrect if this patient qualifies for a dual diagnosis such that the psychological effects of addictive behaviors interact with pre-existing psychological symptoms. Usually, this interaction exacerbates the severity of a patient's pre-existing psychological symptoms.

For example, take the case of a woman who comes to psychotherapy reporting anxiety. A substance-use screening reveals a history of alcohol abuse. While treating this addiction, it will be important to explore both the current and historical contexts surrounding her anxiety. One common scenario is for a female patient to begin using alcohol as a way to feel comfortable being sexual (i.e., as a way to self-medicate guilt and anxiety). However, due to years of excess alcohol use, anxiety has become pervasive. For this patient, anxiety both precedes alcohol abuse and is exacerbated by it. Alcohol cessation will reduce her generalized anxiety but still leave her with sexual concerns that predate her drinking problem. In a similar manner, PTSD symptoms that are exacerbated by cocaine decline with abstinence from the drug but are not resolved. Likewise, cessation of alcohol can decrease the sleep and mood disturbances associated with depression but this does not rid the patient of depression. Leaving pre-existing psychological issues untreated increases the risk of relapse.

Other times, addictive behaviors have the opposite affect on psychological symptoms; instead of exacerbating psychological distress, the addiction actually mask the symptom's severity. The psychological problems reported at the outset of therapy will appear milder than they actually are. For many, an addiction has been serving a self-medication function that masks the full extent of the psychological symptoms. If substance use is recognized and treated, the psychotherapist will be surprised to find that along with a reduction in substance use comes an exacerbation of the psychological condition.

It is well accepted that those most prone to addiction take substances for their effect (e.g., to relax, to release inhibitions). Khantzian's (1997) self-medication hypothesis takes this position one step further by arguing that the preferred substance depends on the symptoms and emotional states that the person wants to manage. The stimulating effects of cocaine can bring energy to a person with depression. Bipolar patients and those with anxiety disorders drink to self medicate uncomfortable affective states. The intensity of a manic episode is reduced with alcohol. Attention disorders are relieved by cocaine use as well as with nicotine. Sedating drugs help moderate PTSD symptoms. Alcohol, nicotine, and stimulants relieve negative symptoms of schizophrenia. Adolescents drink to alleviate anxiety and depression associated with adjustment reactions; these psychological issues cannot be effectively addressed in psychotherapy as long as the patient continues to drink (Brems and Johnson 1997; Khantzian 1997).

Making a differential diagnosis is complicated by the varied interactions between pre-existing psychological symptoms and addiction. In light of this complexity, research has been designed to provide a better understanding of the relationship between specific psychological disorders and substance use. Research by Abraham and Fava (1999) reveals that depression frequently predates development of a substance-related disorder. In a sample of outpatients being treated for major depressive disorders, onset of depression preceded alcohol dependence by 4.5 years and cocaine dependence by 6.8 years. Among polysubstance users, with the exception of LSD, drug use followed the onset of the first reported depression.

Often the exact nature of the interaction between addictions and psychiatric disorders is unknown until the addiction stops. A psychotherapist, who was interviewed about why she did not routinely assess for addictions, expressed regret about not having conducted an addiction assessment with a patient she knew smoked marijuana. This therapist reported that "the bipolar client was engaging in some out-of-character, sexual, acting-out behaviors that I attributed more to being manic, but as it turned out, they were really more about substance abuse." For this patient, smoking marijuana had a disinhibiting effect that led to sexual acting-out and other behaviors that were not in character. These were misinterpreted as simply a manic episode and the patient was rehospitalized. Following this hospitalization, where marijuana abuse was assessed and treated, the patient's manic episodes declined in intensity and frequency.

The previous examples show the different ways in which hidden addictions create on inaccurate picture of the psychological problems patients present in psychotherapy. Sometimes there is no psychological problem but merely an undiagnosed addiction masquerading as a psychological problem. Other times psychological disorders predate addictive behaviors and the unrecognized addiction leaves the clinician with an understanding of psychological symptoms that is exaggerated (addictive substances mimic the psychological symptoms) or minimized (addictive substances act as self-medication). No matter the origin, an inaccurate understanding of the psychological picture due to addiction impedes the effectiveness of psychotherapy.

SUMMARY

Most patients come to psychotherapy reporting depression and anxiety-like symptoms. The co-occurrence of psychological symptoms and addictive behaviors is the rule. The extent of this relationship is striking for some disorders with estimates of co-occurrence ranging from 25 to 58 percent (Brems and Johnson 1997). These figures, although large, exclude the co-occurrence of process addictions and psychological diagnoses. In light of the prevalence of dual diagnoses, any treatment provider must consider whether substance use or a process addiction is in any way complicating the psychological issues that will be the focus of therapy. Given that prolonged use of sedatives is associated with increased anxiety, one would not want to recommend that a patient with panic attacks or social anxiety be given benzodiazepines without first ensuring that this class of drugs is not contributing to the presenting problem. Likewise, a therapist would not want to use a cognitive-behavior or interpersonal therapy for depressive symptoms that are caused primarily by the physiological effects of active alcoholism or withdrawal. In other cases, where addictive behaviors are having a self-medicating effect, psychological distress will be underestimated and, if not recognized, treatment will stall.

10

Transforming the Assessment Process into Treatment

The context for assessing addictions in psychotherapy differs from an addiction treatment center. In the latter, patients have self-defined as being addicted or have been defined by others (e.g., a spouse, the legal system). In contrast, the typical psychotherapy patient is seeking treatment for a self-defined problem that is psychological in nature. A few patients will have vaguely articulated concerns that a behavior is excessive or problematic and turn to psychotherapy as way to decide if this is true or not. A new patient may not give voice to this concern but rather wait to see if the therapist recognizes a problem. Others enter treatment with no addiction issues, but over the course of treatment, behaviors that were once moderate and controlled become excessive and out of control.

The frequent co-occurrence of addictions and psychopathology and the regularity with which addictions go unrecognized in health care settings means that mental health professionals need to be better attuned to addiction issues. Simply being more knowledgeable about the symptoms of addiction and the addictive process will not solve this problem. Practitioners also need to be aware of their own hesitations to recognize and assess for addictions. This requires cognizance of entrenched beliefs about addictions arising out of professional culture (e.g., twelve-step groups are a cult or treatment and can only be conducted by addiction specialists) and supported by social stigmas (e.g., the addict is weak and unmotivated to change). This book has provided an array of formal and informal approaches to screening that can be incorporated into the clinician's general assessment style. The intent of this chapter is to highlight the central points regarding screening and then to illustrate how the results of a screening, when integrated with further knowledge about the addiction, sets the stage for treatment.

Assessment involves gathering information in order to identify a problem, provide a tentative diagnosis, and begin to develop a case conceptualization and treatment plan. While often thought of as occurring before the onset of formal treatment, assessment is not necessarily limited to a discrete number of sessions but can be an ongoing process that is inextricably linked with treatment. But even if a clinician prefers to complete a thorough initial screening before therapy begins, as the therapeutic relationship deepens, it is not surprising to have a patient reveal previously withheld information about an excessive behavior. Often the assessment process itself will have therapeutic consequences. Identifying a behavior that heretofore has not been recognized as problematic can be sufficient to decrease or stop the behavior. But even if this is not the outcome, a good assessment prepares the patient for treatment by facilitating motivation to change the newly identified addictive behavior.

THE ASSESSMENT PROCESS IN LIGHT OF STAGES OF CHANGE

At the completion of a successful assessment, the patient recognizes a problem and is ready to initiate change. Stages of change is a popular organizational scheme that has been applied frequently to substance use treatment. A number of scales are available to assess a substance abusing/dependent person's stage of change. These scales are best suited for those actively seeking addiction treatment (whether referred by oneself or another), which is rarely the case for the typical psychotherapy patient. However, the stage-of-change model remains useful because it provides a framework for creating an assessment process that prepares a patient to use psychotherapy as a place to change an addictive behavior.

Stages of Change

Precontemplation: No perception of a problem or minimal awareness of a problem without any acknowledgment that change is necessary. If a person seeks help, it is not for the addiction.
Typical presentation: Sally enters psychotherapy reporting a growing disinterest in her work and three-year relationship. Sally smokes marijuana three or four times a week and while she has, on occasion, wondered if this is a problem, she does not link her current concerns to her drug use and does not volunteer the information to the therapist.
Contemplation: Recognition of a problem and the need for change but there is no consistent conviction that change is necessary. No attempts to change have been initiated. Ambivalence about the addictive behavior and making a

change is strong. Even though addictive behavior is recognized as problematic, a person can remain in the contemplation stage for prolonged periods. Often, therapists mistakenly interpret a patient's recognition of a problem as indicating the patient is ready to participate in treatment.

Typical presentation: Ted knows he drinks too much. He has even thought about cutting down or quitting. When he comes to therapy for a growing sense of depression, he does not necessarily link this symptom to his alcohol consumption. Unless asked, there is no guarantee that he will mention his concern about drinking. If Ted mentions his drinking, it will be done as a passing comment and, unless the therapist picks up the topic, Ted will not bring it up again. If the therapist asks Ted to talk more about his drinking, he will oscillate between voicing the need to change so that he feels better and his wife doesn't get upset to concluding that his wife is too sensitive and his drinking really is not an issue.

Preparation: Addictive behavior is recognized as a problem and the need for change is acknowledged. Some small, overt changes have been made (e.g., he has told friends he gambles too much, she stops buying alcohol for the house, credit cards are destroyed). Often these changes are short-lived because the patient is not yet fully committed to change or the patient is unaware of effective change strategies.

Typical presentation: Among a variety of other worries, Carol mentions concern about her drinking at the outset of psychotherapy. She says that her roommate, who also drinks, is worried that Carol seems to become a different person after drinking. While she dismisses her roommate's opinion of her behavior, Carol has told her friends never to let her have more than three drinks when they go out. This plan has not worked. Carol is still interested in making a change and will be willing to work on her addictive behavior in treatment as long as the therapist correctly identifies her alcohol abuse.

Action: Concerted efforts are made to change the problematic behavior by changing oneself or the environment. When there are setbacks, the person keeps moving forward and remains motivated. Others begin to notice the behavior change.

Typical presentation: John seeks psychotherapy because he knows he is abusing cocaine and wants to stop. He explicitly asks the therapist for help with the problem, acts on recommendations to attend a self-help group, and reports on his progress in every therapy session.

Maintenance: Change is ongoing along with consolidation of gains while becoming more comfortable living without addictive behaviors.

Too often therapists assume that just because a patient recognizes a problem and is asking for help (i.e., contemplation stage), he or she is ready to change. In fact, patients who are ready to work on addiction issues are in the preparation or action stage. An effective assessment process helps move a patient through the first two or three stages of change so that by the assessment's completion, the patient is ready to take action. In the case of psychotherapy patients, most are unaware that the psychological symptoms for which they seek help are connected to an addictive behavior. Lack of problem awareness characterizes the precontemplation stage. Identification of a potential addiction through formal or informal screening moves the patient out of precontemplation into the contemplation stage.

SCREENING: IDENTIFYING A POTENTIAL PROBLEM

A psychotherapy patient's failure to mention an addictive behavior, may reflect the operation of denial, a concept that has emerged out of addiction treatment centers where patients, with a long history of substance use and unsuccessful attempts to stop, actively minimize or disavow a behavior's destructiveness. Most psychotherapy patients have a very different relationship to their excessive behavior. Addictions are often an integral part of the psychological symptoms they bring to psychotherapy—so integral that the patient does not recognize that psychological symptoms are a function of substance use or excess behavior.

Failure to identify that life problems are meaningfully connected to addictive behaviors occurs for a number of reasons: (1) psychological problems preceded the addictive behavior making them more salient, (2) the addictive behavior is in its early stages so that adverse consequences are limited and/or have not reliably followed the behavior, and (3) the addictive behavior does not stand out because it is considered normative within the family of origin or cultural environment.

When patients do not self-identify an addiction, screening instruments become a practical clinical tool that both facilitate identification and convey to the patient that addictive behaviors are a topic for therapy. A new patient can complete a self-report instrument such as the MAST or AUDIT. Both focus on alcohol's negative consequences with the AUDIT including questions about quantity and frequency of consumption. Or the practitioner can ask a set of structured questions such as the CAGE. The RAPS, developed by taking the most effective questions from a variety of popular brief screening tools, has some advantages over previous instruments given its improved sensitivity with minority populations (Cherpital 1997). Nearly all instruments focus on a single substance, usually alcohol. A few screening tools assess drug and alcohol use simultaneously (e.g., CAGE-AID, TICS) or a range of process addictions (PROMIS). All these tools identify addiction by calling attention to the negative consequences of a given behavior.

Some clinicians feel that any self-report instrument or structured set of questions necessarily impedes the developing therapeutic relationship that, once established, facilitates the gathering of meaningful information. A strong working alliance with an interested and empathic clinician allows the patient to feel more comfortable revealing excessive behaviors and their consequences. These clinicians wait until the time seems appropriate to ask questions that draw from major screening tools. Or, "leading questions" related to lifestyle are asked in order to bring information about excessive behaviors into the therapeutic dialogue. How do you have a good time? What do you do for pleasure? How to you cope with X (a specific stressful situation)? What do you do to relax?

Of course, alternative approaches to screening are not mutually exclusive. A clinician who provides a self-administered screen at the start of therapy can administer a less structured assessment later in treatment. Screenings at different points in treatment provide patients with several opportunities to talk about a behavior. Research indicates that the accuracy of self-reports increases with repeated inquiries (chapter 5).

Clinicians who avoid structured assessments and prefer that information emerge out of the therapeutic dialogue need to listen for subtle signs of addiction such as those discussed in depth for alcohol in chapter 7. Subtle signs that cut across addictions include

1. Remorse or regret about a behavior. "I wish I hadn't said all those things." "I can't believe we got into a fight over such a minor problem." Exploring the context in which regret or remorse occurs can reveal substance use that is occurring excessively or is out of control.

2. Lack of concern over the object of the behavior or the situation in which it occurs. A woman shops but does not care what is purchased; a man drinks but does not care about the type of alcohol.

3. The patient's reflections frequently make reference to a potentially addictive behavior that is seemingly unrelated to the presenting problem. The behavior may be in the forefront of the discussion but more likely it will be in the background of reported events. During every session, exercise weaves its way into the conversation; every social occasion involves a mention of drinking. It is easy to miss the significance of these references because, on the surface, the behavior appears to be a minor detail that is not meaningful connected to the presenting problem.

4. Having peers, a significant other, or a family member with an addiction. For men, peers are an important predictor of an addictive behavior, while for women, a husband's addiction predicts her own. Having a parent with an addiction increases one's own chance for an addiction, although not necessarily the same type.

Remaining attuned to subtle signs of addiction is necessary even if screenings are conducted routinely. No scale is comprehensive given that the newest fad in drugs will not be included. A process addiction can be missed in this initial screening and/or a problem may develop over the course of therapy. A woman, who starts therapy to support her decision to divorce, turns to alcohol to relieve feelings of guilt and loneliness once her husband leaves the house. For a patient like this, attention to subtle signs helps to reveal that a behavior is becoming addictive.

Given that the range of addictive behaviors has expanded, subtle signs can be the only clue that there is an addiction, even after a careful screening. As emphasized in chapter 1, the types of behavior that can occur in an addictive manner are probably limitless. As initially conceived, addictions were confined to a distinct set of objects, that is, substances with mood-altering effects. With recognition of behavioral addictions, a limited number of behaviors that could become excessive and create negative consequences was enumerated (e.g., gambling, sex, exercise). Since then the scope of addictive behaviors has been broadened. Behavior is now referred to as an addictive disorder (e.g., Goodman 1998) or addictive process (e.g., Peele 1985), and emphasis is placed on how one behaves and not on the object of the behavior (e.g., a substance, a slot machine, running). A behavior pattern that has the capacity to powerfully modify subjective experience is considered addictive when: (1) it persists despite adverse consequences, (2) attempts to control the frequency or quantity of the behavior are unsuccessful and (3) there is a subjective sense of craving or compulsion to do the behavior or to have the substance (Shaffer 1999).

Screening tools cast a wide net; not all who score positively or show evidence of subtle signs of abuse will be addicted. The presence of an addiction can only be determined through additional clinical inquiry or a structured diagnostic interview. Another alternative, once an addiction is suspected, is to ask how the patient perceives the behavior. "Do you consider your drinking a problem?" "Have you ever thought you should cut back your computer use?" A patient who is convinced that the behavior is not a problem remains in the precontemplation stage. A patient who expresses concern, no matter how minimal, is moving into the contemplation stage. Either way, the next step is further inquiry into the scope and nature of the behavior to determine if it meets the diagnostic criteria for an addiction.

FROM SCREENING TO DIAGNOSIS

In chapter 3, addictive behaviors were described as occurring along a continuum from nonoccurrence (e.g., abstinence) to addiction. Formal diagnosis (e.g., substance dependence, pathological gambling) spotlights one end of this continuum. However, in the context of psychotherapy, less extreme forms of addictive behavior (e.g., so-called subclinical levels) deserve attention. This is because even low levels of potentially addictive behaviors have adverse effects. Substance use can impede the effectiveness of psychotropic medications, exacerbate or mask psychological symptoms, and bring instability into a person's life. The clinician who concludes that the presenting problems are solely psychological in nature will be left with an inaccurate understanding of the patient's issues, which has implications for treatment planning. Thinking of addictive behaviors as occurring along a continuum supports therapists in exploring any behaviors at risk of becoming addictive to ensure that this behavior is not complicating the patient's life or hindering the effectiveness of treatment.

What defines a behavior as being at risk and in need of assessment? When it comes to alcohol, an at-risk drinker is easily defined. This person consumes more than two standard drinks per day but shows no signs of abuse or dependence (chapter 4). There are no governmental standards defining safe limits for illegal substances or process addictions. When assessing whether these behaviors are at risk, one can follow Shaffer's recommendation that behaviors or substances that "reliably and robustly shift subjective experience" (1997, 1576) have the potential of becoming addictive. With adolescent patients, where clinicians want to determine if experimentation represents an at-risk behavior, Swadi (1997) finds the following question useful: "Is the effect of the substance more important than the adventure of use?"

Next along the continuum are varying degrees of problematic behavior or substance use. If relying on the DSM-IV, problematic use is taken to be synonymous with substance abuse and diagnosed based on a range of negative social and health consequences. In the case of process addictions, a behavior is either problematic or addictive based on the degree to which the behavior meets criteria for an addictive disorder (see chapter 1) or specific process addictions such as pathological gambling in DSM-IV, exercise addiction (Hausenblas and Symons Downs 2002a), or computer addiction (Orzack and Ross 2000). A behavior is defined as problematic if it meets one criteria but less than the requisite number needed for a formal diagnosis.

Another way to distinguish problematic and addictive levels of a behavior is to look at how the behavior occurs. Using alcohol as the example, normal drinkers drink primarily because of the setting (e.g., to be sociable), although sometimes they drink to relax or cope. When drinking becomes the primary means of coping with a problem, then use is problematic. What distinguishes the problem drinker from the person addicted to alcohol is that the alcoholic continues drinking even after the problem that initiated the drinking (e.g., stressful feelings) is gone. This line of thinking can be applied to process addictions. A person may sometimes shop as a way to relax but when the primary motivation for shopping is to manage uncomfortable feelings, then shopping is becoming problematic and potentially addictive.

These various criteria help to distinguish whether a behavior merits a diagnosis of addiction or dependence, can be considered problematic, or is at risk. However, all of these criteria and rules are difficult to keep in the forefront during a session. As a result, when listening for evidence of addiction, the tendency is to resort to the more commonsense view of addiction as any behavior that is occurring excessively. But, as seen in chapter 1's review of diagnostic practices, excess alone is not a reliable indicator of a behavior's addictive potential. For some, even small amounts of substance use or a relatively infrequent behavior creates adverse effects. One drink for an elderly person who has equilibrium problems is too much. Two drinks for a pregnant woman are too many.

During the clinical hour I find it useful to listen to a patient with Shaffer's (1999) three addiction criteria in mind: (1) adverse consequences, (2) loss of control, and (3) cravings. These are simple to remember and make it easy to hear whether a behavior, even an infrequent behavior, warrants attention in therapy. Take the case of a successful businessman in his late forties whose drug use was reasonable and controlled but still problematic. He had a long history of weekly use of either codeine or heroin, which he snorted. He had considered this his unique approach to stress reduction. Despite years of limited and controlled use, upon reaching his mid-forties he decided, for health reasons, to try a more traditional means of stress management. He began training in yoga and meditation. While his drug use declined to once-monthly (a schedule he stuck to rigorously), subjectively he felt more addicted than ever. He found himself constantly thinking about where the drugs were located, imagining where he would be when using them on the designated day at the end of the month, and fantasizing about the high that would follow. This man had a high risk of returning to addiction because, despite using small quantities, being in control, and avoiding negative consequences, he continued to crave drugs.

Diagnosis in the context of a continuum model is more than a matter of deciding if a person meets diagnostic criteria or not. A positive screening, be it formal or informal, is followed by further information gathering in order to clarify the extent of the problem. Further information to be gathered includes: (1) quantity and frequency; (2) negative consequences; and (3) feelings, thoughts, or motives associated with the behavior and its change.

Assessing Quantity/Frequency

Although diagnosis is not dependent on the degree to which a behavior is "in excess," information concerning quantity and frequency still has utility in the assessment process. Often, until asked, patients have not thought much about their behavior and do not have a good sense of how much of a substance they use or the extent to which a behavior is occurring. By facilitating self-awareness, this knowledge can be sufficient to change the behavior.

Questions from the Quantity/Frequency Questionnaire (see chapter 5) address alcohol consumption. Patients are asked the quantity of alcohol consumed on a typical day, average frequency of use per week, and maximum quantity (as a way to check for binge drinking). This questionnaire can be modified in order to assess for other substances and process addictions. For substances other than alcohol, a more meaningful measure of quantity is the financial cost. How much is spent on cocaine weekly is more informative than the number of grams used. For process addictions, quantity is assessed in terms of the amount of time the activity takes and/or the amount of money spent. How often during the week do you gamble and how much money, on average, do you win or lose? What is your biggest win or loss? Whether an addiction is suspected or not, the questions are framed with the assumption that the behavior is occurring. "How much do you drink on a typical day?" "How often do you exercise during the week and for how long?" "What is the longest time you have ever spent gambling?" Recall that for substances, quantity consumed is more informative than frequency. Frequency is strongly influenced by social factors and setting, but quantity is largely individually determined. Binge drinking is common in fraternities, but one young man stops drinking after five drinks in a row while another consumes ten or twelve total.

Quantity and frequency questions have an additional role to play in the assessment of alcohol where safe drinking limits have been set at two standard drinks per day for men and one for women (U.S. Department of Health and Human Services 2000). A patient who routinely drinks above the safe limits is considered at risk for developing problematic use. Before drawing any conclusions, it will be important to remember that definitions of safe drinking vary with age and gender and are based on the assumption that only alcohol is being used. Individual differences and co-occurring addictions are always important factors to consider during the assessment of any addictive behavior.

Assessing Negative Consequences

Continuing a behavior despite negative consequences helps to define it as problematic and potentially addictive. For this reason, most screening tools focus on negative consequences, such as feelings of guilt, others being annoyed or worried, periods of time that are unaccounted for, or not following through on responsibilities. Whether a behavior ultimately qualifies for a diagnosis or not, continuing a behavior despite awareness of its negative consequences indicates that treatment is warranted. Negative consequences can be divided into two types: those that are a direct effect of the behavior or substance use and those that are secondary to these direct effects.

Direct negative consequences usually arise from the addictive behaviors' affect on biological systems. Some biological changes mimic psychological symptoms, which can be confused with anxiety and depressive disorders. Lessening the effectiveness of medications, especially of psychotropics, is another direct negative consequence. Other examples include accidental overdose; hangovers, stomach or liver problems, and brain damage for an alcoholic; leg pain after too much sitting for a gambler; infection from unclean needles used by injection drug users; nose bleeds, lost sleep, sexual difficulties, and weight loss with cocaine use. With process addictions, direct effects are not solely linked to biological changes. Excessive shopping or gambling results in unanticipated levels of credit card debt, while time on the computer leads to neglect of appearance and household chores. Negative consequences arising directly from excess behavior or substance use can disappear simply by reducing or stopping the behavior.

Secondary effects are based on responses to these direct effects and can include guilt about the addictive behavior, arguments about a lack of attention to household responsibilities, or a boss's warning due to declining job performance. As direct and secondary effects begin to accumulate, functional impairments emerge that adversely affect one's sense of well-being, work life, finances, leisure activities, marital and social relationships, and legal matters. Functional consequences rarely ameliorate with change in the addictive behavior and often require psychotherapy.

The direct effects of addiction as well as the resulting functional impairments are often more salient and compelling to both patient and psychotherapist than the addictive behavior itself. When this happens, it is quite possible that treatment will focus on addiction's consequences without recognizing (or treating) the underlying addiction.

Once an addictive behavior is identified, however, it will be important to explore its full range of negative consequences. Two types tend to be overlooked. Because patients usually describe direct and secondary consequences affecting only them, the therapist will want to ask questions to determine if an addictive behavior poses a danger to others (e.g., driving or operating machinery under the influence, neglecting childcare responsibilities, unsafe sexual practices). Therapists also need to be vigilant not to overlook the toll addictive behaviors take on physical health. Any time a behavior is creating functional consequences, an appointment with a physician for a complete physical should be recommended. Given that physicians are no more adept in recognizing addiction than psychotherapists (chapter 4), a patient should be encouraged to explain the reason for the visit.

Developing a Fuller Picture of Antecedents and Consequences

The road to addiction usually begins with a simple behavior that is experienced as gratifying, whether it is directly pleasurable or is a way to remove discomfort. There is a paradoxical nature to the addictive process (Donovan and Marlatt 1988). A behavior that originates in order to exert some control over and cope with certain aspects of life ends up becoming out of control and making life less manageable. For the patient, this paradox is subjectively experienced as ambivalence. Ambivalence characterizes the contemplation stage of change. This ambivalence makes some clinicians want to avoid treating addictions. In the long run, addicted patients probably are no more ambivalent than other patients. As clinicians often discover while working with a nonaddicted patient, as treatment progresses, a patient can become extremely ambivalent or resistant to changing the problem that initially precipitated seeking treatment. What distinguishes this patient from the addicted one is that the addicted patient's ambivalence is overt and expressed at treatment's outset.

Positives and Negatives of Addictive Behavior

The assessment process can help motivate a patient to change. One way it can do this is by serving to highlight a patient's ambivalence and then allowing the patient to give voice to both the negative and positive sides of the addictive behavior. During this exploration, negative consequences are likely to capture the therapist's attention. The altered states associated with substance use and negative psychosocial consequences place patients at greater risk for self-harm and harm to others. These risks can be a source of anxiety that the therapist manages by moving prematurely into an educational role. While education has a role to play in the addiction assessment process, this should be saved until the clinician has a fully developed understanding of the clinical picture. Equally important, premature emphasis on the negatives of addiction impedes a thorough exploration of both sides of the ambivalence.

The allure of an addictive behavior is aptly captured in the title of two books, Knapp's *Drinking: A Love Story* (1996) and Moriarty's *Liquid Lover* (2001). Outside the literary realm, the appeal of addictive behavior has been examined in terms of attachment theory where the addiction, not people, is the primary relationship (Flores 2004). The clinician needs to ensure that the assessment does not concentrate on negative consequences to the exclusion of an equally thorough exploration of the behavior's positive appeal.

It is rarely productive to ask directly: "Why do you do cocaine?" Instead, one asks: "What are the things you enjoy about your drug use?" "*Tell me the pleasure you get from gambling?*" Some patients are jarred by these questions; they have not realized, until asked, that the behavior is no longer solely pleasurable.

Patients who have difficulty with these questions may be better able to describe their experience if questions are phrased in the more emotionally neutral, thought-oriented language of expectations. Expected positive effects predict at-risk behaviors as much as mood-altering motivations: "What is it you expect to happen when you get on the computer?" "Tell me what you imagine it is like to smoke marijuana."

Positive outcomes, like negative consequences, come in many forms. Most patients easily acknowledge the social reasons for substance use. An adolescent will say there is no reason to worry about her drug use; she is just doing it because all of her friends do. A woman drinks as a way to be able to spend time with her husband. A man drinks at his business lunch in order to be a team player. For patients who cannot move beyond normative social explanations for their addictive behavior, one can validate these reasons while emphasizing that drinking to the point of getting drunk (or any other form of behavioral excess) is not required in these situations.

One of the more notable appeals of addictive behavior stems from its mood-altering effects. The self-medication hypothesis proposes that preference for a specific substance develops because of its unique mood-altering properties or its ability to address psychological deficits (Khantzian 1985). Alcohol, Valium, and other sedative-hypnotics alleviate anxiety. Cocaine and other stimulants induce feelings of elation and grandiosity lacking in depressed and narcissistically empty persons. Opiates and other narcotics serve to mute the disorganizing effects of rage and aggression. Most often, the mood-altering effects remove discomfort; however, one should never make assumptions about what qualifies as an uncomfortable affective state. One adolescent woman with a history of smoking marijuana and drinking since she was twelve was two years sober when she relapsed after being admitted to college; she could not tolerate the attention this success brought her.

Some patients have difficulty answering questions about experiences, feelings, motives, and expectations linked to an addictive behavior. These patients and those who focus solely on positive effects or social reasons benefit from detailed inquiries into specific occurrences of addictive behavior using Shea's validity techniques (1999) described in chapter 7. After recalling several specific incidences, patients who were previously blocked begin to get a sense that certain settings, feelings, and thoughts are reliably connected to the addictive behavior. Incorporating the validity techniques of normalization and shame attenuation facilitate this inquiry. With both approaches, questions include reference to a specific thought or feeling state, but a phrase is added that makes a "yes" reply seem normal. "Sometimes when people are angry or stressed, they think that drinking is the only way to feel better." "Given how often you feel bored and aimless, I wouldn't be surprised if you like to use cocaine in order to feel more alive, more engaged with life."

By inviting the patient to explore both the positives and negatives of their addictive behavior, the clinician is less likely to be seen as moralizing or adhering to an "addictions are bad" position. This balanced exploration of pros and cons supports the patient's full expression of ambivalence, which is the task of the contemplation stage. In so doing, the patient feels understood because ambivalence is being acknowledged and accepted, which in turn sets the stage for successful therapy by facilitating the therapeutic relationship.

Benefits and Costs of Change

Parallel to a patient's ambivalence about the addiction, is ambivalence regarding changing the behavior. A good question to ask which recognizes the patient's experience is: *"Tell me which part of you wants to change and which part does not?*

Patients can easily give voice to the advantages of changing. Often significant others have been emphasizing these benefits for quite some time. Work performance will improve; there will be money for things other than drugs, gambling, or shopping; health will improve; and of course, the significant other will be happier. A common cost of change is that all the positive consequences of the addiction are lost and the addiction itself will be missed; for many, the addictive behavior or substance, no matter how disruptive, has been the most reliable and stable relationship and a source of release for many years. To give up the addiction is like losing a good friend, one's past, or a part of oneself (Diamond 2000).

During initial explorations, costs associated with the loss of the addiction are more acutely felt than the benefits. While trying to maintain a balanced inquiry, the provider will want to help the patient consider the attractiveness of nonaddictive behavior and to find meaning and hope in change.

Decisional Balance

A patient's readiness for change is influenced by his or her appraisal of the pros and cons of continuing and changing the addictive behavior. In a dual-diagnosis population, movement into the preparation stage is facilitated by emphasizing the negative consequences of addiction while simultaneously highlighting the benefits of change. Diminishing the appeal of addiction or the cost of changing has little effect on motivation. The latter, cost of change, declines naturally as part of the action stage (Carey, Purnine, Maisto, and

Carey 2002). This process is known as decisional balance (Miller and Roll-nick 2002). A number of scales contribute to assessing decisional balance, but these are limited in scope to alcoholism (Center for Substance Abuse Treatment 2000). The one exception is the Alcohol and Drug Consequences Questionnaire that can be easily modified to examine the pros and cons of changing any addictive behavior (Cunningham et al. 1997). The wide array of feelings and beliefs contributing to decisional balance also can be expressed by simply asking patients to write a letter to their addiction (Diamond 2000). For an illustration of the components of a decisional balance see table 10.1.

When exploring the attitudes and expectations that contribute to a decisional balance, clinicians will want to (1) make sure that what the patient says is personally meaningful, and (2) increase the salience of less conscious or less obvious attitudes and feelings.

Many patients can easily voice the negative consequences of their addictive behaviors; they have been hearing about these from significant others for a long time or they know intellectually that there are problems. Clinicians should not be seduced into believing the patient is ready to change just because he or she can list an addiction's adverse effects or the benefits of change. One patient who says that she may lose her job if she keeps doing drugs, reports this only because friends and her boss have told her so; she has yet to believe this really will happen. The clinician will want to make sure that the patient is not just obligingly giving a list of negatives without having a full appreciation of their implications. With this patient, the therapist would be advised to explore in some detail what is happening at work and the implications of unemployment.

Table 10.1 primarily reflects functional pros and cons of addiction and change. However, ambivalence is often shaped by less conscious attitudes and feelings associated with addictive behaviors' capacity to alter mood or sense of self. When high (be it on a substance or from a behavior), a person feels less vulnerable, less fragmented, more substantial, more real, more connected, etc. By using therapy sessions to better understand the precipitants, contexts, and factors that serve to initiate and maintain addiction, the clinician helps the patient become aware of these less conscious contributions to their decision to change or not.

Table 10.1.   Pros and Cons of Continuing or Changing the Addictive Behavior

Continue the Addictive Behavior		Change the Addictive Behavior	
Pros	*Cons*	*Pros*	*Cons*
Easier to socialize	Wife is angry	Better family relations	More anxiety
Cope better	Tired, don't feel good	Improved finances	Lose friends
Enjoy sex more	Bad role model	Wake up easier	Nothing to do
Feel like a winner			

Often the decisional balance is such that the patient recognizes the harm that arises from continuing the behavior but sees few if any benefits of reducing or eliminating the addictive behavior itself. While stage of change research suggests that movement into the preparation and action phases is best achieved when both the negatives of addiction and the benefits of change are salient, treatment can proceed when only the former condition is met. This patient can be motivated to engage in a treatment where the initial goal is reducing negative consequences (i.e., harm reduction) without necessarily changing the addictive behavior. Often through this process, the patient comes to value the benefits of change and becomes motivated to participate fully in treatment that is the hallmark of the action stage.

Background Information

Other information that facilitates treatment planning consists of the history of the behavior, including family history of related problems; current addictive behaviors in the family; and the role family members, whether addicted or not, play in maintaining the patient's addiction. The age at which the behavior first began and when it became more or less ongoing is also revealing. With substance addictions, sex, and gambling, the earlier the onset, the greater likelihood of addiction. In a similar vein, it is useful to know about periods when the addiction was absent. Knowing whether the person has ever abstained and for how long is critical for treatment planning when the goal is cessation of a substance—especially alcohol or other sedatives. The serious alcoholic who drinks daily can experience severe and potentially life-threatening withdrawal symptoms if alcohol is stopped precipitously while not under medical care.

When the risky or addictive behavior involves substances, asking about other substance use and being attuned to excessive behaviors, both current and historical, is necessary given the high incidence of polysubstance use and cross addictions. Even if an initial inquiry reveals nothing significant, the therapist should remain attuned since a patient who has just acknowledged one addiction may minimize the use of other substances or behavior. When there is evidence of polysubstance use, careful attention should be paid to substances taken from within the same group as a way to prevent accidental overdose due to cross tolerance.

THE ROLE OF INPUT FROM SIGNIFICANT OTHERS: COLLATERAL REPORTS

Whenever possible, assessment in addiction treatment centers includes input from significant others. Collateral reports are considered essential because the addicted person's self-report is assumed inaccurate because of either denial or substance-induced impairments in judgment and cognition. Information provided by significant others is intended to provide a more accurate picture of the scope of the problem and its consequences. Psychotherapists, especially those working with adults in individual treatment, are not in the habit of requesting outside input. The benefits and complications that come with another's input is familiar to those working with families and couples, but in these modalities, the contract includes another person from treatment onset. Psychotherapists who treat children and adolescents regularly have parental input and are more familiar with a model that incorporates participation from persons other than the designated patient.

If a patient is agreeable, input from significant others helps to round out the clinical picture. While generally self-reports of quantity or frequency of addictive behaviors are underestimated but somewhat accurate (chapter 5), the designated patient often has a restricted perception of the consequences. One patient readily agreed that she drank excessively but kept challenging me to come up with consequences. I was able to point out a few, but only when her spouse came in to talk about her self-injurious behavior and increased temper when drunk did she begin to take her alcohol abuse seriously.

Often a patient has some awareness of adverse consequences, but these are limited to the negatives directly affecting him or her (e.g., a spouse's anger, probation at work) and their severity is underestimated.

I was working with a man who readily acknowledged the negative consequences of his periodic drinking; if he ran out of liquor late at night he would impulsively leave the house and drive in an intoxicated state to the only open convenience store located in a dangerous area. Sometimes, when drunk, he would decide to clean up a messy cellar and would endanger himself by lifting overly heavy objects or accidentally dropping things. He was ashamed to admit that when hung over the next morning, he was short tempered with his wife and children. When his wife came to a session, she supported these observations and added some he did not know or had not acknowledged. When he rushed out at night to buy liquor, he left the door of their ground floor apartment open, thus exposing her and the children to danger. Several times his cleaning accidents involved broken glass that left on the floor could injure the children. And once, when she left for work early, he had fallen asleep while taking care of his two year old and was awakened when the babysitter arrived.

Psychotherapists usually have only a patient's report to inform treatment. When working with a patient who appears to be genuinely open and interested in changing, collateral reports seem superfluous. However, it has been my experience that no matter how open and forthcoming the patient, there is something to be learned from a significant other, be it a spouse, parent, boss, or friend, who attends a session to discuss the designated patient's addictive behavior. This significant other confirms or provides a more realistic picture of the degree of excess and flushes out a wider range of negative consequences. Enlarging the range of consequences is one way to make the patient recognize the severity of the problem. This, in turn, enhances motivation to change by helping the patient move from the contemplation to the preparation stage.

CONCLUDING THE ASSESSMENT: DEVELOPING A SHARED DEFINITION OF THE PROBLEM

The assessment process concludes by sharing with the patient what has been learned. This conclusion may emerge out of a formal, time limited assessment, or it may be the result of impressions gathered over a series of psychotherapy sessions. Whether this conclusion includes a diagnostic label depends on the setting, the practitioner's needs, and the patient. Practically speaking, in many cases the addictive behavior will not have a corresponding diagnostic label because it is not included in the DSM (e.g., most process addictions) or the behavior, at this point in time, is only considered to be "at risk." However, the behavior can still be described to the patient as an addiction to exercise, work, etc., or at high risk of becoming addictive. Treatment providers may resist offering labels because doing so resonates too strongly with the insistence of twelve-step philosophy that a patient self identify as an addict: "Hi, I am Dan. I am an alcoholic." Forgoing labels such as substance dependent or addicted also avoids bringing back into the consulting room all of the negative connotations associated with the term *addiction* (see chapter 4).

While effective treatment does not require that a diagnosis or label be shared with the patient, some find it constructive. A diagnosis or label can give a name to an array of behaviors that otherwise are simply taken to mean one is a bad person. The experience of a married woman I treated serves as an illustration. As a polysubstance abuser, she would have sex for drugs, felt chronically depressed when not high, was neglectful of her children, and had finally been sent for treatment after family members came across her stash of painkillers. When all of these different actions, for which she felt great remorse, fell under a single title of addiction, she felt as if her problems were less diffuse and more manageable. This in turn increased her sense of hope.

For others, a diagnosis makes the problem more real, which in turn enhances the motivation to change. The man described above, whose wife's report helped expand the scope of negative consequences, kept from fully recognizing the severity of his alcoholic behavior by keeping the consequences

separated in his mind. Sometimes he drank a lot. Other times he acted errati-
cally. Sometimes he was thoughtless. Other days he was inattentive. All of
these were brought together with the simple statement, "Based on your behavior, it seems clear that you are an alcoholic." He was quiet for a few minutes and then acknowledged for the first time, "I guess I really do have a
problem." Accepting that he had a problem needed to occur before considering changing the behavior. He had moved from the precontemplation to the
contemplation stage.

For others, the commonsense meaning of the term *addiction*, provides a
feeling of being understood. With reference to sexual addictions,

> Patients, however, seem intuitively drawn to "sexual addiction." . . . Whether
> thinking of it literally or merely as a powerful metaphor, many patients see in
> the addiction concept ideas that speak to their own experience—the sense of be-
> ing driven to do something even though they know they will regret it, the feel-
> ing of being high when engaging in sexual acting out, the experience of painful
> withdrawal when trying to control sexual activity (Nathan as cited in Carnes
> 1996, 131).

If the treatment provider has any doubt about the value of providing a label or a diagnosis, the patient can always be invited to provide one. Do you
worry that you might have a gambling problem? Have you ever thought you
were an alcoholic? The slightest indication of concern on the patient's part
provides material to work with. If the therapist feels strongly that there is an
addiction, but the patient indicates otherwise, it is worth asking:

- What would you need to have happen for you to consider that you have
  a problem?
- What concerns do you have about this behavior?

Simply stating that a certain pattern of behavior is problematic, without giving it a specific label, is often sufficient to move a patient out of the precontemplation stage.

Whether or not a diagnosis is provided, at the completion of an assessment
and as a transition to treatment planning, the practitioner and patient develop
a shared definition of the problem. This information is offered in a nonjudgmental manner, staying as close to the patient's experience as possible. Here
is a sample summary for a college student majoring in acting whose marijuana use had become problematic:

> Over the past few sessions you have been telling me that your roommates and
> parents are quite upset at your marijuana use and that recently you have begun

to think it may be affecting you in ways you hadn't thought of. You have done some reading and we've talked about how smoking marijuana may be behind your declining interest in your schoolwork and difficulty sticking to rehearsal schedules. Over the past six months, you told me that you have been more likely to smoke on the weekends and, where before you only smoked once or maybe twice a week, now you smoke almost everyday. We have talked about your family history—your father's history of alcoholism early in your parent's marriage and your older brother's problems with gambling, which suggests that addiction is not foreign to you or your family. You've seen how your brother's gambling has ruined his relationship with his wife and your parents. So now you are uncertain. Maybe marijuana has had more effects than you realized. You have wondered whether you should cut back or stop and see what happens. You're pretty sure that if you do this, your grades would improve. Two months ago, you did try to cut back to your old level of once or twice a week, but that didn't last long. What are your thoughts?

Much can be learned from the ensuing dialogue. But this will not be true for all patients. Some will adamantly refuse to agree with the assessment's conclusion that there is a problem. In these instances, addiction counselors, especially those trained in therapeutic communities, turn to confrontation. While this technique is not respected by most psychotherapists, some patients find traditional "in-your-face" confrontation valuable. For a patient with a chaotic and dysfunctional family history characterized by neglect, careful use of aggression, where the therapist insists there is a problem that requires attention, leaves the patient feeling supported and understood. Confrontation need not be all or nothing; it can be thought of as a gradual process. Instead of choosing between insisting the patient acknowledge a problem and dropping all mention of addiction, the therapist can be persistent in periodically reminding the patient that addiction is a concern and regularly raising questions that bring negative consequences to light. Of course, clinical judgment is called for when deciding which type of confrontation best suits a given patient.

As an alternative to confrontation, Miller (Miller and Rollnick 1991; 2002) developed motivational interviewing as a set of strategies that facilitate a patient's transition from the precontemplation or contemplation stage to the action stage. Based on Carl Roger's work, the approach supports a patient in talking about a behavior and, in so doing, helping him or her begin to connect life problems to this behavior. The strategies that make up motivational interviewing include:

1. Be empathic. Empathy involves understanding a patient's feelings while not approving or disapproving of the behavior. Empathy is critical when it comes to the patient's ambivalence about changing the ad-

dictive behavior. Instead of labeling this as a resistance or lack of motivation, the therapist accepts and understands the ambivalence while still supporting the need to change the behavior.

2. Avoid arguments. Never argue with a patient about whether the problem is an addiction or not. Instead, keep the focus on the consequences of the behavior—both positive and negative.

3. Roll with resistances. Patients with addiction issues have many reasons why their behavior is not a problem. To roll with a resistance often involves a reframing of what the patient says. A patient who insists that his gambling or drinking is not a problem but complains about his controlling spouse who nags him about his behavior can be asked to reframe his wife's nagging as an expression of concern or a desire to have a better relationship. This patient may go on to report the specific complaints that his nagging spouse voices. "She tells me I'm forgetful, that I don't listen to her, and that she doesn't trust me to follow through on things. I mean really, what does she want from me? Her expectations are unrealistic." To roll with this resistance, where the significant other rather than the addiction is presented as the problem, one can simply ask: "What concerns do you have about your gambling? Drinking?"

4. Develop discrepancies. Resistances function to keep the patient's addictive behavior ego-syntonic. Developing discrepancies helps to make the behavior ego-dystonic. One way to do this is to help the patient spell out his or her goals and aspirations and then listen for how current behavior supports or defeats achievement of these goals.

When Addictions Emerge in the Midst of Psychotherapy

Much has been said about how often addictive behaviors remain hidden in psychotherapy. It may be that the patient has not recognized the addiction or that the therapist has been colluding with the patient to keep addiction out of treatment. Another possibility is that reasonable use has escalated as a means to deal with difficult feelings evoked by the therapy. No matter its origin, once recognized, how does a therapist bring an addiction into the treatment? Kaufman (1994) is well aware of the challenge this transition poses. He suggests that to develop objectivity, an outside consultation is recommended. Once the therapist is prepared to intervene, an empathic tone is required with an emphasis on negative consequences of the behavior: "It seems that our recent inability to make progress, particularly in regard to intimate relationships, is related to your drinking and how it affects those who are close to you. Let's talk about how you can stop drinking, so that we can again focus meaningfully on your relationships" (Kaufman 1994, 94).

Except when the addictive behavior poses a serious threat to a patient's health or another person, I think it is best to let patients set their own initial treatment goals even if it is not abstinence. Having such a trial run at changing is an important component of the preparation stage. The goal may be realistic and the outcome successful. If not, failed attempts to meet self-defined goals can help patients move to the action stage where they are ready to follow recommended treatment strategies and goals. When addiction emerges as a theme during ongoing treatment, Kaufman believes that such self-defined goal setting is the only option.

In some cases, continued attempts to change the addictive behavior will not succeed and a referral to more specialized treatment will need to be considered. In other cases, patients will refuse to accept the idea that a behavior is problematic despite clear-cut negative consequences for the patient's life and treatment. When a patient remains in the precontemplation stage, the therapist will need to decide if therapy should be continued. One therapist I interviewed had faced this situation with a man who sought treatment in order to improve his interpersonal relationships. No addictions were reported at the outset of treatment. But, about a year into psychotherapy, addiction became a theme shortly after the patient reported that several men had been fired at work. Further inquiry revealed that they had been spending several hours a day on their computers viewing pornography. Wisely, the therapist asked her patient if he had done the same and the patient acknowledged that while not as extreme, he had developed an interest in cybersex. Over the course of the following month, the therapist was able to assess that this man's behavior was "at risk" of becoming addictive. She also began to wonder if the patient's failure to make much progress on his stated goal—to improve his relationships with women and ultimately, marry—was related to his involvement with cybersex. The patient balked at her assessment of the situation and despite her continued attempts to link his online activities to growing disinterest in dating suitable woman, he refused any suggestion to cut down or cease the behavior. The therapist ultimately concluded that she could not continue treatment and provided the patient with a referral to a specialist in cybersex addiction as well as a colleague who was willing to see him without requiring that he change his cybersex involvement. The patient followed through on neither option and left treatment.

SUMMARY

Too often addictions are set apart from mental health disorders. Addictions are viewed as social problems, moral weaknesses, or bad habits that are not amenable to psychotherapeutic treatment. As a result, addictions are not recognized or, if assessment is mandated, it is done in a pro forma manner and the outcome is filed away ("too far away" as one therapist has said). Earlier chapters of this book reviewed mistaken beliefs about addictions and the history of diagnosis and treatment in order to facilitate an open-mindedness in clinicians regarding the similarity between addictions and other types of psychological disorders. This attitude is necessary if mental health providers are to assess for addictions in a thorough manner.

This chapter has explored the different segments of the assessment process. These can occur in a circumscribed manner over a brief period of time or during a select number of sessions. In psychotherapy, limiting assessment in this way is not the best practice. While some practitioners will routinely assess for addiction in a first session, such initial assessments, no matter how thorough, do not guarantee that an addiction will be recognized. One cannot screen for all possible addictions, and often addiction arises over the course of treatment as a response to handling feelings inside and outside of treatment. In addition, as one gets to know the patient better, and the patient comes to trust the working relationship, new information is revealed. Often, assessment is ongoing and addiction recognition emerges over many treatment sessions. The process described here provides a set of flexible guidelines that can be applied over one or many sessions early, amidst, or well into treatment.

PART II

11

Assessing Hidden Addictions in Psychotherapy: Case Illustrations

The next two chapters bring to life the meaning of hidden addictions and their assessment through case material and reviews of autobiographies of addiction. The thinking of treatment providers who have not (knowingly) worked with addicted populations is predominated by the stereotypes about who is addicted and what an addicted person acts like (chapter 4). The people described in the coming chapters rarely fit these stereotypes. In fact, it is hoped that these individuals' experiences and presenting problems sound familiar because their lives are not very different from those of a nonaddicted psychotherapy patient. Since snippets of transcripts and case summaries rarely convey the richness of the person, I strongly encourage the reading of some of the autobiographies of addiction reviewed in chapter 12. The small details, private thoughts, and simple interactions convey how addiction weaves its way into a person's life and relationships and yet remains hidden from the author, the therapist, and significant others. Although hidden, these autobiographies contain clues to addiction's presence (such as the subtle signs presented in chapter 8). Reading such books can help to hone a practitioner's skill in recognizing addiction.

The patients described below all sought psychotherapy for problems unrelated to addiction. Only in one case did addiction issues emerge in the initial interview. For the others, addictions became apparent during psychotherapy. For the sake of clarity, the case material focuses on the assessment piece. Because this material has been pulled out from the session, the flow of the therapeutic dialogue can seem somewhat disjointed and leave the mistaken impression that the assessment is separated from the therapy process. Despite these impressions, it is important to remember that assessment takes place in the context of ongoing psychotherapy.

About half of the examples given here are taken from case notes I made while I was in the process of becoming aware of how often I, and psychotherapists in general, failed to recognize the co-occurrence of addictions and mental health problems. The other half comes from a time when I was more aware of the issue and experimenting with different assessment formats. I hope that within this range of examples, the reader finds an approach suitable to his or her style.

THE CASE OF SARAH

Sarah was a forty-six-year-old woman who came to psychotherapy shortly after her divorce was finalized. She had been separated from her husband for two years and they shared joint custody of their ten-year-old daughter. As a successful businesswoman, her financial well being was not adversely affected by this divorce. She owned her own home in a neighborhood near her husband's apartment. Sarah initially entered treatment to address unresolved feelings toward her ex-spouse. They maintained frequent contact because of a shared business pursuit and joint child custody. Although she had been instrumental in initiating the divorce because of her husband's temper and emotional distance, now that they were living apart and getting along better she wondered if the divorce had been a mistake.

Sarah had been in psychotherapy with another treatment provider before she was married and we were able to make good progress in relation to her presenting problem. She also brought into therapy problems she was having with her male boss. Because Sarah traveled a great deal for work, we met about three times a month. In the fourteenth session, nestled amidst a number of observations about the previous week, she reported that, "Sometimes I think that maybe I'm drinking too much." If I had not already begun to contemplate the frequent occurrence of addictions in psychotherapy patients, I wonder if I would have pursued this casual aside in more than a cursory manner.

However, because I was attuned to such remarks, I asked Sarah how much she was drinking and how this differed from her usual way of drinking. She was having two or three glasses of red wine (about six to eight ounces each) after her daughter went to bed and she was alone in her room reading. Having wine at night was not new to her, but drinking almost nightly was. I asked about possible motivations for increased drinking; she had none, although she was receptive to the idea that drinking might be her way of handling feelings of loneliness that were surfacing as we addressed her marriage and divorce. I indicated that three drinks of this size exceeded the recommended limit of two standard drinks per day and that her drinking could be considered problematic. A subsequent inquiry into negative consequences revealed none that she could report on except that she sometimes awakened at night to urinate— which did not happen on evenings when she did not drink. If there were no negative effects, I was wondering why Sarah even mentioned that her drinking might be a problem. When asked about her concerns, they focused on her feeling that it was difficult *not* to drink at night. A brief exploration into her drinking history revealed nothing significant—she drank a bit too much in college for brief periods but asked, "who didn't?" She recalled that her parents would have a before dinner drink on a regular basis. No one in her extended family had a history of drinking problems.

Sarah approached her increased drinking in much the same manner as she would an assignment at work—as a problem to be solved. She knew that AA was a place to go if you were an alcoholic, so she attended a beginners AA meeting in a city near her office. She did not want to go to a meeting in her local community out of fear of meeting someone she knew. She left the meeting feeling that those in attendance were not like her and she did not relate to the drinking stories she heard. Any large metropolitan area has numerous meetings so it is possible to find one that is a good fit. When I suggested Sarah try another meeting, she concluded that she just needed to cut back on her drinking. This seemed a reasonable goal; she was the perfect candidate for controlled drinking. She had been overusing for a relatively brief period. There was no evidence of addiction in her family and her drinking was not associated with harmful consequences. We began a moderation management program—thirty days of no drinking. This was pretty easy for her and after the allotted time, she began a different pattern of drinking that we jointly defined as moderate. She no longer drank alone and had no more than two drinks at a party (Kishline 1994; Sobell and Sobell 1993).

Over the next few months, as we continued to work on grief around her divorce, she occasionally reported in on her drinking. It was going well—she was not drinking at all during the week, and when she did drink, it was with friends or at social gatherings on the weekend. She was pleased with the outcome and reported that this "little push" was all she needed; her drinking was under control. She felt physically much better and more present at social engagements. After six months, she continued to report no difficulties with her moderate drinking plan. I recognized that I had very little to do with her overcoming her drinking problem. She ran this part of the treatment herself. This was quite consistent with Sarah's counterdependent stance where she felt threatened any time she was in need of help from another person.

While therapy had been productive during her period of increased consumption, without the wine bottle as her nighttime companion, the depth of feelings around her divorce, and its resonance with past separations and loss, surfaced. Coming to terms with her divorce was complicated by longstanding issues with her depressed mother. By all accounts the therapy and her life had improved; she was socially active—she had dinner with female friends or with parents of her daughter's close friends—but curiously she insisted that she had no interest in dating. Sarah was an attractive, dynamic woman who met many men yet rarely was asked on a date. Attempts to explore her lack of interest in developing a relationship with a man led nowhere, which was in marked contrast to other life issues that we had explored effectively together.

During this period of successful moderate drinking, Sarah left her job in a big corporation to join a fledgling business venture that, in a short period, was bought out by a Fortune 500 company. This was around fifteen months into treatment. Sarah continued to drink moderately, and while issues with her mother were not completely worked through, she felt more separate from her ex-husband. Despite ongoing frequent contacts around their daughter's care, she no longer wondered if she had made a mistake in divorcing him.

At this point, she stopped worked in the city where we conducted our sessions, and she decided to take a "sabbatical" from therapy and do some things she had never done before—be home when her daughter went to school in the morning, volunteer in the community, and develop plans for her own business. My attempts to make this a termination—this is the end of our treatment, or at least this phase of it—was met with marked anxiety as separation issues resurfaced. She assured me she wanted a break and would be back in touch.

About seven months went by when I received a message from Sarah indicating that she "needed" to see me. This was a woman who never "needs" anything from people so I knew something significant had happened. When we meet, she told me she had a drinking problem. It was not unusual for her to have three glasses of wine at a party, but that was not the real problem. I asked about the evenings, given that this had been the time of day when her drinking was problematic. After a brief silence, she guiltily acknowledged that most evenings she would finish off a bottle of wine before falling asleep. We then talked about her period of moderate drinking during the previous year and how it gradually evolved to this high consumption level. She concluded by saying: "I am so glad we kept talking about my drinking in therapy. That increased my awareness and made it hard for me to hide from myself that my drinking has really sky rocketed."

She acknowledged feeling out of control of her drinking and wondered whether this was true for other members of her family. She had just read Susan Cheever's book *Note Found in a Bottle* (see chapter 12), which opened her eyes to the significant role alcohol played in her family. Like Cheever, Sarah learned from her family that evenings were not complete without alcohol. In fact, she had begun to suspect that her father had been an alcoholic. Earlier in treatment she had described her parents as social drinkers and simply saw her father's drinking as a way to relax after work. After reading this book, she recognized that after a few drinks his mood changed, he became sullen and withdrawn, and he would remain this way until going to bed. She wondered if her younger brother was following their father's example.

In Cheever's book, AA played a central role in John Cheever's recovery as well as that of the author. Sarah decided that abstinence was the right goal for her, too. I checked to see if there was any need for medical detoxification, but this did not seem warranted given that she was able to go at least forty-eight hours without a drink and experience no major withdrawal symptoms. She agreed to throw out all of the alcohol in her house (including any products with alcohol) and go to an AA meeting in the evenings around the time she usually began drinking. She was hesitant but agreed to try out a number of different meetings until she found one that was comfortable. Thus began treatment of her alcohol abuse. Interestingly, after two months of abstinence, she briefly expressed some interest in dating. But that soon disappeared. I found out why several sessions later. Sarah had begun smoking—just two cigarettes a day she assured me, but in the evening after her daughter was in bed. While the literature questions the reality of symptom substitution, with addictions one must remain attuned to cross addictions to ensure that one substance or behavior with mood-altering affects does not replace another. For Sarah, alcohol was a way to manage feelings of loneliness, fear of dependence, and a deep-seated uncertainty about her attractiveness to men. This latter anxiety emerged ever so briefly when she began to express an interest in dating once she had stopped drinking completely. But the anxiety quickly disappeared and was replaced by a new friend to relate to in the evening—cigarettes.

Lessons

1. Whenever I think of my work with Sarah, what remains salient in my mind was how surprised I was when she first revealed a drinking problem. I would not have been surprised if she told me she were depressed, anxious, or prone to panic attacks. As a psychotherapy patient, emotional problems could be expected. However, her success in the world, competent functioning, and even her gender was totally inconsistent with my belief about what it meant to have a drinking problem. This experience led me to scrutinize my assumptions about who is addicted and what an addict looks and acts like. I discovered that Sarah had most of the personal attributes that lead practitioners to miss addiction: employed, white, insured, and female (Schottenfeld 1994). A fifth attribute associated with a missed diagnosis is the patient being married. After treating Sarah, I was careful not to let my lifelong assumptions get in the way of recognizing potential addictions in high functioning psychotherapy patients. Having

past this hurdle, I discovered another. When I suspected an addiction, I was not always comfortable exploring it with the patient. As discussed fully in chapter 4, therapists may be hesitant to ask questions about addiction when a patient does not volunteer information about an addiction. There is a fear that by asking questions about substance use, patients, especially high functioning ones, will feel accused of wrongdoing and respond with anger or leave treatment. My experience to date has been that patients do not feel criticized or accused when asked questions about drug and alcohol use; these questions are responded to in the same manner as any other interview question.

2. When Sarah initially expressed concern that she might have a drinking problem, I wondered if there had been any hints or clues in the session that I had missed. If Sarah had not reported her drinking as a problem, would I have been able to recognize it? This sparked my interest in subtle signs of addiction (see chapter 7). Once drinking was self-identified as a problem, I realized that, as Sarah described her evenings, there was mention of drinking-related activities—across a number of different sessions, she mentioned drinking a glass of wine, opening a bottle, or going to the basement and bringing up a bottle of wine. When patients' dialogue makes reference to a specific way of behaving on a number of occasions and in different settings, they may be doing more than bringing the therapist up to date on their activities. They may be wondering if the behavior is something to be concerned about and whether the therapist will notice this concern. Is the patient who always mentions what she was drinking at a party merely giving details or wondering if this behavior is a problem? Psychotherapists will want to listen for frequent references to substance use as well as other behaviors linked to process addictions. This type of listening is more crucial for process addictions because, relative to substance use, people are less attuned to thinking about activities such running, shopping, or being on the computer as potentially addictive. As a result, they are less likely to label them as problematic. For example, a female therapist reported on a male patient who came to her for work-related issues. In treatment it quickly emerged that he wanted to change careers and become a writer. Therapy was focused on this topic when, after about a month in therapy, he off-handedly mentioned visiting a pornographic site after finishing that evening's writing. As a female therapist, she was hesitant to inquire into the details even though on several other occasions he had casually mentioned how advertisements for pornographic sites kept popping up on his computer. When, several months later, she recommended a medication evaluation due to increasing low mood, mild anxiety, and sleep disturbances, the psychiatrist's questions revealed a cybersex addiction.

3. If I had it to do all over again, I would handle Sarah's initial report of a drinking problem more seriously by conducting a more thorough assessment. Reflecting on why I had not been more inquisitive, I discovered a number of important lessons in addiction assessment. First, I took the casualness with which she first reported a drinking problem at face value rather than recognizing this attitude as a mask for her feelings of shame associated with her out-of-control drinking. Shame is a major reason why women keep their drinking a secret. It was only later that I realized that Sarah's wish to attend an AA meeting in another community was motivated by shame at having a problem. I also think I took a relatively laid-back stance, partly in response to Sarah's take-charge approach and partly because addiction was not why she came to therapy. At the time, we were immersed in a meaningful exploration of her separation issues. I felt more comfortable in my well-established role as a therapist compared to the more proactive stance that can be necessary when assessing addictions. One's level of activity can range from asking more questions, educating about substance use, and summing up clinical material to helping a patient locate a twelve-step meeting or intervening to prevent harm that could occur should the addiction continue. Many who practice psychotherapy from a nondirective position feel awkward and have the sense of doing something wrong or intrusive when being more active. One psychologist conveyed how this kind of activity was outside her self-defined role by referring to it as "doing the social-work thing." I wonder how often a practitioner's commitment to his or her therapeutic frame prevents effective assessment and management of a client's addiction.

4. As I noted, after Sarah's initial report of drinking more, she ran her own treatment. She regularly checked in with me and told me how she was doing. She openly acknowledged that having someone to report to help her stick to her plan. This turned out to be just one benefit. On reflection I realized that these regular check-ins helped the topic of drinking become more emotionally neutral. Once associated with shame and self-doubt, drinking became one of the many topics we talked about in therapy. As a result, I think it made it easier for Sarah to call for an appointment when her drinking increased again. While Sarah was in charge of check-ins, in subsequent treatment sessions, I made sure these occurred on a regular basis. I often wait to see if the patient will volunteer the information. If not, I raise a question about the previous weeks' use and associated experiences. I do this weekly for patient's whose behavior clearly is an addiction or is associated with clear-cut adverse consequences. For those whose behavior is excessive or problematic and adverse effects are limited, I do not necessarily check in every

week, but I rarely let more than two or three weeks go by without some discussion of the behavior of concern.

5. I learned with Sarah, and subsequent patients with addictions, that the negative consequences extend far beyond what the patient is able to report. I know now that I was seduced by her functionality and thus accepted at face value her report that there were no clear-cut deficits in her life as a result of drinking a few glasses of wine before bed. In light of limited consequences, her motivation, and family history of no addiction (as reported initially), she seemed a perfect candidate for controlled drinking. But once sober she was able to tell me many ways in which she was less functional when drinking excessively. Once she no longer drank, her relationship with her daughter improved dramatically. She was more patient in the evening—not rushing to get a drink. She was able to hear between the lines—to hear her daughter's emotional needs better. At work, this ability helped her relate to her male boss in a way that allowed her to get her needs met and feel less dominated by him.

The full extent of negative consequences is unknown until the addictive behavior has resolved. Not only was this apparent with Sarah but it has been amply illustrated in autobiographies of addiction. The authors, who are usually abstinent for a number of years before they write their stories, create a narrative where the reader is given access to the chaos created by addiction while the author only has a glimmer of the problems the addiction is creating. If asked about the negative consequences, these authors, like psychotherapy patients, could only provide a limited picture of the addiction's effects.

Psychotherapists need to be aware that inaccuracies in reports about addiction can extend beyond the patient's own behavior. When initially asked about addiction in her family, Sarah truthfully answered that, while her parents drank, this was nothing out of the ordinary. Only after reading *Message in a Bottle* did Sarah consider that it might be problematic that her parents could not go an evening without alcohol. She now recalled that her parents' "drink" consisted of a pitcher of martinis and, although her father (and perhaps brother) responded to alcohol by withdrawing inwardly, she now realized that this behavior did not preclude his being an alcoholic. I suspect that if I had been more comfortable with active questioning (see lesson 3 above), the alcoholism in Sarah's family would have emerged without her reading a book. As mentioned in chapter 7, instead of simply asking if there is addiction in the family, the therapist's questions can be more specific and focus on the patient's perceptions (e.g., Did you ever think your mother drank too much? Your father may not have been an alcoholic, but did his behavior change when he drank?) This approach to assessing a family history of addiction facilitates patients' curiosity about their families' drinking patterns as well as their own.

THE CASE OF TOM

Tom sought therapy for what he described as his "inability to be happy." He was successful in many ways; he made good money as a stockbroker, he had been married for seven years to Sally, and they had an eighteen-month-old son, Jason. The only apparent source of disappointment was his inability to fulfill his dream of becoming a singer. He was a talented singer and had been making a living this way until shortly after his marriage. He found that the long hours and frequent out-of-town travel was not compatible with married life, so he stopped. He had recently purchased a home for his family after some risky investments had paid off. To illustrate how nothing brought him pleasure, he observed that, after closing on his home, all he could think of was how to get rid of it.

He had become increasingly aware of and disturbed by his difficulty taking pleasure in life after his son was born. In initial sessions we talked about his history. We came upon what for him was a critical moment in his past. He was the first born, an engaging and dynamic child showered with attention by his mother and her extended family. The birth of a sickly brother, when Tom was three and a half years old, brought about what he experienced as a total loss of the joy and happiness in life. Not only was he robbed of being the center of attention but, shortly after his brother's birth, the family's financial position required that they move in with his father's parents in another state. This brought on a second round of losses. Tom no longer had his mother's family to turn to for affection and his mother lost her social support network. From Tom's description, she seems to have become overwhelmed by the move and the needs of her sickly infant and would often collapse in exhaustion and depression. Tom was left feeling as if he had no one left in his life, but instead of collapsing inward into a depression, he put on a brave face and tried not to be a bother. Then and now he was functioning well, but he took little or no pleasure from what he did. Tom—as was I—was very engaged and emotionally involved in our discussions of this historical material and how it related to his current life. Therapy was going well by all accounts.

In recounting events in his current life, he occasionally mentioned problems sleeping which resulted in his staying up at night alone in the living room (this activity resonated with feelings from childhood when he would be left outside the bedroom as his parents tended to his sick brother).

Therapist: What do you do when you're alone?

Tom: Sometime I get on the computer and read, but mostly I listen to music and drink beer.

I worked with Tom at a point in my professional development when I had begun to routinely ask about substance use after a patient's initial reference to it and to inquire about any behaviors that were potentially linked to typical process addictions.

Therapist: How much do you drink?

Tom: Maybe a six-pack.

I noted the qualifier "Maybe" and wondered if in fact the figure was more. I chose not to pursue the amount consumed in the moment but did return to it later. I have discovered that asking a second time at a later date often reveals a larger quantity.

Therapist: And how many times a week do you do that?

Tom: I would say two or three times.

Therapist: What other substances do you use besides alcohol?

Tom: Nothing else, just alcohol.

I did not expect that Tom was using other substances. For patients where drug use is suspected, Shea (see chapter 7) recommends a technique knows as denial of the specific. The treatment provider asks about the use of specific drugs rather than ask a general question as I do here.

Therapist: And what do you do on the computer?

I was curious about whether his drinking was associated with an overinvolvement with the Internet or a cybersex addiction.

Tom: Read editorials. I enjoy political stuff.

Therapist: How many hours a night do you do that?

Tom: No more than two.

Therapist: Any pornography?

Ideally, as I did with drinking, I could have made a gentle assumption (chapter 7) and asked, "How often do you visit pornographic sites"?

Tom: Oh, sure. It's hard to avoid. But I usually pass it by.

Therapist: When don't you pass it by?

Tom (*smiling*): When I'm mad at my wife. But that doesn't happen too often.

At this point, I decided to use the AUDIT to better assess the amount of use and negative consequences of his drinking. I did not formally assess for a computer addiction or cybersex addiction because neither seemed to be an issue. It is of note, however, that later in treatment, after alcohol abuse was recognized and his drinking declined, I listened carefully for any change in his computer-related behavior, given the evidence that as one addiction declines, behaviors prone to becoming addictive increase. As it turned out, as Tom drank less, he became more aware of angry feelings at his wife, and in turn, he spent more time visiting pornographic sites that were used for sexual gratification.

Results of the Tom's AUDIT

1. How often do you have a drink containing alcohol? 4 or more times a week
   Score: 4
2. On a typical day that you drink alcohol, how many drinks do you have? 1–2
   Score: 0
3. How often do you have six or more drinks on one occasion? Weekly
   Score: 3
4. How often during the past year have you found that you were not able to stop drinking once you started? less than monthly
   Score: 1
5. How often during the past year have you failed to do what was normally expected from you because of drinking? Never
   Score: 0
6. How often during the past year have you needed a first drink in the morning to get yourself going after a heavy drinking sessions? Never
   Score: 0
7. How often during the past year have you had a feeling of guilt or remorse after drinking? Yes, but not in the past year
   Score: 1
8. How often during the past year have you been unable to remember what happened the night before because you had been drinking? Never
   Score: 0
9. Have you or someone else been injured as a result of your drinking? No
   Score: 0
10. Has a relative or friend or doctor or other healthworker been concerned about your drinking or suggested you cut down? No
    Score: 0

Total Score: 9

A score of 8 or more on the AUDIT is considered evidence of problem use for men, which means that Tom's drinking behavior qualified as problematic. In the clinical interview, Tom indicated that he drank at least six beers two or three times a week, which also is consistent with the pattern of a binge drinker. Despite there being two ways in which Tom's drinking behavior could be considered problematic, his responses to the AUDIT indicated relatively little in the way of negative consequences. Only on an intermittent basis does he feel out of control of his drinking. Further inquiry into feelings of guilt and remorse revealed that he felt guilty about having had too much to drink at a work-related holiday party when he became overly effusive about a fellow coworker's attractiveness.

Whether one administers assessment tools at the start of treatment or during, there will be patients whose drinking patterns are well above the recommended limits but who have few or no negative consequences to report. Recall that assessment tools cast a wide net; some patients who score positively will turn out not to have any problems. One task of subsequent therapy sessions with Tom was to determine if his AUDIT score had yielded an accurate picture.

Tom had mentioned in an early session that his maternal aunt, who he was close to in his childhood years, had been alcoholic and ultimately stopped drinking through the help of AA. I decided it would be important in upcoming sessions to learn more about other family members and Tom's drinking history. To do this does not require that the focus of therapy change dramatically. Questions can be asked at the start of a session or they may emerge naturally out of the clinical dialogue. Tom made it easy by asking for the results of his AUDIT at our next session.

> Therapist: The AUDIT indicates that your weekly consumption is above recommended limits and can be considered problematic. More specifically, the way you drink fits with a pattern of binge drinking.
>
> Tom (*pauses before replying*): Problematic. . . . I don't see any problem. Do you?
>
> *I had been thinking about Tom's AUDIT and wondering if adverse effects were as absent as they appeared. Did his wife really not mind? Was he effective at work the day after a binge? Tom was a big guy, so perhaps this much alcohol did not have much effect. I decided to remain attentive to any negative consequences. In addition to assessing negative consequences, whenever a behavior appears addictive, it is important to consider whether it is serving some function. The AUDIT does not address the function of drinking. Tom was a man with strong feelings and I suspected that his drinking was a way of managing or addressing certain affective states. If this were true, then we would be unable to talk about the full range of his experiencing and, as such, the effectiveness of therapy could be adversely affected.*
>
> Therapist: The effects of drinking take many forms. Some are very individualistic.
>
> Tom (*thinks for a moment*): I don't see any problems; if anything, it helps me get a good night's sleep.
>
> *Sleep disturbances are common with alcoholics. In treatment, alcohol is presented as way to resolve the problem when, in many instances, it is the cause. I was still curious about potential problems created by his drinking and associated behaviors (staying up late, not going to bed with his wife, occasional use of pornography). I doubted it would be productive to ask directly; "Do you see any negative effects of your drinking?" given that twice Tom had volunteered that he did not recognize any. Instead, using Shea's denial of the specific, I provided Tom with some areas where negative consequences might be found.*
>
> Therapist: Your wife doesn't mind?

Tom: She's really tired at the end of the day. She has to get up early to get to work, so after the baby goes to bed, she's had it. She doesn't seem to mind if I stay up later.

Note that there is no mention of her feelings about his drinking.

Therapist: But how does she feel about your drinking a six-pack or so several times a week?

Tom: Well she's told me I can't sleep with her if I have more than a beer or two because I tend to be a restless sleeper and that disturbs her. Ever since Jason was born she is listening with one ear and never sleeps as soundly.

Still, the focus is on sleep without saying if his wife has a response to his drinking on its own. This is an area to be explored further.

Therapist: And your work? What's different after a night of drinking?

Tom: Nothing that I've noticed.

Those with traditional training in the addictions field might consider these disavowals of any problems as evidence of denial. Tom may be minimizing the effects or he may just be unaware. Asking such questions often gets a patient to wonder about whether drinking is a problem in these areas. At this point, I thought I would try further to stimulate his thinking by suggesting a number of effects that he had not considered.

Therapist: I do wonder though if drinking affects you physically; in our first session, you told me you put on some weight and are having difficulty taking it off despite exercising. As you know beer has lots of calories. I also wonder if drinking is having a more subtle effect—it takes away some of your vitality. Alcohol can do that. While we haven't talked about it in therapy so far, when we first met you talked about wanting to get back into singing and how your decision to stop may have been made impulsively; while you wanted to stop traveling, there may be more local opportunities than you realized. So far you have been unable to make any movement to explore that option. I wonder if your drinking is having an effect here, too.

Tom listened attentively and neither denied nor accepted my ideas.

In therapy we continued working on sadness and empty feelings associated with feelings of loss as a child. But there was one difference. In every session I continued to assess for addiction. I listened for negative consequences and possible functions of his drinking, and I made sure that his drinking was a topic for some part of almost every session by asking how much he drank and how often he drank the previous week. He remained convinced that he did not have a drinking problem. I did not disagree but continued to raise questions that could reveal the effects drinking had on his life. He had begun to recognize that drinking had a few limited effects, but he remained ambivalent about whether these were truly problematic. While considering the possibility that drinking made if difficult for him to lose the ten pounds he had gained, he was healthy and ran several miles a day. His family was thriving and his wife was now pregnant with their second child. He admitted that it was hard to get up some mornings, but his work life was sufficiently flexible that this did not pose a problem.

During the next few sessions, when I asked about the previous week's drinking, I also tried to get a better sense of the context in which it occurred. Recall that Tom considered his drinking simply as a means to help him sleep. I was interested in knowing whether he had any sense that drinking was serving a function or was motivated by more than its sleep inducing benefit. A question that often gets patients to think about the function of their drinking is "Tell me what you enjoy about drinking." Most people begin drinking for social reasons or because they enjoy it. Once having tried alcohol, a person can discover that the addictive behavior has other benefits (e.g., alleviates anxiety and self-criticism). Over time, the purpose of the behavior shifts from being sociable/pleasurable to alleviation of discomfort.

> Therapist: Tell me about the enjoyment you get from having six beers by yourself in the evening?
>
> Tom: I never really thought about that. It makes me think back to when I was a teenager and in college. Drinking was really fun. You'd get together with a bunch of guys and hang out, drink beer, watch some sports or maybe play basketball. (*silence*)
>
> You know, ever since we spoke about how being alone at night is like how I was left alone outside my parent's door when they were with my brother, I have been thinking . . . I'm not sure I enjoy that time alone. I'd rather be with my wife. But I can't because I can't fall asleep and once I drink, I'm more likely to snore and wake her.
>
> Therapist: What does six beers do that two or three does not?
>
> Tom: You know, after a few beers I feel good. I feel relaxed. But I don't stop. Drinking more, it's almost like I am running away.
>
> *A behavior that occurs to create an effect is not necessarily addictive. But, one sign of addiction is continuing the behavior after the desired effect is achieved.*
>
> Therapist: Running away from what?
>
> Tom: I don't know.
>
> Therapist: What about when you actually go for a run?
>
> Tom: There, too. Sometimes I get that same feeling and I keep running until exhaustion takes over.
>
> *Up until this comment, I had not really thought that Tom's running could be addictive, but this comment, which suggested that running (like drinking) was serving to avoid certain feeling, emphasized the need to stay attuned to his exercise behavior. I made a mental note to consider giving him the Exercise Dependence Scale (chapter 6).*

The next session provided further opportunity to develop an understanding of the functions and motivations served by his drinking and to assess negative effects. As he talked about drinking eight or nine beers on Wednesday and Thursday nights but only two or three on the other nights of the week, I took the opportunity to inquire about whether he saw any reason for why he drank so much on some nights and not others.

> Therapist: What's your sense of why you drink a six-pack on some nights and just a few beers on the other nights?
>
> Tom: That's a good question! Most nights it's hard for me to fall asleep, but you know what? I don't drink like that every single night.
>
> Therapist: So what do you think is going on?
>
> Tom: I'm not really sure.
>
> Therapist: Why don't you go back to the last evening you had at least six beers and tell me in detail what happened from the time you got home.
>
> *This is a variant of one of Shea's validity techniques known as "behavioral incident questioning." In order to bring an event to life, there is a detailed inquiry into a specific incident. When used in therapy, I ask the patient to recall a specific incident in detail and then ask questions when more information would be desirable.*
>
> Tom: Well, I got home at 4:30 and told the babysitter she could leave. Then I played with Jason and Sally came home.
>
> Therapist: You went right to playing?
>
> Tom: Well, no, I took Jason upstairs and changed into sweats and then we played on the bedroom floor.
>
> Therapist: Tell me what you did with Jason.
>
> *By asking these questions, I am indicating to Tom that I really want to know the details. With more details, the feelings and thoughts that occurred at that time are more likely to be revived.*
>
> Tom: You know, just horseplay on the floor and then piling up a huge tower of blocks and knocking them over. He has such a great laugh. Sally got home around 5:30. . . . You know what, that's when something began to feel different. I got this kind of bothered feeling. I don't know how to describe it any better than that. I just know it was not comfortable.

Exploration of this event ultimately led us back to the abandonment he felt with his mother. Tom would be happily playing with Jason for an hour or so before Sally arrived home from work. The passion with which Jason greeted his mother's arrival and her pleasure in him aroused strong feelings in Tom about how he lost the adoring and passionate relationship with his own mother. He was also losing Jason's attention in that moment. Later in treatment, when drinking had declined, he became aware of other feelings that felt more shameful to admit—he felt competitive with and jealous of Jason for getting the love he had lost and angry at his wife for being more interested in Jason than him.

This session illustrates how addiction assessment and therapy weave together where each facilitates the other. While the session was productive in terms of the therapy, it is important to mention that these realizations and insights had absolutely no effect on Tom's drinking. While articles have been written about the successful alleviation of addiction through therapy alone (e.g., Johnson 1992; Smaldino 1991), frequently addictive behavior takes on a life of its own. That is, the addiction has its own reinforcing effects that serve to maintain the behavior even after the initial motivating conditions are resolved or removed.

In the next session, Tom again spoke about feelings toward his mother. Since the beginning of therapy, very little had been said about his father other than that Tom believed his father, like himself, had denied himself work that would be more satisfying for the sake of making money for the family.

> Therapist: You've talked a lot about your mother since we began, but I know very little about your father.
>
> Tom: Remember his first love was coaching, but he had to get a job with an insurance company so that his growing family—there were three kids by then—had health insurance and enough money. Even so, he was a hard worker. His father, my grandfather, was a kind of mean guy and his mom was rather distant. They were very different from my mother's family who were so warm and giving. I think that's why it was so hard when we moved in with my father's family.
>
> Therapist: What are some things you remember about your father?
>
> Tom: I remember we used to go fishing. Just him and me. It was our private time together. Also, I remember when he came home from work. When I was a kid, he would call before leaving work and ask whomever answered to be sure there was beer in the refrigerator.
>
> *Tom's nonverbal expression at the moment conveyed that, for the first time, he saw that his drinking might have something to do with his father.*
>
> Therapist: How much beer?
>
> Tom (*smiling*): We would put a six-pack in and he usually drank it all. But he wasn't like my aunt. She would get loud, silly, kind of warm and fuzzy. Not my Dad; we just had dinner and then he went to bed.
>
> *Tom's maternal aunt was considered the family drunk. Her behavior fit one of the stereotypes of what a drunken person is like. His father's response to alcohol did not fit this picture. As a consequence, his father's drinking had never been considered an issue.*

At this point I felt I had enough information that I could provide Tom with an effective summary statement. I collected my thoughts and began the next session as follows.

> Therapist: Over the last couple sessions, since you filled out the AUDIT, I have learned a lot more about your drinking. You started drinking when you were in your teens, around thirteen. There is alcoholism on your mother's side of the family and your father, too, may have been an alcoholic. You've begun to notice that you don't enjoy drinking alone and that your drinking can have some

adverse effects. While at first you thought drinking had no effect on your marriage, you've begun to suspect that alcohol does take time away from your wife and affects your relationship. The other day, much to your surprise, you fell when drunk. Since we have been talking about your drinking, several times you've mentioned wanting to cut back but you have not been able to do so.

Tom: Yeah, I hear you. It's funny what you say about my father maybe being an alcoholic. He told me the other day that his father was an alcoholic. I never knew that. And now I wonder if my father was, too. Do you know I drink the same brand of beer? Maybe there is something to what you say.

Therapist: What would you like to do?

Tom: What are my options?

I told Tom that it might be a good idea to attend an AA meeting. Some, like Tom, may be surprised to know that people can attend AA meetings while still drinking. The twelve-step philosophy says to bring the body and the mind will follow. Sometimes this happens and attendance alone leads to a desire for abstinence. For others, by simply attending open meetings or newcomers' meetings, they hear others attest to the negative consequences of drinking that the patient had not previously self-identified. These revelations, when brought back into therapy, help motivate the patient to move from the precontemplation or contemplation stage into action. Tom agreed to try a few meetings. He enjoyed them but found little with which he could identify. He focused on people's reports of "disasters" due to drinking—job loss, divorce, fights—none of which applied to him. Although, Tom returned from these meetings convinced that he was not an alcoholic, he expressed an interest in cutting down on his drinking. I was willing to go along with this plan but considered it a part of the assessment process rather than the treatment. I was not confident his plan would succeed because he was not a good candidate for controlled drinking: although his history of problematic drinking was short lived, he had begun drinking early and there was alcoholism in his family. However, this experiment seemed acceptable in light of the fact that his current drinking was not associated with major risks. I also felt strongly that if I insisted on abstinence at this point, he would leave treatment.

Tom defined his goals, which were to have no more than two beers or glasses of wine nightly. If he drank more it could only be once a week. I indicated that I also wanted him not to drink twenty-four hours before a session. The rationale was that it was necessary that he is fully present in treatment and for this to happen, he needed to be alcohol-free. A second function of this twenty-four-hour rule is to assess the patient's control over drinking. On the AUDIT (item 4), Tom had indicated that once a month he had difficulty stopping drinking once he started. From descriptions of his drinking, I knew this occurred more often than he admitted to. Inability to stick to the twenty-four-hour rule would make his difficulty controlling his drinking more observable. From this point on, each session began by checking in on the success of the plan we developed.

During the next several weeks, as he stuck to his plan, Tom began to reveal some more of the negative effects of his drinking. Tom indicated that his wife was not as neutral about his drinking as initially implied. While Tom had emphasized originally that she was upset about his sleeping problem and had some mild feelings about their not going to bed together, he now revealed that she was angry about his drinking; she was anxious that if anything happened to her or Jason at night (she was now pregnant with their second child), he would not be able to function effectively. Interestingly, when, later in the same session, I asked directly if, with his new drinking plan, he had noticed any changes, he still reported seeing few negative effects of his drinking. I asked why he did not consider making his wife anxious a problem; this ultimately opened up previously unacknowledged feelings of anger and disappointment about his marriage. I don't think he had been hiding these feelings but rather, until he reduced his drinking, along with its self-medicating function, these feelings were not available for him to report on. Several weeks later Tom volunteered information on a definite benefit of less drinking; he felt energized and was completing his work more efficiently. He had even looked in the newspaper for local singing auditions. Despite a growing list of drinking's effects, Tom remained in the precontemplation stage given that he had yet to acknowledge that drinking was a problem.

After five weeks of sticking to his plan, Tom called to say he was running late and wondered if he should even bother to come in. I indicated that he should keep the appointment. He arrived looking tired and disheveled. In the course of saying he overslept, he admitted that he had gotten very drunk the night before. He went from there to talking about some sexual problems with his wife when I stopped the conversation and asked why he had broken our rule: twenty-four hours of no drinking before a session. He glared at me. The rest of the session was not easy as he tried to blame me for making him come in, felt angry with his wife for not being more supportive, and mentioned his hatred for his mother for leaving him feeling so empty.

I began the next session by exploring Tom's feelings about *not* drinking.

Therapist: What do you think life would be like if you didn't drink?
   Tom (*after a very long pause*): It scares me to be without alcohol. It's about my father. It's our connection. It's all I have of him to take with me.

This turned into a very productive session in terms of understanding his relationship with his father and his ambivalence about becoming an adult and taking his rightful place in the world. However, as before, this personal growth was not altering his drinking behavior. We had a strong working alliance, so after careful consideration, I thought it was time to be more direct about how I saw his drinking. In a casual and warm voice I said, "You know, I think you are a drunk and the only viable solution is to stop drinking." His look could kill. He mumbled that he would think about what I had said and the session ended.

Tom drank heavily during the week but began the next session by telling me more of the story of his drinking.

> Tom: I just don't understand why I can't stop. I had two beers the other night and felt just fine and then went on to have four more. I don't know why. But there is one thing I do know. You are one smart lady to call me a drunk and to not let me get away with breaking that twenty-four-hour rule. You know what I am and you were not afraid of it. During this past week, I've been doing a lot of thinking and I believe I came to therapy because I was worried about my drinking.

Therapists worry that labeling a patient will be met with anger or flight from treatment. While someone who is under the influence and confronted about his behavior may act aggressively, research shows that patients in health care settings are unlikely to exhibit such behavior (Dhossche 1999). For Tom my willingness to refer to him as a drunk meant I was not afraid of his alcoholism and this made him feel safer to face more of the truth and begin to consider that his drinking was in fact problematic. In fact, Tom went so far as to say that his drinking was probably the main motivation behind his coming to therapy in the first place. Tom is not alone. Quite often patients will initiate treatment because of concern about an addictive behavior but not volunteer this concern until the psychotherapist has asked relevant questions or identified addiction as a problem. With Tom's acknowledged concern about his drinking, he was moving into the contemplation stage.

Lessons

1. One of the benefits of routinely assessing for addictions is that treatment can be more effective. If addiction is a way to avoid or manage difficult experiences and feelings, active addiction means that these will not be a part of therapy. In the previous case, therapy with Sarah was productive but ultimately limited as long as she masked her loneliness and fear of men with alcohol and then cigarettes. Therapy with Tom was far from neutral; it was filled with strong emotions and insights. An inkling of the full range of anger he felt toward his wife began to emerge when he first cut down on his drinking. With this change, a new goal emerged in therapy. Instead of self-medicating his anger with alcohol or running, Tom needed to learn how to handle his anger and communicate it effectively to his wife. From both Sarah and Tom, I

learned that just because treatment is going well does not mean that addictions are absent.

2. In Tom's therapy, I also learned that support and understanding have their limits. Referring to Tom as a drunk is not exactly the same as confrontation, but psychotherapists sometimes need to be direct in describing a patient's behavior as problematic and labeling it as such. Likewise, if a patient's behavior suggests that he or she has broken a contract, such as no drinking twenty-four hours before a session, this must be discussed in therapy. Sometimes it is difficult to know if the rule has been broken. Even though the signs are ambiguous (e.g., the patient's eyes look different, the quality of the relationship feels unusual, there is the faintest smell of alcohol in the room), once a therapist suspects the contract has been broken, he or she needs to risk being wrong and neutrally report on what is being observed. Not doing so enables the patient's continued use. In Tom's case, I was initially hesitant to say he needed to stop drinking. My silence replicated his mother's failure to recognize that he was hurting as a child. In the same way as when he was a child, he hid in therapy, resorting to hyperfunctionality (i.e., being a good patient) and never acknowledging that he was in pain or worried about being an alcoholic.

3. This case, like others that follow, illustrates how it is not a simple matter to distinguish the assessment process from the treatment. The two frequently merge. Looking from the outside, Tom's initial trial of controlled drinking could look like a part of treatment. However, I saw it as part of the assessment. This trial period of reduced intake provided a way for Tom to recognize his lack of control and the effects his drinking had on himself and his family. This period also helped Tom to see some of the functions of his drinking that were related to an inability to express anger at his wife.

4. How addictions are assessed in psychotherapy is in large part a matter of personal style. Some will prefer to ask many questions within a single session in order to gather information quickly about the bare outlines of the behavior and its consequences and motivations. Others are comfortable letting the picture emerge over time. Personal preference is fine when the patient is like Tom. His drinking is problematic but there seems to be no immediate risk to oneself or another. Tom's wife was not threatening to leave because of his drinking; his boss was not about to fire him. This is quite different from the case of an adolescent college student whose binge drinking is associated with property damage and drunk driving. When addictions pose risk of harm to oneself or others, psychotherapists must actively assess the problem and develop a treatment plan. This plan may involve a reduction in the addictive behavior.

or, if the patient does not agree to this goal, then treatment needs to focus on reducing the risk of potential harm.

5. As illustrated with Sarah in the previous case, the scope of negative consequences expands with a reduction in the addictive behavior. The negative consequences that a patient acknowledges or is aware of when an addiction is fully active are those that are creating observable changes in the patient's world (e.g., falling asleep on the couch, breaking things). Negative consequences that involve an absence or loss are harder to recognize until after the addictive behavior ceases or declines. Once Tom reduced his drinking, he was able to realize that alcohol sapped the vitality he needed to move ahead with singing.

THE CASE OF GEORGE

George, a man in his late sixties, came to therapy seven months after retiring from his lifelong position as an accountant. He had never been in therapy before but had called for an appointment on his wife's insistence that he deal with what she referred to as his depression. This was his second wife, Bella, who was fifteen years younger than George. Bella was still working fulltime as a nurse and had concluded that her husband was depressed after taking a series of courses on geriatric psychiatry. He was cooperating with her request to get help but was puzzled because he did not report feeling depressed. When asked why his wife thought he was depressed, he replied that whatever she had said had made no sense to him. At best he could acknowledge that he had been more irritable and more likely to snap at her in recent months. He thought it would be useful if his wife came for a session or two so that she could describe the problem. Bella met with us at the next session. She confirmed George's observation that he was more irritable or "snappy" than he used to be. Other than this general observation, she was the one who seemed annoyed at George who, since retiring, was able to sleep late and fill several days a week volunteering for organizations he valued while she continued to work full time. George said he was quite content with his schedule after years of rising early and working all day. Their age difference and the resulting differences in lifestyles suggested that couples therapy was warranted, but Bella declined the offer saying she preferred, for the moment, to work on these issues in her own individual treatment.

George was not very psychologically minded and yet, despite the absence of a defined focus, he expressed interest in coming to treatment regularly. He seemed to profit from talking about the events of the week, such as his volunteer activities, reflecting on his somewhat strained relationship with his children from a previous marriage, and trying to understand the reasons for his "snapping" at his wife.

Bella arose each morning at 6:00 AM to exercise before starting a ten-hour shift at a local nursing home. Because of her long shifts and his more flexible schedule, George had the responsibility for cleaning up the house before leaving in the late morning, shopping for food on the way home, and then preparing food each evening. His wife had very specific food preferences that required almost daily shopping and a good deal of preparation time. Before retiring from work, they shared the cooking responsibilities. He acknowledged that he preferred the old way but recognized that with their current lifestyles, it made sense for him to have these responsibilities. When I asked Tom if his "preference" for the old way meant he felt some anger about the current situation, he initially said that he really didn't have that strong of a feeling about it, he only "disliked it." A preliminary attempt to explore how to talk to his wife about his dislike of the cooking arrangements was dismissed as unnecessary. He thought he might seem "snappy" because he became uncomfortably hot when working in their small kitchen.

I asked George a lot of questions in order to get beyond an objective report of "news of the week" to his thoughts and feelings. In order to bring his day more to life, I turned to Shea's behavior incident technique (see chapter 7) in the hope that this would help him recall his thoughts and feelings from the day in more detail. I asked George to describe his shopping and cooking thoroughly.

Therapist: Tell me more about your shopping and preparing dinner.

George: What do you want to know?

Therapist: Well, for example, tell me what happened yesterday. When did you leave X [the place he volunteers for]? Where did you go shopping? What did you buy?

George: I finished up around four and went to the big new market they built just down the street. I had to get a lot of fresh vegetables since my wife doesn't like to eat meat very often. I got fresh lettuce to add to the salad makings we had at home already and zucchini, onion, mushrooms, and red peppers for the wok. Then I went home.

Therapist: How did you get home?

George: I like to walk in nice weather; it's about twelve blocks, but when I got home yesterday, my knees were really aching from carrying all those bags.

I wondered if his irritability might be connected to physical discomfort.

Therapist: What did you do then?

George: I would have liked to sit down for a while and rest, but I needed to get the food into the refrigerator and anyway, Bella would be home in a couple hours and I needed to start preparing the vegetables. So I poured myself a drink and began to chop the vegetables for the wok.

Therapist: What kind of drink?

George: It was a hot day so I had a beer.

Given that George is over age sixty-five, drinking more than one beer a day is considered risky drinking behavior. Alcohol over this amount can be problematic because it increases risks of falls, injuries (George does a lot of cutting), and compromises the effectiveness of medications. For these reasons, and the fact that his presenting complaints could potentially be alcohol-related (depression, decreased control of his anger), I decided to ask more about his drinking.

Therapist: How much did you drink after that beer?

George: Oh, let's see. I would say three more.

Therapist: Is that typical?

George: It all depends. I can have another beer or two after dinner while I am watching TV or reading.

Therapist: Does Bella drink with you?

I ask in order to see if both of them are drinking above recommended limits and if drinking plays a role in their relationship. I am especially curious about Bella's drinking because she never mentioned George's drinking during the few sessions when we all met together. If George was an alcoholic, it would be important to find out whether Bella played a role in his drinking.

George: No, she doesn't like to drink. The only time she drinks is to have a glass of wine when we're at a restaurant.

Therapist: What else do you drink besides beer?

This question reflects a gentle assumption. I am assuming that he drinks more than beer. This is preferred to asking a question that can be answered with a "yes" or "no," such as, "Do you drink only beer?"

George: Depends a lot on the weather. In the fall and winter I am more likely to have a glass of scotch.

Therapist: Just a glass?

Using a gentle assumption, it would have been better to ask, "How many?"

George: Pretty much the same as beer. Two or three over the evening.

I could have asked about the size of these drinks but decided I could come back to that. In a subsequent session, when I did ask, it turned out that he liked an Australian beer that came in large cans equal to two beers and that he drank Scotch from jelly jar glasses where the amount of each drink was closer to two standard drinks.

Therapist: Is that the most you ever drink?

Again, it would have been better to avoid yes-or-no questions and ask, "What is the most you ever drink?" instead.

George *(thinks for a moment)*: Yeah, I can't recall when it was more than that.

Therapist: And how often do you have two or three drinks?

George: Every day.

Therapist: Tell me, how long have you been drinking on a regular basis like this?

George: On and off my whole life. But I would say I have been drinking more on a daily basis since my retirement. I don't have to get up early anymore and I enjoy just relaxing in the evening.

*This amount of alcohol on a daily basis is well above the recommended level
and suggests the possibility that George has developed a physical dependence
on alcohol.*

Therapist: Is there ever a day that you don't drink or drink less?

George (*smiles*): Yes, that happens. Last Sunday we spent the whole day with
friends who don't drink.

Therapist: So you had no alcohol that day?

George: Let me think. No, as I recall, I had a nightcap, some Benedictine.

*If physically dependent on alcohol, George would develop signs of withdrawal
within twenty-four hours. These could involve disorientation and hallucinations or be mild such as slight hand tremor, headache, or flulike feelings. I remained concerned that George might be physically dependent. At this point in
the session, I decided not to ask any more questions because I sensed that
George was beginning to feel defensive. I decided to tell him why I was asking.*

Therapist: I am asking all these questions because for a man over sixty-five the
recommended daily limit of alcohol is no more than one beer or one shot of
scotch. Drinking over these limits can have psychological effects like those
you've reported, such as being more irritable. In older adults there is increased risk of adverse physical effects like stomach and liver damage and alcohol reduces effectiveness of medications.

George: I don't think that's the case for me. I was at my physician last week and
he told me I was in good health, just a little heart murmur. The big problem
is my knees.

This was George's way of saying that he was not concerned about his
drinking. Reference to his knees reminded me that I needed to ask if the
physician had given him any medication. Mixing pain medication with this
amount of alcohol would be dangerous. With older patients who are taking a
number of medications, it is good to use the medication section from the Alcohol Related Problems Survey (ARPS) (chapter 8). This was not necessary
with George who had good recall about the few medications he was taking. It
turned out he was not taking any painkillers or other medications where alcohol was contraindicated. At this point in the session, it would have been
good to ask if he had an opportunity to tell his doctor about how much he
drank (e.g., "Did your doctor ask you about alcohol and drug use?") given
that physicians, like psychotherapists, do not routinely assess for addictions.

I was concerned about George's alcohol consumption, so during the next session I returned to the topic with the goal of assessing for any negative consequences. One can weave the assessment into the treatment hour by waiting for
some related topic to emerge or one can chose to initiate the discussion. Many
therapists, especially those who are trained to let the patient take the lead, feel uncomfortable with this more directive role. I am one of those therapists, but I was
sufficiently concerned about George's drinking that I initiated the discussion.

Therapist: We ended last time talking about your drinking. Since then, I wonder what other thoughts or reactions you've had to that discussion.

George: I didn't think about it too much, although I did notice that there was one night when I had four beers before bed.

For patients who do not define an addiction as a problem, the therapist's interest often becomes their own. Without being explicitly asked, George had begun to monitor his own intake. As is common, subsequent reports of consumption are often larger than the initial report.

Therapist: What happened after four beers?

George (*with a slight smile*): I don't recall; I fell asleep on the couch watching TV.

Therapist: Does that happen if you drink less than four beers?

George: A lot of nights I fall asleep and Bella has to wake me up to go to bed. It's probably the beer. I mean Bella remarked a few Sundays ago that I came to bed when she did and that was the Sunday when I just had a nightcap.

Therapist: Any other ways you notice that drinking affects you?

Better to have asked, "What other ways does drinking affect you?"

George: Not really.

He answered rather quickly, leaving me with the impression he didn't want to think about my question, so I tried again.

Therapist: That was pretty quick. Take a moment to think. Other than falling asleep on the couch, what effect does drinking have?

George (*pause*): Nothing I can think of.

Another approach to assessing for negative effects is to ask the person to imagine what their life would be like if the addictive behavior were absent.

Therapist: Let's think about this another way. What are you *not* doing at night because of your drinking?

George (*pauses to think*): I'm less likely to spend a lot of time on the computer. That's about it.

Recall that George is not very attuned to his inner life so, at best, I was hoping he would recognize some change in his behavior. This hope may have been optimistic given that the amount of alcohol George drinks likely affects his cognitive capacities and clouds self-awareness. Shea's behavioral incident technique for exploring a specific evening of drinking can be helpful with some patients (e.g., Tom), but to be effective the person needs to have good recall and, when intoxicated, I did not think this was the case for George. Instead, I took another approach. Negative consequences that are linked to the presenting problem are most likely to engage the patient's attention and, in George's case, I suspected there was a connection.

Therapist: I am wondering if your drinking has anything to do with your snapping at Bella. You've told me that you don't like having sole responsibility for the food shopping and cooking. If you had it your way, you'd just load up the freezer with food and heat it up each evening. Both you and Bella said that you are more likely to "snap" at her in the evenings. You attributed this to getting overheated in the kitchen, but I am wondering if you are more annoyed at Bella about the food arrangements than you realize. You don't feel it's ac-

ceptable to be angry, because, as you say, it is reasonable for you to have this responsibility. Could it be when you drink some of your anger gets out?
George: Before I retired Bella and I rarely fought. I don't like to fight. So maybe you're right; maybe I can get a little angry because I have had something to drink. You know, it's funny—your last question just brought something to mind. What don't I do because of drinking? The dishes. If I fall asleep, Bella usually does them.

The subsequent session explored other times that George got "snappy" with Bella. In the vast majority, he had been drinking. He agreed that handling anger was a topic he would like to work on in therapy. At the same time, I repeated to George that I remained very concerned about his level of alcohol consumption and wondered if three beers were clouding his consciousness and that we had yet to get an accurate picture of how much he drinks and the consequences. Having recognized that drinking had some affect and being a man who was comfortable with numbers (a retired accountant), I thought George would be motivated to get a better picture of his drinking behavior. I asked him to keep track of the number of drinks and their size. For the next several weeks, he brought in carefully prepared charts showing for each day of the week how many drinks he had and the size of each drink. As often happens, the initial response to recordkeeping was a reduction in drinking. George's drinking declined over the first two weeks but then climbed again to its original level. The average amount was higher than first reported; three drinks per day was a minimum and, taking into account drink size, he sometimes was having up to six standard drinks a day. The amount seemed sufficient and long-term (at least seven months) that I would be hesitant to ask him to stop out of fear he would go into withdrawal. I told George my concerns and enumerated the negative consequences that had emerged over the sessions (falling asleep, creating distance with his wife, weight gain, exacerbation of a balance problem, and potential long-term health consequences). George said he knew he drank more than he should. He had gotten on the computer and taken an online test. (Such assessments are readily available online and many patients have reported filling them out after drinking becomes an issue in therapy.) Still, he expressed no desire to stop drinking. He was quite adamant about this point. However, he acknowledged that it would be good to cut back. For him, cutting back still involved drinking more than the recommended one standard drink per day for a person his age. I agreed to this as an acceptable starting point in light of the harm-reduction model (see below) and George and Bella's plans to move to a new part of the country after Bella was offered an excellent position in hospital administration.

As it turned out, we were able to dramatically cut down George's drinking before he left. While George enjoyed the effects of alcohol, he found it important to have something in his hands all evening. We ultimately landed on a plan where George alternated an alcoholic beverage with water or juice. This effectively cut down his alcohol consumption but, more importantly, it greatly lengthened the time over which a set amount of alcohol was consumed. This had the effect of significantly lowering his blood alcohol levels. As a result, he was more alert in the evenings, less likely to fall asleep on the couch, and ended up doing the dishes more often.

Lessons

1. As discussed extensively in chapter 3, a psychotherapist should not rely on a physician to assess for or recognize drinking problems or other addictions. Although medical training often contains education about addictions, physicians are no more likely than psychotherapists to recognize addiction in their patients. George had a long-standing relationship with his physician, but this doctor had no knowledge of the extent of George's alcohol use. However, once an addiction is recognized, a physician should be included in the treatment. Any addiction can have physical consequences, although these are most salient for substance-based addictions. Thus, whenever a psychotherapy patient has an addiction, it is essential to recommend a physical. Even if a patient goes for a physical, there is no guarantee that there will be an inquiry into the addictive behavior. For this reason, patients should be asked explicitly to bring this information to the physician's attention. While always good practice, recommended visits to a physician are necessary for any substance-using patient who is taking medications so that the physician is well aware of any negative interactions or muting of the medication's effectiveness. Once I recognized the extent of George's drinking, I received written permission to contact his physician to ensure that he was informed and to determine that the lab work revealed no adverse physical effects of drinking.

2. Reports from significant others (i.e., collateral reports) usually provide useful information about the extent of drinking and its consequences (see chapter 10) because the significant other is much more distressed by the addictive behavior than the one who has the drinking problem. I was surprised that Bella did not mention George's drinking in the session we had together. Because of their move, I was unable to meet with them again as a couple. The importance of understanding why a significant other does not report a partner's addiction is addressed in the "Case of Aida" below.

   Significant others, like physicians and psychotherapists, do not always interpret the behavior they see as an indication of addiction. Bella saw George's problem as depression and anger and not alcoholism. This example suggests that when therapy involves relationship problems, one cannot dismiss the possibility that the presenting problem is connected to an addiction. Couples therapists will want to consider asking their patients routinely about addictions or, at least, they will want to be attuned to the possibility that addiction is contributing to their problems. Certainly for couples presenting with sexual difficulties, it will be important to consider involvement with cybersex. In individual therapy, when working on patients' relationship problems, therapists will want to make sure that the relationship is not complicated by an unrecognized addiction.

3. The addiction-treatment culture is infused with the goals set by twelve-step programs; the only acceptable treatment outcome is nonuse. From this perspective, a psychotherapist who continues working with a patient who has no interest in stopping the addictive behavior is considered an enabler. Psychotherapists are not immune to these pressures. In talking to therapists who do not specialize in addiction treatment but who, out of necessity, have treated addictions in patients who came for psychotherapy, I have found that this group experiences enormous uncertainty and guilt if they continue to treat a patient, like George, who does not want to quit the addictive behavior.

Based on the information I had, in my opinion George was an alcoholic. It would have been best if he did not drink, but certainly he should be consuming no more than one drink a day. He was uninterested in either alternative. At this point I had the option to terminate treatment, insist he drink reasonably, or try to develop a plan with him and work toward limiting any harm that would arise because of his continued alcohol use. George had no interest in the first two options so I took the latter approach. This meant informing his physician about his drinking, helping him learn how to express anger without using alcohol, and reducing the specified harm of his drinking (e.g., falling asleep on the couch, memory impairment).

Harm reduction is an alternative treatment philosophy for addictions (see chapter 2). This philosophy states that successful treatment can occur by reducing the harm created by addiction. Often this involves reducing the addictive behavior, but if the patient is opposed to this option, then treatment focuses on taking actions to reduce the harm itself (e.g., clean needles for heroin users, not driving while intoxicated). With this approach, treatment is still considered a success, even if the behavior continues unabated, as long as harm is reduced. While harm-reduction and twelve-step treatments are presented as being opposites, it is important to know that treatment informed by harm reduction does not require abandoning the goal of abstinence. Through reducing harm and with time, a patient may decide that being rid of the addiction is a good alternative. The effectiveness of harm reduction and controlled use models of treatment is addressed in a research review by Saladin and Santa Ana (2004).

A harm-reduction philosophy also informs the assessment process. For patients who do not want to stop (such as Tom and George), reduction in use and/or associated harm facilitates gathering information necessary for a full assessment. By focusing on the harm created by a behavior and then taking steps to reduce the harm, patients develop a new perspective on actions they have taken for granted, which is a first step in enhancing motivation to change the behavior itself. This kind of assessment can reveal whether a patient has control over substance use (can they stick to the agreed upon limits or not?). If the addictive behavior is reduced even temporarily, the patient often is better able to understand the functions served by the behavior. For George, drinking served two functions: it was a way to mute his anger at his wife's requirement that he take on most household responsibilities after retirement, but it was also a means to express his anger by being able to "snap" at her and not feel the associated guilt. Most importantly, an assessment informed by harm-reduction philosophy is considered a collaborative effort where patient and therapist work together to define the problem, discover the risks, and set the goals.

THE CASE OF JACOB

Jacob was a twenty-one-year-old, tall, and lanky man. We began treatment six months after he had begun his first job after college, working in the human relations department of a large manufacturing company. His stated reason for coming to therapy was that he was feeling lonely because he could not "connect up" with a girl. Otherwise, he thought his life was in good shape; he had a nice place to live and his job was going so well that he had been recently promoted. Jacob was smart and witty and had amicable relations with both of his parents, who were divorced, and a strong network of male friends. When asked about his dating history, he indicated that he had never had much success with girls in high school or college. The few times a relationship had extended beyond the first date, the girl usually made some excuse to break it off after several months.

When asked to elaborate on his social life (i.e., "Tell me how you have fun"), he talked extensively about his weekend athletic activities with his male friends. After an afternoon of basketball or rock climbing, they would go out in the evening as a group. Many of his friends had girlfriends who would join them and bring along some of their single female friends. As is typical of this age group (see the section titled "Late Adolescence" in chapter

8), he freely revealed that most weekend evenings included heavy drinking to the point of being "wasted." While his openness suggested no sense of shame or concern about this behavior, I wanted to clarify the extent of his drinking in order to assess if any other substances were involved.

Therapist: Tell me more about your drinking.

For a very brief second, Jacob gave me a curious look. Up until now, we had been talking in general about his social life, and he sensed this was a shift in focus from his agenda.

Jacob: We get together at a friend's place or maybe my place about eight or nine o'clock and have a few beers. Sometimes we just end up staying there, or later we'll meet up with some of their girlfriends and their friends at a dance place. We usually start with beer. Sometimes we have whiskey or martinis.

Therapist: You said that sometimes you get "wasted." What does that mean?

Jacob (*showing his first overt sign of discomfort*): That means we could just pass out watching sports or we could still be standing, out dancing, but the next day not remember stuff that happened.

Jacob's description indicated that "wasted" included drinking to the point of blacking out (which is not passing out but a loss of memory for what happened while intoxicated).

Therapist: How often do you get wasted that way?

Jacob: Probably once each weekend.

At this point in my learning about addictions, I knew not to take information for granted, such as assuming I knew the size of a "a drink" or how long a weekend lasted. I wondered if drinking was limited to only weekends. But I chose not to ask at this point in the session. I sensed that Jacob was feeling uncomfortable talking about his drinking in this level of detail, so I decided I would just listen for the information or ask at another time.

Therapist: You and your friends just drink?

A better question would have been "What other substances do you and your friends use?" (i.e., a gentle assumption).

Jacob: Mostly. What I really like is to have a few drinks and then down a Valium. Then I feel really good.

Therapist: Really good?

Jacob: I mean I really like to dance, you know, be physical and move around. I can be really loose with a Valium. And it's more fun talking to girls.

Because of dangerous cross-tolerance effects that significantly increase the risk of overdose, I make it a policy to mention what happens when alcohol mixes with other sedatives. However, clinical judgment is needed to determine if it is necessary to say this in the moment when the topic first is mentioned. While education about drug effects can be an important part of the assessment process, it can be a mistake to take on an educative role too quickly because the patient can experience this as moralizing or shaming and become less open about substance use. Clinical judgment should determine whether the risk merits an immediate discussion or whether it is possible to wait until a fuller picture of the patient and substance use emerges and the working alliance is more developed. In Jacob's case, I never had to ask. He went on to assure me that his drug use was not a danger.

Jacob: While that Valium makes for more fun, we don't do anything dangerous. We're really careful about what we do. My friends and I have an agreement. When we get wasted, no one is allowed to drive until they get sober.

I assumed this group of friends was responding to what they had learned in high school prevention programs. While the intent of their agreement was to avoid negative consequences, I wondered how a group of people high on drugs and alcohol was able to assess sobriety. I supported their intent and briefly explored how this decision was made.

Therapist: So you all look out for each other. How do you decide if someone is too wasted to drive?

Jacob: Someone has to be able to walk a straight line back and forth. The truth is that a lot of nights we just party at a friend's house and crash there.

Jacob went on to describe what he knew about drug interaction effects. He had what seemed to be a pharmacist's level of knowledge of how to use one substance to enhance or counteract the effects of another. This knowledge attested to his interest in drugs and the possibility that he actively worked to minimize negative consequences.

Therapist: You certainly know a lot.

Jacob: Yes, I was pre-med for a while in college.

Therapist: You changed your mind?

Jacob: I think that my parents wanted that more than I did. Plus I had a hard time fitting in at college. The pre-med types were kind of preppy and I wasn't. I found a few guys like myself, and we did a lot of pot, and my grades sucked so I quit premed and went into business and computers.

Therapist: What other drugs did you do in college?

As discussed in the "Adolescent" section in chapter 8, distinguishing age-appropriate experimentation from addiction for this age group is an assessment challenge. Using drugs or alcohol alone rather than as part of a social activity is one warning sign. Evidence that drugs and alcohol are used to facilitate adjustment is another.

Jacob: A lot. When I stopped smoking at the end of my freshman year, I couldn't sleep and I felt anxious all the time. My family physician gave me some sleeping pills and another doctor gave me some Valium. That's when I learned about how much fun it was to mix Valium and alcohol. I almost overdosed once as a result, and that set me straight for the rest of college.

I wondered if these physicians ever assessed their adolescent patient's history of drug use.

Therapist: When did you start drinking and taking Valium again?

Jacob: Let's see . . . sometime after I moved here.

In light of this timing, it would be worth exploring in therapy whether his substance use is a way to manage feelings associated with major life transitions and associated feelings of not fitting in.

In the next session, I was able to establish that Jacob's weekend drinking qualified as binge drinking. He would have five or more standard size drinks (a 12 ounce can of beer, 1.5 ounces of 80 proof liquor) in a row or, if less, alcohol's effects were enhanced by sedative use. As he elaborated on his evenings out, I listened carefully for evidence of negative consequences or risk of harm to others and continued to do so in subsequent sessions. Jacob valued being physically fit and was confident that his drinking and drug use had no adverse effects. In fact, his substance use motivated his physical activity; a night out was just what he needed to motivate himself to go running the next day. Given that exercise is a behavior that can be addictive, I did ask how far he ran and how often. He liked to run long distances (up to six miles), but he limited this to twice a week so as not to injure his knees. I have been surprised at the number of patients who manage their substance use by exercising away any adverse physical effects. They interpret being physically active as evidence that substance use has done no harm. To understand this relationship further, see Ann Marlowe's autobiography (1999) in which she emphasizes the ironic coexistence of excessive drug use (in her case, heroin) and health-affirming activities such as exercise and careful diet monitoring. I made a note to remain attuned to any negative consequences Jacob may have experienced from substance use or exercise.

Within three weeks of starting treatment, a woman who he had been interested in—it was his growing feelings for her that resulted in his seeking therapy—returned his interest. Their relationship involved talking daily on the phone but, because she lived out of town, they got together only on weekends. When together they spent most of their time in her apartment drinking, smoking marijuana, and having sex. I wanted to understand the role drugs were playing in this relationship.

Therapist: What do you think it would be like if you and Joanna did not smoke or drink?
Substance use was such a given in his social life that at first he didn't know how to answer the question. Jacob knew more about drugs and alcohol than his own feelings. But my curiosity piqued his, and the next session he reported an initial awareness of intense social anxiety that alcohol alone did not alleviate. Up until this point, he had only been able to acknowledge that it was likely he was feeling anxious around women, but he considered this more of an idea rather than a reality that fit his experience.
Jacob: I have been thinking about what you asked last week. You know I think that girls really do make me anxious. I mean I know Joanna really likes me; she tells me so, but if she doesn't call me back when she says she will, I begin to worry that she doesn't want to be with me anymore. And with sex I am worried that I am not going to be adequate, like I won't be able to keep an

erection. That happens sometimes. Other times I come way too quickly, but Joanna tells me she doesn't mind.

With these initial reflections, the social anxiety that he had self-medicated with drugs and alcohol became a topic in therapy. At this point Jacob was "thinking" more about being anxious than fully feeling it. However, as we continued to talk, his awareness continued to grow and he recognized the extent of self-doubt and self-criticism when around women and that substances helped to "stop the constant pressure in [his] head" when with a girl. While substances helped calm his anxiety, Jacob also worried about his sexual performance, which likely was being adversely affected by his substance use.

The relationship with Joanna did not last very long. She seemed quite different from the alluring and highly intelligent women with whom he had wanted to become involved. Her life appeared to be characterized by unexpected and disruptive events. Jacob responded by trying to make her life more workable, which may have been indicative of a compulsive helping relationship (see discussion of the Shorter PROMIS Questionnaire [SPQ] in "Lessons" section below). She ended the relationship abruptly as if he was the source of the chaos. Jacob described himself as "devastated"—a mix of feeling anxious and lonely. To address these feelings, and perhaps maintain a sense of connection to Joanna, he added smoking marijuana to his drinking and sedative use, which remained contained to the weekends. He did report several bouts of overeating at this time and connected this to a vague sense of wanting to fill himself up where Joanna's absence had left a hole. Given polyaddictions, I checked in on his running, which had increased to long-distance runs up to four times a week as he continued to prove to himself that his substance use was not having an adverse affect on him.

At this point, I brought together my observations about his addictive behaviors and their consequences. Whenever possible, it facilitates motivation if addictive behaviors can be linked to the problem that brought the patient to treatment.

Therapist: A large part of your reason for starting therapy was your desire to get what you wanted—a relationship with a woman. During your relationship with Joanna, you have become acutely aware of what you only suspected before; while you feel confident with your friends and at work, when you are around women you become filled with self-doubt and criticism. Drinking and drugs help you avoid these feelings and allow you to be more comfortable with a woman. But this is a sort of catch-22. If you have to be high to relax around women, this means you probably need to be with a woman who also uses drugs and, as you saw with Joanna, that can make for a pretty unpredictable relationship with emotional highs and lows. You emphasized that using substances is not really creating any problems for you; you are as physically fit as ever and your friends make sure no one is put in harms way. But your substance use has other effects. Because alcohol and Valium have sedating effects, they may be affecting your sexual performance. Plus, as you have said, you don't always recall what happens; you are not really present when you are so high, and a few times you've observed that you were not as productive at work as you used to be. While substance use is still only on the weekends, it looks like you may be trying to manage uncomfortable feelings during the week by binge eating and running more, which increases the risk of an injury. Both of these, as you know, are not good for your health.

Jacob: I hear what you're saying, but I really don't think it's a big deal. But I'll think about it.

Despite this lukewarm response, Jacob reported in the next session that he had attended an AA meeting with a female friend whose drinking clearly qualified as alcoholic in his mind. Because of drinking she had been placed on probation at work due to chronic lateness, a boyfriend had left her, and her parents were about to cut off contact with her if she did not agree to attend AA or enter treatment.

Jacob: Those meetings are really something. People there have had a really rough time—lost their jobs, their homes—they're not like me. My friend is worse off; her family says if she keeps drinking they won't have anything to do with her. I think that's a bit extreme. Maybe she needs to stop using for a while, but that's not for me.

Once a patient is willing to consider that there might be a problem, twelve-step participation can facilitate movement from the contemplation to action stage by helping a patient recognize aspects of his or her own behavior in what others are sharing at meetings. Because I believe that AA and other twelve-step groups can facilitate the assessment and treatment of addictions (Freimuth 2000), I often suggest to my patients that they go and take from meetings what makes sense to them. But twelve-step programs are not for everyone; there are many alternative means to overcoming addiction (Fletcher 2001). Despite distinguishing himself from others at the meeting, Jacob did report that he had cut "way back" on his drinking and smoking marijuana and had stopped sedative use all together.

Therapist: So what do you think reasonable use would be for you?

Jacob: I think I just need to cut back and drink less.

Therapist: What would that look like?

It is important that a patient provide a specific plan.

Jacob: Well over the past two weeks I have been trying to only drink a couple, two or three beers, and if I do Scotch, to limit it to just one chaser. And no Valium or other stuff like that.

Therapist: What's that like for you?

As discussed in chapters 3 and 4, psychotherapy patients often have difficulty connecting addictive behaviors to negative consequences and, as a result, they come to therapy reporting the negative consequences but not the addiction. This may be denial but it can also reflect a number of other cognitive processes (chapter 4). Because recognition of negative consequences helps to define a behavior as problematic and to enhance motivation to change, it is important to return to this topic any time there is a change in the addictive behavior (i.e., whether an increase or decrease).

Jacob: Actually, the pressure in my head is not so bad. I mean I notice myself get uncertain about whether a girl I find attractive will talk to me, but I can live with that and not get wasted.

Therapist: So what do you think about making a plan to drink less?

Jacob: Sure, that sounds good to me. I'll just stick to what I am doing.

Jacob missed the next two sessions (see lesson 5 below).

Jacob: Sorry about the last few weeks. Work was wild; some weeks there is almost nothing to do, but last week I had three deadlines. And with all that going on, I hardly had anything to drink. No pills or pot. I got wasted last Saturday, but I don't even think I drank the weekend before that.

Therapist: What's that been like for you?

Jacob: Well, it feels sort of good.

Therapist: What feels sort of good?

Jacob: I don't know. It's easier to go to work on Mondays—I'm not so tired. I have to say I am kind of proud of myself.

Therapist *(smiles in support)*: Anything else you've noticed?

Jacob: It's hard to describe, but I feel more focused and I don't think I realized what a strain it is to run with a hangover. Running is so much easier now.

Therapist: And what about running and eating?

This is important to ask in light of Jacob's tendency to replace one addiction with another.

Jacob: I'm not running so much, but I did play a load of basketball this weekend. Once, I think it was Saturday night, I must have bought two pounds of cheese and just eaten it all.

Therapist: . . . and dating?

Jacob: Actually, I have not been going out much. I haven't felt like it.

By isolating himself, Jacob had found a new way to avoid uncomfortable feelings around women.

At this point, Jacob's addictive behaviors were fewer in quantity and frequency, and we could work more effectively on his presenting problem. By connecting his substance use to the presenting problem, Jacob was able to experience and give voice to a wide range of worries he had about getting involved with a woman. Upon reducing substance use, he was able to recognize that there were negative effects in other domains such as his work life, which he had originally believed was unaffected by his substance use. Also, Jacob became aware of how he used substances and behaviors to manage most of his strong feelings (positive or negative) by overdoing it, whether by drinking, running, or eating.

Jacob did not remain in treatment very long, but he would return periodically every six months to check in and discuss any current concerns in his relationships or work life. Jacob's drinking remained at a moderate level. He stopped taking sedatives altogether and smoked marijuana a couple times a month. Within the year, he was happily living with a woman who drank moderately.

Lessons

1. Jacob came to me relatively early in my education about addictions and psychotherapy. While I recognized the importance of gathering information about his drug use and other excessive behaviors, I was not as proactive as I might be today. I felt hesitant to ask too many questions in every session for fear this would hinder our working alliance, and yet Jacob had a number of potentially addictive behaviors that were in need of assessment. A good deal of the information did emerge gradually over a number of sessions. Given that Jacob was open and relatively nondefensive about his drug use, bingeing, and exercising, he would have been a good candidate for a structured assessment tool. In light of evidence of multiple addictions and the possibility that his relationship with women involved an element of compulsive helping, the SPQ (discussed in chapter 6) would have been a good instrument. I expect this simple and easy to administer assessment tool would have yielded much for us to talk about.

2. Jacob volunteered information regarding his mixing of alcohol with other drugs that have depressant effects. This combination is the most common source of accidental overdose. Good practice recommends that any time a patient appears to be drinking near or over daily recommended amounts, an inquiry should be made into other types of substances used with special attention given to prescribed medications or substances that have depressant effects. As a result of cross tolerance, drinking moderately (a drink or two daily) may mask an addiction if substances with sedating effects are also being used.

3. In addition to cross tolerance, a good addiction assessment looks for the possibility of polyaddictions such as are assessed on the SPQ. This is important for several reasons. During treatment, one addiction can replace another or a potentially addictive behavior that is nonproblematic at the start of therapy becomes problematic as the main addiction is addressed. Also, it is possible that no single behavior or substance use qualifies as addictive, but when taken together, their effects serve a self-medicating function. As a result, an inaccurate picture develops of what requires treatment. In Jacob's case, addictive activities (substance use,

eating, running) medicated his intense anxiety and fear of incompetence around women. While one could guess from his presenting problem that Jacob had such anxieties, they were not fully available to Jacob's experience until the addictive behaviors were reduced.

4. Therapists, not surprisingly, like to feel that interventions are effective. This can make addiction treatment difficult because often one's interventions appear to be far from effective—the addictive behavior continues on. A similar dynamic can emerge in the assessment process where patients dismiss the treatment provider's interest in the nature of potentially addictive behaviors and their negative consequences. Jacob had a typical response to my summary of his problem, which linked his substance use to his difficulty developing relationships with women: "I hear what you're saying, but I really don't think it's a big deal." Therapists can become disheartened by such reactions and may stop the assessment process too early. Instead they should remain attuned to more than the immediate verbal response. Addicted patients rarely trust the therapist's interest in their addiction (especially when the patient did not come to therapy with addiction as the stated problem). Patients are often unsure if the therapist will become another moralizing and controlling spouse or parent. Thus, it is important to keep in mind that, although one's interventions and concerns are dismissed outwardly, this does not mean they have been ineffective. Careful attention to the patient's behavior and experience during the coming weeks in therapy can provide encouragement to continue with the assessment process. The result won't always be dramatic, as with Jacob who began attending AA meetings. Instead, during the next session, the therapist might hear about a night of no use, a slight reduction in use, an inkling of empathy for a spouse who is worried, or a greater willingness to volunteer information about negative consequences.

5. The transition from assessment to treatment can be seamless as long as it does not occur prematurely. I took Jacob's attendance at some AA meetings as a sign that he was ready to do something about his drinking. Consequently, I asked him if he was ready to make a plan to drink less. I believe I acted prematurely, as indicated by his missing the next two sessions. I was asking Jacob to change before developing a mutually agreed upon picture of the negative consequences. A detailed picture of the negative consequences plays an important part in motivating change. While it was true that I was only asking Jacob if he was ready to make a plan, questions are often taken as commands, and Jacob was still somewhere between the precontemplation and contemplation stage. In fact, his drinking stayed at a lowered level those two weeks, suggesting that he was contemplating a change but was not ready to

make it public. A major cause of treatment failure is that therapists assume too quickly that a patient is ready to make a change (action stage) when he or she is still in an earlier stage of change (see chapter 10).

THE CASE OF TRACY

Tracy was referred to me by an addictions counselor who had been helping her maintain abstinence after a seven-year history of substance dependence. After two years of successful sobriety, he felt she would be a good candidate for psychotherapy where she could address her long-standing depression and find help for her current marital crisis. I performed a rather thorough formal intake with Tracy that included a detailed discussion of her addiction history. At that time, she was thirty-six years old and lived with her husband, whom she was considering divorcing, and their three daughters, ages nine, eleven, and fourteen. She worked three days a week in a retail clothing store. College was the first time she had tried drugs but only on an experimental basis. Throughout her marriage, she had abused alcohol, but only on social occasions; she never drank alone. She had tried cocaine with her husband, but she found it unpleasant. Her drugs of choice were tranquilizers and pain relievers, which she first became exposed to after a shoulder injury. She began to make the rounds to different physicians where she would complain of pain or general anxiety and they would prescribe these drugs to her. Her husband finally had to confront her addiction when he came home from work one evening to find her passed out on the bed and she could not be aroused. She denied that this was a suicide attempt. Tracy was initially treated as an inpatient and then was treated in an outpatient, day treatment program.

When first hospitalized, she was medicated with a combination of antidepressants that helped to stabilize her mood, and she had continued with these as an outpatient. After three months of this intensive treatment, she was followed by an addictions counselor whom she saw weekly and then bimonthly. She had remained successfully abstinent for two years. All of her treatments had been informed by twelve-step philosophy. She believed addiction was a disease and that abstinence from all nonprescribed substances was the only viable goal. She attended twelve-step meetings three to four times a week.

As Tracy introduced me to her life, I listened for evidence of other excessive behaviors. She liked to exercise but found it difficult to do so regularly. When she did exercise, she did so in moderation. She liked to shop, and money was a major source of conflict in her marriage. It was hard to tell whether Tracy was overspending. Some times it seemed as if she was dealing appropriately with the fashion needs of adolescent daughters and that the source of conflict stemmed from the couple's differing values about money.

She was addicted to cigarettes and openly ambivalent about it. There was some evidence of compulsive behavior. Sometimes she would stay up late at night organizing closets and drawers. She took no pleasure from the activity, although she did like the finished product. She knew that she was overdoing it (the behavior was ego-dystonic), but she continued it anyway.

She described her problem as "not knowing who I am." She actively participated in the first few months of therapy, where she used sessions to vent her anger and frustration about her marriage and her sense that she was trapped there because she could never manage on her own financially. She reported feeling less depressed and overwhelmed but, as the focus turned more to herself, she became less certain about what to talk about in a session. She came from an emotionally chaotic family where there was great deal of acting out (although there was no evidence of substance abuse). With her own children, she consciously endeavored to give them a consistent home life and provide the kind of nurturance she never received. Even at the height of her drug use, she made sure the house was clean, dinner was served, and help with homework was provided. She worried that divorce would take away the stability she wanted to give her children. She saw her compulsive neatness as part of her attempt to counteract the disorganized home from which she came.

Since starting psychotherapy, she had spoken of wanting to stop smoking cigarettes. She worried about her health and feeling guilty if she got lung cancer and deprived her children of a mother. After several attempts, she successfully gave up cigarettes. She was immensely proud of her accomplishment but, at the same time, she began feeling more depressed and lost. She found that cigarettes were soothing, and laughed at her thought that although they were just smoke, they provided her with some sense of being substantial. Without them, she felt even emptier. It was around this time, ten months into weekly psychotherapy, that she returned from a two-week vacation and began the session as follows:

Tracy: I had to make an emergency appointment with the psychiatrist before going on vacation because I was feeling really "hyper."

A long-standing issue between us was that Tracy never contacted me between sessions. She was intrigued by the idea that other patients might call. Instead, she would talk to her sponsor, go to the psychiatrist who was overseeing her medication, or tell me, after she was no longer having strong feelings, that she thought about calling but didn't. For example, she only told me about a cancer scare after the test results had come back negative.

Therapist: Why did you call him and not me?

Tracy: I don't know; I really can't recall. Was it really two weeks ago? Oh, I know. I was certain it was the medication. Remember, he increased the dosage of A [one of her antidepressants] at the last visit, and I have never felt it was right. I had been feeling racy and almost out of control. He said the medication wouldn't do that, so maybe it was just a response to all the preparation it took

to get the family organized and packed for vacation. Or maybe it's not smoking. God, I want a cigarette. Do you think I can have a cigarette?

Therapist: What happened with those hyper feelings when you were away on
vacation?

Tracy: They were still there, but there was a lot of reason to feel that way. I can't
stand staying with my in-laws. They keep asking how Doug [her husband] and
I are doing, and I lie and say everything is OK. What else can I say? I mean,
you know, there are loads of problems, but if I were to say anything, they'll just
blame it on me. I'm the one who was hospitalized. I'm the drug addict. Doug
can drink all he wants and he's still Mr. OK. Plus, we're in such close quarters
there. It's hard to hide from the kids how angry I am at Doug for not pulling his
weight and not standing up to his mother when she criticizes the kids.

Like many in recovery from addiction, Tracy had a long history of withholding
information and lying to cover up her drug use. She continued to withhold some
information from me by not calling when in crisis. With her in-laws and children,
she understood that this monitoring was designed to protect herself and her chil-
dren from hurt. While intellectually recognizing that being fully truthful on all oc-
casions was not required, any time she kept emotionally loaded information to
herself, and thus was less than fully honest, it stirred up old feelings.

Therapist: It's hard to know what's private and what is being kept as a secret.
And when it's kept private does that mean what you say is a lie? It used to be
almost second nature to you when you were using to keep secrets and tell lies
about where you were and what you were doing. Remember how hard it was
for you when you were sneaking outside to have a cigarette and wondering if
your kids would find out?

This recognition had contributed greatly to her motivation to stop smoking.

Tracy: Do you think it's a problem that I take B [a second antidepressant] all at
one time?

Apparently, these reflections on lies and secrets are an impetus to reveal
something she has been hiding. Of course Tracy knows the answer to this ques-
tion, so instead of asking the following question, I should have encouraged her
to make explicit what she knows by asking, "What do you think?"

Therapist: How is it supposed to be taken?

Tracy: Three times a day—morning, noon, and night.

Therapist: But you don't always do that . . .

Tracy: Remember, I told you before that I forget the noon pill a lot of the time.
It's the only one I take during the day, and I'm never in the same place. I'm
either too busy with work or out running errands, so by the time I remember
it's already around dinnertime. So, when I remember, I take two so it ends up
just being three a day.

Therapist: What happens when you take two together?

Tracy: It makes me feel less depressed . . . well, not really, maybe it makes me
feel more in the present, more . . . I don't know . . . it's not necessarily a good
feeling but a few months back when I talked to the psychiatrist about my
problem remembering to take the noon pill, he said not to worry; he didn't
think it would have any adverse effects.

Apparently, the psychiatrist had no concern about her routinely doubling up on the medication and as a result, the potential abuse of the medication did not come out in her session with him. She had broached the subject in our session, but only as a question. From the outside, one might conclude that Tracy's failure to acknowledge abuse of her medication means she is in denial. While patients with a long history of lying and hiding their addiction can learn to hide the addiction from themselves, too, chapter 4 discussed how often the defense mechanism of denial is an interpersonal process. This is nicely illustrated here as well. Tracy seems to want to tell the psychiatrist about her medication abuse, but when he dismisses her concern, she joins him. Is she denying the problem or merely cooperating with what he wants to talk about?

Therapist: And sometimes you take all three at the same time?

Tracy: It just sort of happened by accident. Like I said, because I forget during the day, it got to be a routine of taking two pills in the evening. Taking more than prescribed just seemed normal; the paper from the pharmacy says if you miss a pill, take it as soon as you remember. I was following directions, making up for the missed pill. But I am not sure that was really true, or at least it is not true anymore. It's more deliberate now. A couple of times I've noticed that I remember at noontime but don't get around to taking the pill. Other days I skip both morning and noon and I take all three at once. I don't know how it affects me. I just know I want to feel different in any kind of way I can. I just want a change from whatever it is and taking all three does that. Sounds like a slip, doesn't it?

Lessons

1. When patients with a long and stable recovery from addiction come to psychotherapy, it can be easy to forget about their addiction history and overlook the return of addictive behavior. Thus, whenever I treat a patient with a history of addiction, I like to get as much background information as possible. Those with histories of recovery longer than Tracy's can and do relapse. Sometimes the slip will involve the same substance or behavior, or the addiction will appear in a new form.

   For Tracy, the slip came with her preferred form of abuse—prescription medications. I don't think that it was arbitrary that she began misusing her medication in an addictive manner around the time she stopped smoking. Substances had been her way of managing her sense of self. Without cigarettes, she turned to mismanaging one of her medications. It was not clear if the medication's biological properties helped her in some way (the effect of taking three simultaneously was not described as pleasant), or whether the act of misusing something simply helped to consolidate her sense of self. Ann Marlowe (1999) writes about how heroin gave her a sense of identity. She is certain that this effect

was not due to the drug's high but rather was a function of the special-ness, "outlawry," and "transgressive glamour" that using heroin gave her (272). For Tracy, it was better to be a "bad" person than a nobody.
2. Just because a medication is prescribed does not mean it is immune to abuse. Taking medications in a manner other than prescribed—be it more or in intervals other than prescribed—is equivalent to substance abuse. Tranquilizers and pain relief medications, such as synthetic opioids, are the most likely to be abused. Weight control substances, such as those prescribed to counteract the effects of weight gain due to antidepressants, also are prone to abuse. For Tracy, her psychotropic medication became the substance to abuse. Misuse of prescription medications is not con-fined to do those with an addiction history. Elizabeth Wurtzel (2002) de-scribes in her autobiography her initial decline into addiction through abuse of Ritalin that was initially prescribed by her therapist to overcome difficulty completing the writing of her book *Bitch*.

Psychotropic medications are prescribed by psychiatrists, psy-chopharmacologists, or general practitioners, which means that usually medication is managed by someone other than the psychotherapist. As a result, psychotherapists are prone to assign responsibility for careful monitoring of the medication to the professional who does the prescrib-ing. This is not the best practice. It is true that most psychotherapists will know some things about their patients' medications: the name of the medication, the daily dosage, and, perhaps, the patient's thoughts about its effectiveness. But knowledge about medication needs to extend be-yond this minimum. The treatment provider should have a list of all medications, both prescribed and over-the-counter, that a patient is tak-ing. In the case of older patients, the list can be quite extensive, and this is where the checklist from the Alcohol Related Problems Survey (ARPS) (see chapter 8) comes in handy. Other information to be recorded and inquired about periodically is how the medication should be taken, when it is actually taken during the day, if this schedule is ad-hered to, and its potential side effects. Patients should be reminded to tell the therapist about any upcoming visits to the prescribing physician, and after the visit they should inform the therapist about any changes in their medication regimen. These questions convey to the patient that, although not the prescribing doctor, as the psychotherapist you are interested in medication and consider it a topic for discussion during sessions.
3. Psychiatrists who complete routine, structured interviews as part of an in-take are apt to recognize addiction in their new patients. However, once a relationship has developed, they can, as occurred with Tracy, fail to recog-nize a patient's abuse of the medication they have been prescribing. Even

blatant signs can be overlooked—especially when the patient seems to be functioning well in other areas, as was Tracy at the time this occurred. When Wurtzel (2002) runs out of prescribed Ritalin too quickly, she puts in a call to her psychiatrist for an early refill, making up some well-crafted excuse for why she is out of the drug so soon. The psychiatrist does not question her patient, who is a successful author, and calls in the refill.

Psychotherapists cannot assume that the prescribing physician will recognize problems in how a medication is being used. Tracy was not taking too much medication, she was just taking it in a manner other than prescribed with an intention to change how she felt. When she mentioned to her psychiatrist that she was doubling up on medication on a regular basis, he explored this no further because either he forgot her addiction history in light of her current level of functioning or he knew that the recommended practice is to take a forgotten pill. Further blinding him to a potential problem were the symptoms she was complaining about, which did not make sense in light of the medication's effect. Thus, when he normalized her concern, Tracy cooperated and went along with his line of questioning. Only in psychotherapy, when the session turned to the topic of truth and lying, did she blurt out, in the form of a question, her concern about how she was misusing her medication. At this point, Tracy revealed that she had been routinely doubling up and sometimes even taking all three of her pills at one time.

THE CASE OF AIDA: FACILITATING TREATMENT FOR AN ADDICTED SIGNIFICANT OTHER

One of the benefits of routinely assessing for addiction is that the assessment process itself raises patients' awareness of potentially addictive behaviors in themselves as well as others. One rather remarkable statistic to keep in mind is that for any given patient, there is a 43 percent chance that a spouse or blood relative has a diagnosable addiction (The Recovery Institute 1998). Aida came to therapy for difficulties in her marriage and, within a few sessions, it became clear that her husband, Pat, had a drinking problem. As is typical, she was aware of the consequences of his drinking, and these were a major source of distress in the marriage. However, Aida had not defined drinking itself as a problem. While her husband's alcoholism certainly was not the sole marital issue, any chance of the marriage improving was dependent upon his addressing the problem.

When Aida came to therapy, she had been married to Pat for twelve years, and they had agreed not to have children. When they met, they were both making a modest living as dancers supplemented by part-time day jobs, but Pat's performing career ended abruptly due to an injury. This happened shortly after they were married. He had become a dance instructor but had never been very successful and, over the past five years, had continued to lose students to the point where now he taught one or two lessons a week. Aida had been the main income earner for years. After the marriage and Pat's injury, she continued dancing for another five years, at which point she returned to school to get a business degree. Upon graduation, she received an excellent job offer from a large corporation. Aida adored Pat. When he was attentive, she felt loved and adored in return. However, the loving periods were becoming fewer and further between. He was increasingly withdrawing into himself. At these times, he would become sarcastic and short tempered. Aida in turn would fly into a rage. She attributed the failure of his career as a teacher and their growing conflicts to his depression and his refusal to get help. As an adolescent and early in their marriage, after his injury, he had been prescribed antidepressant medication and had been in psychotherapy. He felt both had failed to help him. She thought he might consider couples therapy, but first sought treatment for herself in order to clarify whether she wanted to stay in the marriage and to learn to manage her anger.

In talking about one of their more recent fights, Aida mentioned in passing that Pat had gotten so angry that he had thrown a glass of wine at her.

Therapist: Is this kind of behavior on Pat's part typical of your fights?
Aida: More so lately. But I've gotten angry and thrown things, too.
Aida had no problem criticizing Pat, but any time she suspected that someone else would be critical of him, she would protect him. Here she tries to normalize his aggressive behavior.
Therapist: Why more so lately?
Aida (*pauses*): He has been drinking more.
Therapist: Tell me more about his drinking.
Aida (*smiling*): You know, Pat, he's Irish. His whole family probably drinks a bit too much. Pat has been drinking almost the whole time we've been married. But it hasn't been a problem. He would have a drink or a few beers in the evening. But that's changed. Now I think he starts having a few beers during the day. Sometimes I think he could be drunk by the time I get home from work.
Therapist: Do you drink with him?
Aida: Actually, no. I don't like to drink.
Therapist: What other drugs have you or Pat used?
Aida: When we were both dancing, I have to admit we used a fair amount of cocaine. It helped control my appetite and be able to work during the day and have enough energy to dance at night. But that was a long time ago. Pat never liked it or any other drugs. He's begun to put on weight, probably because of his drinking, but he doesn't seem to care.

Therapist: Any drug use now?

Aida: No. I don't even like to take aspirin.

Therapist: How much do you think Pat is drinking?

Aida: This is kind of embarrassing to say, but I went through the trash and counted cans and bottles. He mostly drinks beer—sometimes more than a six-pack. But I think he drinks other alcohol, too.

Therapist: How do you feel about Pat's drinking?

Aida: When he's been drinking, I just feel he's different. Like he's not really there. I get scared and then angry that he's abandoning me. Now that I think about it, maybe the reason he keeps losing students is that he's drunk during the day.

Although Aida did not present Pat's drinking as a source of their marital problems, it is clear from her behavior that she has had some worries about Pat's drinking. In this exchange, Aida is beginning to recognize that Pat's drinking may have harmful consequences.

I have often wondered why a patient will describe the flaws of a significant other and fail to mention his or her drinking. This is always worth exploring. Sometimes, when drinking has been a consistent part of the marriage, gradual changes in drinking patterns are not emotionally registered until someone asks about them. In Aida's case, she obviously had some concern about Pat's drinking, otherwise she would not have been in the trash counting his beer cans. However, until we talked about it in therapy, she had not fully recognized the extent of her growing concern. This was due partly to the fact that she had attributed the changes in Pat's behavior to his depression and had not considered the possibility that his growing depression was alcohol-related. More importantly, Aida had reasons not to fully recognize Pat's drinking problem. These became apparent in a later session as we explored the pros and cons of Pat's drinking.

From these initial sessions, it was clear that Aida's feelings of abandonment and resulting rages needed to be addressed in her individual therapy. Aida also concluded that she could not leave Pat; she worried what would happen to him without her. She truly loved him despite the problems and wanted to stay in the marriage. Pat was open to considering marital therapy with another therapist, but he remained adamant that he did not need individual treatment. To be successful, marriage counseling would require that Pat's alcoholism be addressed, and this meant that Aida, too, would need to define his drinking as a significant problem.

One of the outcomes of an individualized addiction assessment is a decisional balance reflecting the pros and cons of the addictive behavior and its cessation (see chapter 10). With Aida I began to develop a decisional balance that reflected her experiences of Pat's drinking. The addicted person's significant other is much more aware of the negative outcomes of the behavior than

Chapter 11

the benefits. (In contrast, the addicted person is more aware of the benefits than the problems). Aida could quickly list the cons of Pat's drinking: it impeded him from making a living, his thinking became fuzzy and he just didn't seem to be himself when drunk. The latter scared Aida and made her feel like she was losing him. This feeling of loss was compounded by his actually being less attentive to her. If a patient has difficulty fully recognizing the negative consequences of the other's addictive behavior, there is the Significant Other Checklist that is being developed for this purpose (Kirby, Dugosh, Benishek, and Harrington 2005).

The positive aspects of his drinking were more difficult to recognize so to help Aida become aware of the benefits she found in Pat's drinking, I began to ask questions along the following lines: "What did she enjoy about him when he was drunk?" "Why might she be afraid to have Pat stop drinking?" "What might happen if he were sober that can't happen now?"

A subtle benefit of Pat's drinking emerged in therapy while exploring Aida's relationship to her father. While not an alcoholic, he was prone to angry outbursts that terrorized her. To counter such feelings, as an adult she liked being in control. As long as Pat was a drunk, she could remain righteously indignant about his inadequacies and, therefore, it was her responsibility and duty to run their life. Intellectually, she quickly grasped her need for control, although it took a long time for her to realize that consequently she was acting like the controlling father she disliked intensely. The other positive outcome of Pat's drinking related to the fear she felt in relation to her father's anger. Pat was generally easy-going and quite mellow, especially when drunk (as long as she was not arguing with him). He was more critical of her and prone to initiate arguments when sober.

The extent of Aida's ambivalence about Pat's drinking emerged as we talked about the pros and cons associated with his being sober. When sober she found him incredibly adoring. He was witty and smart and she enjoyed both traits enormously. She claimed that there could be no negatives to his sobriety, but it just took time for these to become apparent: if Pat were to remain sober, he would get a job and have his own money. This would mean he would be less dependent on her and would have the means to leave her. This led us to Aida's dependency on Pat and her sense that she was safe with him because, as along as he was a drunk, he would never leave her.

The resulting decisional balance looks as follows:

Continue the Addictive Behavior:
   Cons: Pat is less attentive, his thinking is fuzzy, and he is not himself or feels like a stranger; she feels abandoned; he responds more strongly when she gets angry
   Pros: Aida feels safe being in control of the relationship; Pat is less likely to be critical of her and initiate a fight

Change the Addictive Behavior:
   Cons: he would be more of his own person and have the means to leave her; she would be jealous and fearful of losing him
   Pros: he is sweet; Aida feels adored

Although I asked Aida directly about the pros and cons of Pat's drinking and not drinking, most of the more meaningful responses emerged over a series of sessions where the focus was on Aida's personal issues. The only difference between Aida's therapy and that of someone without an addicted spouse was that I drew out the implications of her dynamics for the marital relationship in general and for Pat's continued drinking in particular. Even though Aida came to see Pat's drinking as a problem and overtly expressed the desire that he stop, based on the above decisional balance, it would be surprising if Aida would whole heartedly support his efforts to become sober. Unless each individual in this relationship makes changes in his or her behavior, this couples' marriage will be difficult to alter.

I recommended Aida and Pat to a supervisee who was a rather unconventional therapist whom I thought Pat might like. He did and they began working together first as a couple and then later Pat agreed to individual treatment to address his drinking and depression. Aida began to attend Al-Anon and found it useful, although she struggled with the notion of detachment, which she experienced as abandoning Pat to a life of being a drunk. She continued in individual therapy, asking for help with her anger, her relationships with men in general, and to make sure she could support Pat's sobriety.

Lessons

1. Pat's unsuccessful treatments for depression since adolescence led me to wonder if these were more examples of failed treatment due to an unrecognized addiction. Pat's use of sedating substances could have long preceded his marriage to Aida. What a number of psychiatrists and psychotherapists had concluded was simply depression could have been the side effect of his alcoholism or a depression, complicated by addiction. It is possible that Pat's perception that previous treatments had been ineffective may have been a reflection of the fact that Pat's addiction was hidden, and treatment planning was based on the assumption that depression was his only problem.

2. Aida's presentation in therapy was a reminder that spouses and significant others can miss addiction in their loved ones. They overlook addictions for much the same reasons that therapists fail to see addictions in their psychotherapy patients—the person's behavior does not fit the stereotype and/or the consequences of the behavior are more salient and troublesome than the behavior itself. Aida was distressed by Pat's failure

as a dance instructor and his withdrawal, which she initially attributed to his history of having been diagnosed as depressed. A striking example of a spouse's failure to see an addiction was provided by a colleague who performed an initial interview with a woman, similar to Aida, who was distressed because her husband was, as she described it, "just not there for me." Unlike Pat, whose "not being there" simply involved being inattentive, this husband would actually disappear unexpectedly for a whole day. The wife brought her husband into treatment reporting that once or twice a month he would disappear for a weekend afternoon. She feared he was having an affair, but he insisted that this was not true. He explained that he needed some time to be with the guys to fish, go to a bar, or watch sports. She had spoken to some of his friends who confirmed that they had been together at these times. In the first session, the wife explained the final straw that brought them to couples therapy. He had left on a Saturday morning before she woke up, and he had not returned that evening. He had never failed to return before. By calling his friends and speaking to their wives, she found out that he was in Las Vegas. She turned to the therapist and said, "See what the problem is?" The therapist thought he saw the problem and was about to answer when she replied, "He keeps abandoning me." She had no idea he was addicted to gambling.

3. In working with Aida, I was reminded that overtly expressed desires to change do not necessarily indicate that the person is at the action stage and ready to make a change. This can be true for individuals who enter therapy asking for help with addictions as well as for significant others who are affected by the addiction. The expressed need for change may simply be the vocalizing of socially expected responses. "If I am an addict, of course, I would want to give up my addiction." "If my husband drinks, what kind of wife would I be if I did not want him to stop?" In order to know if these expressed wishes to change (whether made by the addicted person or the significant other) reflect readiness for action, it is important to create a decisional balance diagram as part of the assessment process. As occurred with Aida, the initial diagram that emerges during intake is often just a skeleton compared to what will take shape over the course of therapy. The success of treatment involves an awareness of ambivalence and how it can interfere with a successful outcome.

12

Autobiographies of Addiction

Seeing an addiction "live" is one of the best lessons in learning how to recognize its presence. The following autobiographical and fictional accounts of living with and recovering from addiction sensitize the clinician to its many faces. Each brief review highlights what can be learned from the book about addiction assessment. Patients, too, can benefit from reading one or more of these texts. The experiences described by these authors can serve as a mirror for patients who have yet to recognize their addiction—for whatever reason. Seeing themselves in these texts can be the first step toward recognizing a problem or the final step that facilitates the patient's entrance into treatment.

KARYN BOSNAK—*SaveKaryn:*
ONE SHOPAHOLIC'S JOURNEY TO DEBT AND BACK

Karyn—a young white female in a metropolitan area—is a likely candidate for psychotherapy. In fact, if she had been, her shopping addiction may have been averted. Karyn experiences intense separation anxiety when she leaves her mother in Chicago and moves to New York City where she has taken a job working in television. Once there she begins shopping. One can imagine hearing in psychotherapy her meanderings about whether she should or should not purchase an item. A therapist may not make much out of these thoughts other than that Karyn is trying to discover her likes and dislikes now that she is living on her own. Unless a detailed history had been taken, a psychotherapist would never know that she had once spent her college tuition money on clothing.

Her growing credit card debt, which is of some concern to her, becomes a major worry when Karyn loses her job. As in other autobiographies, she realizes that her addiction has become a central component of identity. "Without a job, and without being able to pamper myself like I was used to, I slowly started to lose grasp of who I was. It might sound stupid, but I began to realize how much I identified who I was with where I worked and what I looked like" (285). She realizes that perhaps all is not lost; if she sells her purchases, she can get a better sense of who she is and at the same time, pay off her debt. Shortly after she begins selling her possessions on eBay, she decides, as a lark, to develop a website entitled SaveKaryn that asks people to make small donations to help pay off her debt. (This is a true story!) News of her website spreads across the Internet and within weeks thousands of people are visiting it; money slowly but consistently is adding up. The e-mails she receives and her responses make for fun reading. In the end, Karyn becomes a bit of a celebrity and is debt free. The reader is left to wonder whether this experience has allowed Karyn to develop a sufficient sense of self that she won't, once again, go looking for it outside herself in the form of some other addictive behavior.

AUGUSTEN BURROUGHS—*DRY*

Dry is one of many autobiographies that tells the story of a successful overachiever who is addicted. Burroughs, a boy wonder in advertising, comes from the kind of terrifically dysfunctional background that one would expect to read about in a novel rather than an autobiography. His parents gave him to his mother's therapist to raise; the therapist, in turn, overlooked the relationship the boy developed with the pedophile who lived in the barn!

Upon a threat of losing his job after weeks of coming to work late and smelling of alcohol, Burroughs agrees to his employer's demand that he go to rehab. His initial response is the typical one—negative, he does not belong there. But he finally concedes to treatment. One of his first assignments is to write down the history of his drinking. It starts at age seven with NyQuil, his first bottle of wine at age twelve, smoking marijuana after that, and drinking to intoxication nightly by age eighteen. The most surprising revelation is that he is allergic to alcohol and takes Benadryl (ten to fifteen times a day) in order to drink. While psychotherapy patients are unlikely to be in late-stage alcoholism, as is Burroughs, his response to putting forth his drinking and drug history is relevant to any addiction assessment. He is amazed at what he has reported. "I've never actually *quantified* before" (Burroughs 2003, 57).

> I think for the first time I can see, right up there on the board, that I do drink much more than normal. And the pills I have to swallow to drink. . . . I almost can't help but feel like it's possibly a good thing I am here. Or rather, that this has been drawn to my attention, made serious and not a joke (59).

By the end of thirty days in rehab, he is walking the walk and talking the talk, although he keeps wondering if he really means it or, consistent with his advertising background, is simply selling himself and others on his change. Upon return home, he does all the right things. He goes to an addiction recovery group and begins therapy with an alcoholism counselor. Life feels great; he is recognizing his feelings for the first time, and while rehab warned him that all these good feelings (know in AA as the "pink cloud") are temporary, he hopes they are real and forever. He does not drink, but he is far from sober. He, too, replaces one addiction with another.

He begins a relationship with Foster, a recovering crack addict in his therapy group. Intimate relationships with group members are forbidden; the reader observes Burroughs' thinking as he works to make this acceptable (e.g., they have sex but "not really" since he "didn't look"). Foster becomes his new addiction, needing frequent daily contact, which feels very similar to the way Burroughs used to drink. He does other things in an addictive manner as well. "It's Saturday, noon, and I've been chain smoking and drinking coffee alcoholically since seven this morning" (180).

The author observes it all but continues his behavior. Burroughs never denies that his behavior may be addiction-like but he does minimize what it means for his life and the potential negative implications. He leaves AA and the reader joins him in the hope that he is right—he can have this wonderful man, a wonderful relationship, and do it on his own. Then Foster relapses and Burroughs' best friend and former lover becomes ill and dies, after which Burroughs' returns to drinking. The book ends with his year of sobriety—back in AA and redefining his professional life, presumably with Foster out of the picture.

SUSAN CHEEVER—*NOTE FOUND IN A BOTTLE: MY LIFE AS A DRINKER*

Susan Cheever drinks her way through dating, marriage, affairs, parenting, and attending AA meetings. All the time she finds something other than alcoholism to explain the source of her difficulties. During her first marriage while reflecting on how her professional life and marital relationship is going nowhere, Cheever writes, "If you had suggested that there was a connection between what we drank and what was happening to us. . . . Robert and I would both have been amazed. We drank the way everyone did, or so we believed" (Cheever 1999, 111). How could she be an alcoholic if her recently sober father has a glass of white wine waiting for her when they meet for lunch? She even attends AA meetings with her father. She loves the stories she hears but always finds a way that she is different from other alcoholics. The man who drank himself through Yale and is now a successful banker tells a story of being arrested for drunk driving. She has never been arrested. "There was always something in every story that allowed me to keep my distance from the idea that I might be an alcoholic" (123). Is she simply in denial? By providing the details of her history, the reader discovers how excessive behaviors become the family's norm and subsequently one's personal norm.

And so she continues to drink never knowing that "the problem I had with men, with marriage, even with my work had anything to do with drinking. . . . I thought that drinking was a wonderful way I had of dealing with my problems" (158). While Cheever does not refer to being in therapy, one can imagine her entering treatment to address the chaos in her relationships or her worries about her daughter without explicitly mentioning her excessive use of alcohol. Yet a therapist familiar with the possibility would hear in her stories of daily life how often alcohol made an appearance.

The book also elucidates that the most significant negative consequences of an addiction are apparent only when the addictive behavior ceases. In describing her family's secrets (which include her father's bisexuality), she decides that the real secret is drinking and its real impact is just being discovered: "What alcohol does is hidden until the very end and even when it's exposed it hides. I don't think my father ever knew . . . how much drinking had distorted our family life. I am just now beginning to know" (187). Cheever's reflections should help the clinician recognize that a patient's failure to connect an addictive behavior with its negative consequence is not necessarily a result of the patient's wish to hide something (i.e., is in denial). Rather, some patients *really* do not know the adverse effects that result from addictive behaviors until long after the behavior ends.

JAMES FREY—*A MILLION LITTLE PIECES*

Frey is not likely to be a psychotherapy patient with a hidden addiction. Still, the book has much to teach psychotherapists about the brutally compelling nature of addiction, the extremes one will go to keep it going, what happens during detoxification and rehab based on a twelve-step model, and how a person can successfully recover from late-stage addiction to alcohol and crack without following the twelve-steps. In the dialogues between Frey and his therapists, the reader learns the common criticisms that patients raise about such self-help programs (e.g., AA is a substitute addiction; is addiction really a disease?) and how those who adhere to twelve-step philosophy respond to these.

The book begins with Frey coming to consciousness in the back of a plane, covered in blood with teeth missing, and having no idea of how he got there or what happened to him. He is on his way to a rehab in Minnesota. The book is less about what happens in such settings and more about Frey's internal monologue and growing relationships with the wide variety of people who share his stay in this treatment program. We learn that the "Fury" which Frey dissolves with substances is at least partially linked to his early years of unrelenting pain from undiagnosed ear infections. There is much disturbing material in this book, but perhaps the most upsetting is the afterward where Frey briefly describes what happened to all the people in the rehab whom Frey and the reader have gotten to know.

PETE HAMILL—*A DRINKING LIFE: A MEMOIR*

Unlike many of these autobiographies, Hamill is not a child with a successful father or a privileged background. This is the story of a boy with an alcoholic and often unemployed father who grows out of the poverty of his childhood to become a successful sports reporter while, at the same time, growing into the drinking life of his father. Hamill struggles to become who he is professionally, and then he struggles to get sober. Like Susan Cheever's *Note Found in a Bottle*, this book shows that, from the child's perspective, an alcoholic parent's drinking is experienced as an integral, regular, and hence normal part of daily life. Drinking is a way to relax, celebrate, mourn the dead, and bond with the living. For the clinician, reading this book leaves one questioning what denial really means. Is it really a defense mechanism? Or is denial a cognitive distortion that is created from what was learned in the family? For Hamill, the latter seems to hold. It takes him a long time to recognize that alcohol is destroying his life but once he does, his family history and its meaning is reinterpreted.

MARIAN KEYES—*RACHEL'S HOLIDAY*

Rachel's Holiday is not an autobiography but a fictional account of a twenty-seven-year-old Irish girl's addicted life in New York City and her two-month stay in a rehab in her home country of Ireland. There are many fictional accounts of addiction (another compelling one is Carrie Fisher's semi-autobiographical *Postcards from the Edge*). This book contains a number of useful lessons for family members struggling with how to handle a significant other's addiction. The book not only gives the reader a good sense of what happens in a rehab experience (without having to deal with some of the brutal images in Frey's autobiography), but it also provides the story of Rachel's recovery with an excellent illustration of the vicissitudes of denial and the multiple ways of not knowing the implications of one's addiction. By identifying with Rachel's struggles, those with active addictions can become more open about their addiction and its consequences.

The story, which is written from Rachel's perspective, begins with her sense that she is merely a recreational user. Only as the story unwinds is the true extent of her addiction revealed. Even well into rehab, she insists that she is not addicted even though she increasingly recognizes that those around her (who similarly continue to insist that they are *not* addicted) are in denial. In group psychotherapy, Neal, a husband and father, has always insisted that he is completely different from his father whom he despises for having beaten his mother. In one session, he is exposed to the reality that he has become just like his father—a wife-beating alcoholic. Watching this interaction, Rachel begins to understand the true meaning of denial. Only much later does Rachel see the reality of what she has done to those she loves most—her best friend, Brigit, and her ex-boyfriend. The book deftly illustrates the ambivalence of voices within the addicted person's head—a moment of awareness of the mess she has made of her relationships and life is immediately followed by rationalization, minimizing, and externalization as ways to rid herself of the overpowering surge of guilt and shame which comes with such realization.

Rachel's friends and family struggle with their own ambivalences about whether or not to confront her. Families with addicted members will identify with this part of the story. They often hint and complain, but they find it much more difficult to sit down and say, "You have a drinking problem and you need to get some help." In the book, Rachel's roommate and boyfriend often ask about her drug and alcohol use and kindly request that she stop. It is only after the roommate discovers Rachel comatose in bed, having overdosed by taking too many sleeping pills while high on alcohol and cocaine, that her parents are called in and she goes to rehab. This series of events leaves friends and family angry with Rachel, but they also feel guilty about not having been more proactive. As part of the rehab experience, her friends come to confront Rachel with how they experienced her and her drug use. Rachel responds by becoming furious and she spends a good part of the rest of the novel ruminating about how she will get back at them.

This part of the book is useful to significant others who avoid confronting a loved one who is addicted because they cannot tolerate the other's hate and anger. By living through Rachel's anger at her friends, the reader is helped to realize that this rage is not personal and recognizes its defensive function. Rachel does recover from her addiction and her rage and, after months of sobriety, she is ready to thank her ex-roommate and boyfriend for what they did for her and to acknowledge how difficult it must have been.

CAROLINE KNAPP—*DRINKING: A LOVE STORY*

This autobiography describes the gradual disintegration of a woman who maintains a successful journalistic career throughout her addiction. Knapp's alcoholism is complicated by periods of anorexia whose co-occurrence with addiction is common. Two particularly interesting features of this book for psychotherapists are her ongoing psychotherapy and the realization, after she is sober, that her father, a psychoanalyst, was likely an alcoholic.

Knapp does not write in detail about the psychotherapy she began shortly after completing college and continued during the period covered in the book. Reading between the lines, though, it is hard to know if the therapist recognized the extent of his patient's drinking and its consequences. Knapp's description of how she broached the subject in therapy is typical of a patient who is worried about having an addiction and is hoping, wishing, and/or fearing that the treatment provider will recognize the problem:

> Every now and then I'd tell him I was drinking too much, or I'd mention something in which too much wine had played a role, most often a fight with Julian, but I usually skirted my way around the details, justified or minimized the extent to which alcohol was involved. If he brought the subject up again the next week, or asked me how the drinking was going, I'd say "Oh, it seems to be more under control," and drop the subject (Knapp 1996, 172).

The therapist joins his patient in ignoring the problem until one day Knapp begins a session with a straightforward description of her concern. "I said, 'I think I'm having a real problem with alcohol'" (172). The full implication of this direct statement is minimized by it being said without emotion despite her fear as she says it. She goes on to describe the previous night's argument with her boyfriend, Julian. Therapy during the past year often addressed these fights, but this time she offers a new piece of information—"Alcohol is always involved when we fight. I'm drunk every single time" (172). Knapp ultimately asks the therapist if he thinks she will need to stop drinking, and he responds in the affirmative.

His gentle but direct response has a major effect. She attends her first AA meeting and, while it is several years before she commits to stopping drinking, she has acknowledged that there is a problem and has moved from the precontemplation to contemplation stage. Although the reader can never know what actually occurred in her therapy sessions, Knapp's description leaves one wondering what would have happened if the therapist had been more inquisitive in response to her periodic references to drinking and fighting. What if he had not accepted her minimalization of drinking's import?

Would she have left treatment? Would she have been able to tolerate these incursions into her denial system and enter a rehab sooner? Is Knapp actually in denial or, by not addressing addiction actively, are she and the therapist colluding to keep her alcoholism a secret?

Another interesting dimension of this well-written book concerns Knapp's discovery that her father struggled with alcoholism. Knapp's father introduced her to alcohol when she was a teenager. Their relationship seems fraught with discomfort, and it is easier for the two of them to be together when there is a drink between them. Growing up, Knapp saw her father come home to a drink every evening. Like Susan Cheever's family, drinking every day was a normative part of Knapp's family life. No arguments followed, no black outs or broken dishes ensued. She observed her father's drinking but drew no conclusions about it. Only in sobriety, when Knapp asks her father's friend about it, does she discover that her father struggled with the idea that he was an alcoholic.

A critical interview question that may indicate alcoholism is whether a close family member has a drinking problem. Had Knapp been asked during treatment if there was alcoholism in her family, she, like Sarah in the previous chapter, would have answered "no." Instead of a yes-or-no question, an assessment of family addiction is best approached with an alternative set of questions that explores a family's rituals and traditions around drinking and drug use. In the process, both therapist and patient may discover a previously unidentified drinking problem.

KATY LEDERER—*POKER FACE: A GIRLHOOD AMONG GAMBLERS*

Katy Lederer had little in the way of family life. Her father, an English professor at a boarding school, and brother could do little to stop her mother's drinking. They never seemed to have enough money—especially in relation to the affluent people around them. This was a family in disarray except for those few times when they all sat down together to play cards.

Her mother leaves Katy and her marriage to try acting in New York City where Katy's overly large brother (an overeater?) is involved in the seedier side of gambling. Ultimately, the family, minus the father (who has overcome his financial worries by becoming a successful writer and lecturer), reunites in Las Vegas where the brother has become a successful poker player and sports gambler. Katy's older sister moves up the ranks of poker players while their mother is in the background doing the books for the sports gambling operation. Katy tries her hand too, but ultimately she leaves to become a writer.

Other than the occasional arrest and sleepless night, this book does not drag the reader through an array of negative consequences. It does show how different addictions run in the family, and it introduces the reader to many sides of gambling, including sports betting. The author successfully conveys the excitement and appeal of gambling. Most importantly, one learns the difference between an amateur gambler and a successful gambler. The former plays with ego and hopes for luck, while the professional gambler wins at cards because of a great deal of study, lots of discipline, and a little luck.

ANN MARLOWE—*HOW TO STOP TIME: HEROIN FROM A TO Z*

For Ann Marlowe, heroin is her way to handle fear of death; when doing heroin, the inevitable forward movement of time stops. Managing fear of death even explains why "junkies are always running out of dope." She describes the connection in the following manner:

> First you displace your fear of death onto the dope, where the impending disaster, once you call it by the name heroin, is easier to face. And then you displace your fear of dope into the fear of not getting it. The fear of drugs running out is manageable—the fear of time running down isn't. All your anxieties come to rest on the single question of getting dope, which, while strenuous in its own fashion, is easier to negotiate than your mortality (Marlowe 1999, 132).

The reader will learn a great deal about the ins and outs of acquiring heroin (e.g., it is purchased by the dollar-amount bag and not by quantity) and using heroin (e.g., how to avoid an overdose). What is unique about this book is that the heroin-using population is a group that is likely to be in psychotherapy: primarily white, middle- and upper-middle-class young men and women. This group snorts the drug, although a few move on to injecting it. Their demographics are quite different from the stereotypic heroin user whose life is ruined by the drug.

Marlowe's heroin use starts halfway through her four-year psychoanalysis—a reminder to therapists that even with an assessment of addiction at the start of therapy, it is necessary to remain attuned to signs of addiction over the course of treatment. While Marlowe suggests that the introduction of heroin into her life was a "black mark against my analyst, . . . I am now open to the possibility that it was self-medication directed at the painful process" (257). Marlowe is intellectually engaged in her analysis but never develops a transference. Her analyst understands the absence of transference in historical terms when, in fact, it may be a result of her growing relationship with heroin. Drug use does affect the outcome of her psychoanalysis. She learns new things about herself (e.g., she recognizes her competitiveness), but she does not feel them or do anything about them until "after quitting dope, when [her] oddities appeared to [her] in sharper relief" (259).

Heroin is the substance on which all addictions were initially modeled. Being physiologically addictive, it was assumed that some heroin use would inevitably lead to addictive use. As discussed in chapter 2 and as demonstrated by Marlowe, one can manage to use heroin in a moderate fashion over a prolonged period and continue to function effectively, although ultimately she does begin to show signs of being addicted. To her this means that there are no heroin-free times or places in her life. She gets high before a date, starts doing heroin in the morning, or takes it when she goes camping or running.

Her description of heroin's high is a reminder to therapists to ask about the current pleasure a patient receives from a substance. She equates heroin's initial high to "the deep satisfaction of your first cup of coffee in the morning" that is never experienced in the second cup. "And heroin use is one of the indisputable cases where the good old days really were the good old days. The initial highs did feel better than the drug will ever make you feel again" (9). In therapy, this kind of question can engage a patient's curiosity about why they continue to use a substance despite the loss of the special pleasure it once brought. The patient may draw the same conclusion as Marlowe: "Doing dope doesn't sound like so much fun in my account. In retrospect, it wasn't. It was just a little more fun than the other life, lived without dope" (145).

As illustrated in the case histories in chapter 11, addiction and rigorous exercise are not mutually exclusive. Marlowe helps make the connection explicit. Like shooting baskets, a good tennis game, a long distance run, or a serious martial arts practice, "Heroin provides the all-absorbing, anxiety deflecting presentness, which we can also find in sports" (16). She wonders if having experienced the "oblivion of athletics" makes one more vulnerable to addiction.

JOHN MORIARTY—*LIQUID LOVER: A MEMOIR*

Moriarty has tried to get sober before. This book tells of the time he was successful. As the title conveys, Moriarty has an intimate relationship to his liquor referred to as Vitamin V. But he is not faithful to this or any lover, as this book reveals how addiction within the gay community can become interwoven with sexual behavior.

Moriarty comes to alcohol and sex (as well as cocaine and prescription drugs) as a solution to problems from childhood and awkwardness in social situations. They free his "mind from the pounding drum of insecurity and fear" (Moriarty 2001, 113). He truly is puzzled by how drinking turned from a socially acceptable activity to an addiction. "I try to remember when drinking became the focus of my life. When it evolved from a social activity to an act that defined every day of every month. . . . I worry that I drink too much. I worry that I drink too often. I worry that I worry too much about drinking. . . . And through it all, I drink" (45).

As is common in such memoirs, his turning point comes with a suicide attempt. This book is less a linear story of addiction and recovery than an internal monologue that conveys his enjoyments and struggles with addiction and his unmet longing for a real love relationship. Spirituality (not AA) plays a significant role in this man's recovery, but it does not get in the way of his conveying the intense value he finds in living a sober life and the patience one needs to get there.

ELIZABETH WURTZEL—*MORE, NOW, AGAIN*

Elizabeth Wurtzel is a Harvard graduate and well-known author of a bestseller entitled *Prozac Nation* (1994). Wurtzel has a history of experimenting with substances. She did heroin daily for weeks and then stopped. Although she reports taking cocaine only once a week, in between these times, she was always waiting and planning for the next hit. She reminds the reader that it is not how much or how often that defines addiction. "Addiction is when you want to stop doing something and can't" (Wurtzel 2002, 20).

Over the course of the book, Wurtzel visits many health and mental health professionals. She fools most of them. From reading this book, providers will be reminded about how easy it is to miss an addiction while at the same time learning about some of the subtle signs that reveal a hidden addiction.

At the start of the book, she is in therapy with a psychologist while being followed by a psychiatrist for medication. Her therapist, recognizing she is high in sessions, refuses to continue treatment until she stops abusing substances. She begins working only with the psychiatrist, Dr. Singer, who is referred to as an addiction specialist. After not using for four months, she has a brief relapse and then stops again. In an attempt to deal with her continued cravings, Dr. Singer modifies her antidepressant regimen and adds some Ritalin into the mix as a way to "curb my interest in doing other drugs and . . . give me the stimulation I needed without putting my health or life at risk" (25).

Continuing treatment over the phone with Dr. Singer, Wurtzel goes to Florida to write. One day she complains about the medication and the solution offered by the psychiatrist is to take less of the medication more often during the day. This requires cutting the pills into pieces, but the cuts are messy and some portion is left behind in powdery form. Wurtzel snorts this remaining portion. Soon she is snorting up the prescribed amount. She feels no need to mention this to anyone; she is merely taking her medication. Given the appeal cocaine has for her, it is not surprising to discover that Wurtzel begins snorting more than the prescribed amount of Ritalin. She runs out of the prescribed medication sooner than expected, but she finds ways to get more.

This part of the book illustrates many of the scams addicted persons use in order to get more of a regulated substance. For example, she convinces the pharmacist that he has miscounted, and he sends her sixty pills more; she tells her psychiatrist that the pills were lost and a new prescription is provided.

Life goes downhill. She still can't write; she is arrested for shoplifting; she becomes gaunt; and she has stomach trouble, a constant runny nose, and sores on her legs from cutting and picking. Her family becomes concerned and recommends a physical. The physician finds nothing wrong. Visiting Dr. Singer back in New York City, she reveals the open sores on her legs, which are simply diagnosed as trichotillomania. There is no mention of her substance abuse. Wurtzel goes on coolly to describe how, if you don't fit the dope addict stereotype,

> Doctors are not hard to fool. . . . How would this doctor at the Cleveland Clinic who has never seen me before, be able to figure out that I am not in my natural state of antsy anxiety. I've had sessions with Dr. Singer, who used to run a drug treatment program, where she did not know I was high. If you carry if off well, they won't be able to tell. . . . They don't suspect. Why should they? (93).

There are many other enlightening reflections on the nature of addiction in this book. One of the more notable relates to what Wurtzel refers to as postmodern denial, which I have observed in a number of high functioning adults with an addiction:

> It used to be that you'd actually say that you weren't a drunk, sometimes you had a few too many, but nothing outlandish. Nowadays you can't get away with that; knowledge of the nature of dependency is too pervasive. So you start to have people like me, people who say, I am an addict and I like it, try and stop me (59).

The challenge with these patients is to discover the negative consequences that will help motivate their interest in changing.

Wurtzel's book has a happy conclusion, although to get there requires many unsuccessful treatments and forays into other obsessions and addictions.

Appendix

Overview of Major Addictive Substances

ALCOHOL

Drug name: ethanol (ETOH)
Some popular names: brew, booze, juice, hooch
Method of use: swallowed
Potential for physical dependence: high
Potential for psychological dependence: high
Effects: reduced inhibitions, impaired judgment, slurred speech, impaired memory and learning, impaired coordination
Direct negative consequences: organ damage, especially liver and heart; fetal alcohol syndrome; black outs; increased accidents; reduced effectiveness of medications; increased risk of overdose when mixed with depressants; anxiety, depression, severe withdrawal syndrome

CANNABIS

Drug name: marijuana, hashish, TCH
Some popular names: grass, pot, weed, dope, reefer, joint, ganja, sinsemilla
Method of use: smoked, less commonly swallowed
Potential for physical dependence: low
Potential for psychological dependence: moderate
Effects: relaxed, good feeling, hilarity, reduced inhibitions, hunger, altered perception,
Direct negative consequences: lung damage; agitation; paranoia; amotivational syndrome, mistakes

COCAINE

Drug name: cocaine
Some popular names: coke, snow, blow, crack
Method of use: snorted as a powder; crack is smoked, less often swallowed
Potential for physical dependence: possible
Potential for psychological dependence: moderate for cocaine, high for crack
Effects: alertness, increased concentration and sense of well being, diminished appetite
Direct negative consequences: insomnia; anxiety; depression; lung, sinus and nasal passage damage

SEDATIVE/HYPNOTICS/DEPRESSANTS

Drug name:
1. barbiturates
2. benzodiazepines
3. methaqualone
Some popular names:
1. Seconal, Amytal, phenobarbitol, yellow jackets, reds, goodballs
2. Valium, valleys, Atavan, Xanax, Tranxene
3. Quaaludes, ludes, spoor
Method of use: usually swallowed, sometimes injected
Potential for physical dependence: high
Potential for psychological dependence: high
Effects: relaxation, drowsiness
Direct negative consequences: impaired performance and judgment; confusion, slurred speech, memory impairment, respiratory distress; increased overdose potential when mixed with alcohol

STIMULANTS

Drug name:
1. amphetamines/methylphenidate
2. methamphetamine
3. MDMA
4. PCP
5. caffeine and ephedrine

Some popular names:
1. Dexedrine, Ritalin, Adderall, speed, uppers, pep pills, bennies, black beauties
2. crystal (meth)
3. Ecstasy, X, Adam
4. angeldust, dust

Method of use: swallowed or may be injected
Potential for physical dependence: possible for 1, 2
Potential for psychological dependence: high for 1, 2
Effects: alter, energized, appetite loss, grandiosity
Direct negative consequences: nervous, irritable, sleepless, panic, hallucinations, heart attack, strokes, heart arrhythmia

OPIOIDS/NARCOTICS

Drug name: opium, morphine, heroin, synthetic drugs that resemble opium (e.g., Percodan, OxyContin, codeine, fentanyl, Vicodin, Demerol)
Some popular names: junk, smack
Method of use: swallowed or injected
Potential for physical dependence: high
Potential for psychological dependence: high
Effects: euphoria, rush, pain relief, laissez-faire attitude, sleepy, decreased appetite
Direct negative consequences: increased risk of infection when injected, high risk of overdose, constipation, uncomfortable withdrawal syndrome, respiratory depression, coma

HALLUCINOGENS

Drug name:
1. psilocybin
2. mescaline
3. phencyclidine
4. ketamine

Some popular names:
1. LSD, acid, purple haze
2. magic mushrooms
3. PCP; PCP mixed with marijuana—supergrass, killer hog

Method of use: swallowed; PCP is smoked, snorted, or injected
Potential for physical dependence: possible
Potential for psychological dependence: unknown
Effects: altered perceptions/altered sense of reality; visual hallucinations;
    sense of insight; detachment,
Direct negative consequences: fear, anxiety, paranoia, flashbacks, psychosis,

INHALANTS

Drug names:
1. cleaning agents, solvents, adhesives
2. amyl/butyl nitrite
3. nitrous oxide
Some popular names:
1. gasoline, airplane glue, paint thinner, dry cleaning fluid
2. poppers, snappers, locker room
3. laughing gas, whippets
Method of use: inhaled, sniffed sometimes from cotton, ampoules, plastic/paper bags
Potential for physical dependence: unknown
Potential for psychological dependence: unknown
Effects: euphoria, reduced inhibitions, light headedness
Direct negative consequences: impaired reflexes; slowed thought; lack of co-
    ordination; violent behavior; nerve damage, suffocation, kidney failure,
    heart arrhythmia, anoxia

References

Aanavi, M. P., D. O. Taube, D. Y. Ja, and E. F. Duran. (1999). The status of psychologists' training about and treatment of substance abusing clients. *Journal of Psychoactive Drugs* 31: 441–44.

Abraham, H. D., and M. Fava. (1999). Order of onset of substance abuse and depression in a sample of depressed outpatients. *Comprehensive Psychiatry* 40: 44–50.

Adams, J., and R. J. Kirby. (2002). Excessive exercise as an addiction: A review. *Addiction Research and Theory* 10: 415–38.

American Psychiatric Association. (1994). *Diagnostic and statistical manual of mental disorders (4th Ed.)*. Washington, DC: Author.

Ananth, J., S. Vanderwater, M. Karnal, A. Brodsky, R. Gamal, and M. Miller. (1989). Missed diagnosis of substance abuse in psychiatric patients. *Hospital and Community Psychiatry* 40: 297–99.

Babor, T. F., M. Hofmann, F. K. Del Boca, V. Hesselbrock, R. E. Meyer, Z. S. Dolinsky, and B. Rounsaveille. (1992). Types of alcoholics I: Evidence for an empirically derived typology based on indicators of vulnerability and severity. *Archives of General Psychiatry* 49: 599–608.

Bamber, D., I. M. Cockerill, S. Rodgers, and D. Carroll (2000). "It's exercise or nothing": A qualitative analysis of exercise dependence. *British Journal of Sports Medicine.* 34: 423-430.

Beck, A. T., F. W. Wright, C. F. Newman, and B. Liese. (1993). *Cognitive therapy of substance abuse.* New York: Guilford.

Becker, L. K., and B. Walton-Moss. (2001). Detecting and addressing alcohol abuse in women. *Nurse Practitioner* 26: 13–25.

Berenson, D., and E. W. Schrier. (1991). Addressing denial in the therapy of alcohol problems. *Family Dynamics of Addiction Quarterly* 1: 21–30.

Blanco, C., P. Moreyra, E. V. Nunes, J. Saiz Ruiz, and A. Ibanez. (2001). Pathological gambling: Addiction or compulsion. *Seminars in Clinical Neuropsychiatry* 6: 67–176.

Blow, F. C., K. J. Brower, J. E. Schulenberg, L. M. Demo-Dananberg, J. P. Young, and T. P. Beresford. (1992). The Michigan Alcoholism Screening Test-Geriatric Version (MAST-G): A new elderly specific screening instrument. *Alcoholism: Clinical and Experimental Research* 16: 372.

Bosnak, K. (2003). *SaveKaryn: One Shopaholic's Journey to Debt and Back.* New York: HarperCollins.

Boys, A., and J. Marsden. (2003). Perceived functions predict intensity of use and problems in young polysubstance users. *Addiction* 98: 951–63.

Bradley, K. A., J. Boyd-Wickizer, S. H. Powell, and M. L Burman. (1998). Alcohol screening questionnaires in women: A critical review. *Journal of the American Medical Association* 280: 166–71.

Brems, C., and M. E. Johnson. (1997). Clinical implications of the co-occurrence of substance use and other psychiatric disorders. *Professional Psychology: Research and Practice* 28: 437–47.

Brown, R. L., T. Leonard, L. A. Saunders, and O. Papasouliotis. (2001). A two-item conjoint screen for alcohol and other drug problems. *The Journal of the American Board of Family Practice* 14: 95–106.

Brown University Digest of Addiction Theory and Application. (2002). Polysubstance Use Common Among Patients in Treatment, vol. 21, pages 1 and 6. Retrieved on January 20, 2004, from www.medscape.com/viewarticle/433226 ?srcmp=psy-051702.

Burroughs, Augusten. (2003). *Dry.* New York: St. Martin's Press.

Cadoret, R. J., E. Troughton, T. W. O'Gorman, and E. Heywood. (1995). Adoption study demonstrating two genetic pathways to drug abuse. *Archives of General Psychiatry* 42: 1131–36.

Carey, K. B., D. M. Purnine, S. A. Maisto, and M. P. Carey. (2002). Correlates of stages of change for substance abuse among psychiatric outpatients. *Psychology of Addictive Behaviors* 16: 283–89.

Carey, K. B., and L. M. Teitelbaum. (1996). Goals and methods of alcohol assessment. *Professional Psychology: Research and Practice* 27: 460–66.

Carnes, P. J. (1996). Addiction or compulsion: Politics or illness? *Sexual Addiction and Compulsivity* 3: 127–42.

Carroll, J.F.X., and J. J. McGinley. (1998). Managing MICA clients in a modified therapeutic community with enhanced staffing. *Journal of Substance Abuse Treatment* 15: 565–77.

Center for Substance Abuse Treatment. (2000). *Enhancing Motivation for Change in Substance Abuse Treatment.* (Treatment Improvement Protocol Series). Bethesda, MD: Substance Abuse and Mental Health Services Administration.

———. (2004). *Issues in the Treatment of Women.* (Treatment Improvement Protocol Series). Bethesda, MD: Substance Abuse and Mental Health Services Administration.

Chan, C., and H. Grossman. (1988). Psychological effects of running loss on constant runners. *Perceptual and Motor Skills* 66: 875–83.

Charlton, J. P. (2002). A factor-analytic investigation of computer "addiction" and engagement. *British Journal of Psychology* 93: 329–44.

Cheever, Susan. (1999). *Note Found in a Bottle: My Life as a Drinker.* New York: Simon and Schuster.

Cherpitel, C. J. (1995). Screening for alcohol problems in the emergency room: A rapid problems screen. *Drug and Alcohol Dependence* 40: 133–37.

———. (1997). Brief screening instruments for alcoholism. *Alcohol Health and Research World* 21: 348–51.

Cherpitel, C. J., and W. B. Clark. (1995). Ethnic differences in performance of screening instruments for identifying harmful drinking and alcohol dependence in the ER. *Alcoholism: Clinical and Experimental Research* 19: 628–34.

Christenson, G. A., R. J. Faber, M. de Zwaan, N. C. Raymond, S. M. Specker, M. D. Ekern, et al. (1994). Compulsive buying: Descriptive characteristics and psychiatric comorbidity. *Journal of Clinical Psychiatry* 55: 5–11.

Christo, G., S. L. Jones, S. Haylett, G. M. Stephenson, R.M.H. Lefever, and R. Lefever. (2003). The Shorter PROMIS Questionnaire: Further validation of a tool for simultaneous assessment of multiple addictive behaviours. *Addictive Behaviors* 28: 225–48.

Chung, R., S. M. Colby, N. P. Barnett, D. J. Rohsenow, A. Spirito, and P. M. Monti. (2000). Screening adolescents for problem drinking: Performance of brief screens against DSM-IV alcohol diagnoses. *Journal of Studies on Alcohol* 61: 579–87.

Cicala, R. S. (2003). Substance abuse among physicians: What you need to know. *Hospital Physician* (July): 39–46.

Cloninger, C. R. (1987). Neurogenic adaptive mechanisms in alcoholism. *Science* 236: 410–416.

Cooper, A., D. L. Delmonico, and R. Burg. (2000). Cybersex users, abusers, and compulsives: New findings and implications. Pp. 5–30 in *Cybersex: The dark side of the force,* ed. A.Cooper. Philadelphia: Brunner-Routledge.

Cooper, A., C. Scherer, S. S. Boies, and B. Gordon. (1999). Sexuality on the Internet: From sexual exploration to pathological expression. *Professional Psychology: Research and Practice* 30: 154–64.

Cooper, M. L., M. R. Frone, M. Russell, and P. Mudar. (1995). Drinking to regulate positive and negative emotions: A motivational model of alcohol use. *Journal of Personality and Social Psychology* 69: 990–1005.

Cunningham, J. A., L. C. Sobell, D. R. Gavin, M. B. Sobell, and R. C. Breslin. (1997). Assessing motivation for change: Preliminary development and evaluation of a scale measuring the costs and benefits of changing alcohol or drug use. *Psychology of Addictive Behaviors* 11: 107–14.

Dean, J. C., and F. Rud. (1984). The drug addict and the stigma of addiction. *International Journal of Addictions* 19: 859–69.

De Coverley Veale, D.M.E. (1987). Exercise dependence. *British Journal of Addiction* 82: 735–40.

DeJong, W. (2001). Finding common ground for effective campus prevention. *Psychology of Addictive Behaviors* 15: 292–96.

Denning, P. (2000). *Practicing harm reduction psychotherapy: An alternative approach to addictions.* New York: Guilford Press.

Dhossche, D. M. (1999). Aggression and recent substance abuse: Absence of association in psychiatric emergency room patients. *Comprehensive Psychiatry* 40: 343–46.

Diamond, J. (2000). *Narrative means to sober ends: Treating addiction and its aftermath.* New York: Guilford.

Dodes, L. (2003). *The heart of addiction.* New York: Quill.

Donato. T. (2003). Measuring risk among non-PG's: A new look at the SOGS. *The Wager* 8. Retrieved on January 16, 2004, from www.thewager.org/current.htm.

Donovan, D. M., and G. A. Marlatt. (1988). *Assessment of addictive behaviors.* New York: Guilford.

Dunbar-Jacob, J. (1993). Contributions to patient adherence: Is it time to share the blame? *Health Psychology* 12: 91–92.

Evans, W. N. (1998). Assessment and diagnosis of the substance use disorders (SUDs). *Journal of Counseling and Development* 76: 325–32.

Faber, R. J., and G. A. Christenson. (1996). In the mood to buy: Differences in the mood states experienced by compulsive buyers and other consumers. *Psychology and Marketing Special Issue: Aberrant Consumer Behavior* 13: 803–20.

Faber, R. J., G. A. Christenson, M. de Zwaan, and J. Mitchell. (1995). Two forms of compulsive consumption: Comorbidity of compulsive buying and binge eating. *Journal of Consumer Research* 22: 296–304.

Faber, R. J., and T. C. O'Guinn. (1992). A clinical screener for compulsive buying. *Journal of Consumer Research* 19: 459–69.

Fingarette, H. (1988). Alcoholism: The mythical disease. *The Utne Reader* (November), 64.

Fisher, Carrie. (1987). *Postcards from the Edge.* New York: Pocket Books.

Fleming, M. F., M. P. Mundt, M. T. French, L. Baier Manwell, E. A. Stauffacher, and K. F. Lawton Berry. (2002). Brief physician advice for problem drinkers: Long term efficacy and benefit-cost analysis. *Alcoholism: Clinical and Experimental Research* 26: 36–43.

Fletcher, A. M. (2001). *Sober for Good.* Boston: Houghton Mifflin.

Flores, P. J. (2001). Addiction as an attachment disorder: Implications for group therapy. *International Journal of Group Psychotherapy* 51: 63–82.

———. (2004). *Addiction as an attachment disorder.* New York: Jason Aronson.

Forchuk, C. (1984). Cognitive dissonance: Denial, self-concepts and the alcoholic stereotype. *Nursing Papers* 16: 57–69.

Foroud, T., and T. K. Li. (1999). Genetics of Alcoholism: A review of recent studies in human and animal models. *American Journal of Addictions* 8: 261–78.

Fouquereau, E., A. Fernandez, E. Mullet, and P. C. Sorum. (2003). Stress and the urge to drink. *Addictive Behaviors* 28: 669–85.

Freimuth, M. (2000). The conjoint model for working with psychotherapy patients in 12-step programs. *International Journal of Group Psychotherapy* 50: 297–314.

Goldberg, M. E. (1995). Substance-abusing women: False stereotypes and real needs. *Social Work* 40: 789–98.

Goodman, A. (1993). Diagnosis and treatment of sexual addiction. *Journal of Sex and Marital Therapy* 19: 225–51.

———. (1998). *Sexual addiction: An integrated approach.* Madison, CT: International Universities Press.

———. (2001). What's in a name? Terminology for designating a syndrome of driven sexual behavior. *Sexual Addiction and Compulsivity* 8: 191–213.

Gordon, J. R. (1998). Harm reduction psychotherapy comes out of the closet. *In Session: Psychotherapy in Practice* 4: 69–77.

Grant, B. F. (1997). Prevalence and correlates of alcohol use and DSM-IV alcohol dependence in the United States: Results of the National Longitudinal Alcohol Epidemiologic Survey. *Journal of Studies on Alcohol* 58: 464–73.

Grant, B. F., and D. A. Dawson. (1999). Alcohol and drug use, abuse, and dependence: Classification, prevalence, and comorbidity. Pp. 9–29 in *Addictions: A comprehensive textbook*, ed. B. S. McCrady and E. E. Epstein. New York: Oxford.

Greenberg, J. L., S. E. Lewis, and D. K. Dodd. (1999). Overlapping addictions and self-esteem among college men and women. *Addictive Behaviors* 24: 565–71.

Grohol, J. M. (2003). Internet Addiction Guide. Retrieved December 18, 2003, from http://psychcentral.com/netaddiction/.

Hamill, P. (1994). *A Drinking Life: A Memoir.* Boston: Little, Brown and Co.

Hanna, E. Z. (1991). Attitudes toward problem drinkers, revisited: Patient-therapist factors contributing to the differential treatment of patients with alcohol problems. *Alcoholism: Clinical and Experimental Research* 15: 927–31.

Hansen, G. R. (2002). In drug abuse, gender matters. *NIDA Notes* 17: 3–4.

Hasin, D. S. (1991). Diagnostic interviews for assessment: Background, reliability, validity. *Alcohol Health and Research World* 14: 293–303.

Hasin, D. S., M. A. Schuckit, C. S. Martin, B. F. Grand, K. K. Bucholz, and J. E. Helzer. (2003). The validity of DSM-IV alcohol dependence: What do we know and what do we need to know? *Alcoholism: Clinical and Experimental Research* 27: 244–52.

Hausenblas, H. A., and D. Symons Downs. (2002a). Exercise Dependence: A systematic review. *Psychology of Sport and Exercise* 3: 89–123.

———. (2002b). How much is too much? The development and validation of the Exercise Dependence Scale. *Psychology and Health,* 17: 387–404.

Herd, D., and J. Grube. (1996). Black identity and drinking in the U.S.: A national study. *Addiction* 91: 845–57.

Hesselbrock, M. N., and V. M. Hesselbrock. (1997). Gender, alcoholism, and psychiatric comorbidity. Pp. 49–71 in *Gender and alcohol: Individual and social perspectives (Alcohol, culture, and social control monograph series)*, ed. R. W. Wilsnack and S. C. Wilsnack. New Brunswick, NJ: Rutgers Center of Alcohol Studies.

Hodgins, D. C., and K. Makarchuk. (2003). Trusting problem gamblers: Reliability and validity of self-reported gambling behavior. *Psychology of Addictive Behaviors* 17: 244–48.

Howard, M., C. McMillen, L. Nower, D. Elze, T. Edmond, and J. Bricout. (2002). Denial in addiction: Toward an integrated stage and process model—qualitative findings. *Journal of Psychoactive Drugs* 34: 371–83.

Jellinek, E. M. (1960). *The disease concept of alcoholism.* New Haven, CT: Hillhouse Press.

Jersild, D. (2002). *Happy hours: Alcohol in a woman's life.* New York: Perennial.

Johnson, B. (1992). Psychoanalysis of a man with active alcoholism. *Journal of Substance Abuse Treatment* 9: 111–23.

Johnson, J. G, R. L. Spitzer, J. B. Williams, K. W. Kroenke, M. Linzer, D. Brody, et al. (1995). Psychiatric comorbidity, health status, and functional impairment associated with alcohol abuse and dependence in primary care patients: Findings of the PRIME MD-1000 study. *Journal of Consulting and Clinical Psychology* 63: 133–40.

Johnston, L. D., P. M. O'Malley, and J. G. Bachman. (2003). *Monitoring the Future national survey results on adolescent drug use: Overview of key findings, 2002.* (NIH Publication No. 03–5374). Bethesda, MD: National Institute on Drug Abuse.

Johnson, M. D., T. J. Heriza, and C. St. Dennis. (1999). How to spot illicit drug abuse in your patients. *Postgraduate Medicine* 106: 199–200, 203–206, 211, and 214.

Jones, B. T., W. Corbin, and K. Fromme. (2001). A review of expectancy theory and alcohol consumption. *Addiction* 96: 57–72.

Kalichman, S. C., R. R. Johnson, V. Adair, D. Rompa, K. Multhauf, and J. A. Kelly. (1994). Sexual sensation seeking: Scale development and predicting AIDS-risk behavior among homosexually active men. *Journal of Personality Assessment* 62: 385–97.

Kalichman, S. C., and D. Rompa. (2001). The Sexual Compulsivity Scale: Further development and use with HIV-positive persons. *Journal of Personality Assessment* 76: 376–95.

Kandel, D. B. (1982). Epidemiological and psychosocial perspectives on adolescent drug use. *Journal of the American Academy of Child and Adolescent Psychiatry* 20: 328–47.

Kaufman, E. (1994). *Psychotherapy of addicted persons.* New York: Guilford.

Kessler, R. C., R. M. Crum, L .A. Warner, C .B. Nelson, J. Schulenberg, and J. C. Anthony. (1997). Lifetime co-occurrence of DSM-III-R alcohol abuse and dependence with other psychiatric disorders in the National Comorbidity Study. *Archives of General Psychiatry* 54: 313–21.

Keyes, Marian. (1998). *Rachel's Holiday.* New York: Harper Collins.

Khantzian, E. J. (1985). The self-medication hypothesis of addictive disorders: Focus on heroin and cocaine dependence. *American Journal of Psychiatry* 142: 1259–64.

———. (1997). The self-medication hypothesis of substance use disorders: A reconsideration and recent applications. *Harvard Review of Psychiatry* 4: 231–44.

Kirby, K. C., K. Leggett Dugosh, L. A. Benishek, and V. M. Harrington. (2005). The Significant Other Checklist: Measuring the problems experienced by family members of drug users. *Addictive Behaviors* 30: 29–47.

Kishline, A. (1994). *Moderate drinking: The moderation management guide for people who want to reduce their drinking.* New York: Guilford Press.

Knapp, Caroline. (1996). *Drinking: A Love Story.* New York: Dial Press.

Knight, J. R., L. Sherritt, S. K. Harris, E. C. Gates, and G. Chang. (2003). Validity of brief alcohol screening tests among adolescents: A comparison of the AUDIT, POSIT, CAGE, and CRAFFT. *Alcoholism: Clinical and Experimental Research* 27: 67–73.

Knight, J. R., L. A. Shrier, T. D. Bravender, J. Farrell, J. Vander Bilt, and H. J. Shaffer. (1999). A new brief screen for adolescent substance abuse. *Archives of Pediatric Adolescent Medicine* 153: 25–30.

Kohut, H. (1987). *The Kohut seminars on self psychology and psychotherapy with adolescents and young adults,* ed. M. Elson. New York: Norton.

Kraus, L., and R. Augustin. (2001). Measuring alcohol consumption and alcohol-related problems: Comparison of response from self-administered questionnaires and telephone interviews. *Addiction* 96: 459–71.

Ladd, G. T., and N. M. Petry. (2002). Gender differences among pathological gamblers seeking treatment. *Experimental and Clinical Psychopharmacology* 10: 302–9.

Larimer, M. E., and C. Neighbors. (2003). Normative misperception of the impact of descriptive and injunctive norms on college student gambling. *Psychology of Addictive Behaviors* 17: 235–43.

Lederer, K. (2003). *Poker Face: A Girlhood among Gamblers*. New York: Crown.

Lejoyeux, M., V. Tassain, J. Solomon, and J. Ades. (1997). Study of compulsive buying in depressed patients. *Journal of Clinical Psychiatry* 58: 169–73.

Leonard, K. E., and P. Mudar. (2003). Peer and partner drinking and the transition to marriage: A longitudinal examination of selection and influence processes. *Psychology of Addictive Behaviors* 17: 115–25.

Lesieur, H. R., and S. B. Blume. (1987). The South Oaks Gambling Screen (SOGS): A new instrument for the identification of pathological gamblers. *American Journal of Psychiatry* 144: 1184–88.

Leshner, A. I. (2001). Addiction: A brain disease with biological underpinnings. *Voice* 6: 1–3.

Lilenfeld, L. R., and W. H. Kaye. (1996). The link between alcoholism and eating disorders. *Alcohol Health and Research World* 20: 94–99.

Margolis, R. D., and J. E. Zweben. (1998). *Treating patients with alcohol and other drug problems: An integrated approach*. Washington, DC: American Psychological Association.

Marlatt, G. A., ed. (1998). *Harm reduction: Pragmatic strategies for managing high risk behaviors*. New York: Guilford Press.

Marlatt, G. A., A. W. Blume, and G. A. Parks. (2001). Integrating harm reduction therapy and traditional substance abuse treatment. *Journal of Psychoactive Drugs* 33: 13–21.

Marlowe, A. (1999). *How to stop time: Heroin from A to Z*. New York: Basic Books.

Marzuk, P. M., K. Tardiff, A. C. Leon, M. Stajic, E. B. Morgan, and J. Mann. (1992). Prevalence of cocaine use among residents of New York City who committed suicide during a one year period. *American Journal of Psychiatry* 149: 371–75.

Matano, R. A., C. Koopman, S. F. Wanat, S. D. Whitsell, A. Borggrefe, and D. Westrup. (2003). Assessment of binge drinking of alcohol in highly educated employees. *Addictive Behaviors* 28: 1299–310.

Matano, R. A., S. F. Wanat, D. Westrup, C. Koopman, and S. D. Whitsell. (2002). Prevalence of alcohol and drug use in a highly educated workforce. *The Journal of Behavioral Health Services and Research* 29: 30–45.

Matthews, C. R., L. A. Schmid, A. A. Conclaves, and K. H. Bursley. (1998). Assessing problem drinking in college students: Are counseling centers doing enough? *Journal of College Counseling* 12: 3–9.

Mayfield, D., G. MacLeod, and P. Hall. (1974). The CAGE Questionnaire: Validation of a new alcoholism screening instrument. *American Journal of Psychiatry* 131: 1121–23.

McClellan, A., L. Luborsky, G. Woody, and C. O'Brien. (1980). An improved diagnostic evaluation for substance abuse patients: The Addiction Severity Index. *The Journal of Nervous and Mental Disease* 168: 26–33.

McLaney, M. A., F. DelBoca, and T. Babor. (1994). A validation study of the Problem-Oriented Screening Instrument for Teenagers (POSIT). *Journal of Mental Health* 3: 363–76.

Menninger, J. A. (2002). Assessment and treatment of alcoholism and substance-related disorders in the elderly. *Bulletin of the Menninger Foundation* 66: 166–83.

Miele, G. M., K. D. Trautman, and D. S. Hasin. (1996). Assessing comorbid mental and substance use disorders: A guide for clinical practice. *Journal of Practical Psychiatry and Behavioral Health* 2: 272–81.

Miles, H, A. Winstock, and J. Strang. (2001). Identifying young people who drink too much: The clinical utility of the five-item Alcohol Use Disorders Identification Test (AUDIT). *Drug and Alcohol Review* 20: 9–18.

Miller, G. A. (1994). *The Substance Abuse Subtle Screening Inventory manual: Adult SASSI-2 manual supplement.* Spencer, IN: Spencer Evening World.

Miller, W. R., and S. Brown. (1997). Why psychologists should treat alcohol and drug problems. *American Psychologist* 52: 1269–79.

Miller, W. R., and S. Rollnick. (1991). *Motivational interviewing: Preparing people to change addictive behavior.* New York: Guilford.

———. (2002). *Motivational interviewing: Preparing people for change.* 2d ed. New York: Guilford Press.

Mitchell, J. E., J. Redlin, S. Wonderlich, R. Crosby, R. Faber, R. Miltenberberg, et al. (2002). The relationship between compulsive buying and eating disorders. *International Journal of Eating Disorders* 32: 107–11.

Moore, A. A., J. C. Beck, and T. F. Babor. (2002). Beyond alcoholism: Identifying older, at risk drinkers in primary care. *Journal of Studies on Alcohol* 63: 316–24.

Morahan-Martin, J., and P. Schumacher. (2000). Incidence and correlates of pathological Internet use among college students. *Computers in Human Behavior* 16: 13–29.

Moriarty, J. (2001). *Liquid Lover.* New York: Alyson Publications.

Myerholtz, L. E., and H. Rosenberg. (1997). Screening DUI offenders for alcohol problems: Psychometric assessment of the Substance Abuse Subtle Screening Inventory. *Psychology of Addictive Behaviors* 11: 155–65.

Myrick, H., and K. Brady. (2003). Editorial review: Current review of the comorbidity of affective, anxiety, and substance use disorders. *Current Opinion in Psychiatry* 16: 261–70.

National Center on Addiction and Substance Abuse at Columbia University, The. (1994). *Rights of Passage: Substance Abuse on America's Campuses.* New York: The National Center on Addiction and Substance Abuse at Columbia University.

———. (1998). *Under the rug: Substance abuse and the mature woman.* New York: The National Center on Addiction and Substance Abuse at Columbia University.

———. (2000). *Missed opportunity: National Survey of Primary Care Physicians and Patients on Substance Abuse.* New York: The National Center on Addiction and Substance Abuse at Columbia University.

National Institute of Drug Abuse. (2003). Retrieved on September 28, 2003, from www.nida.nih.gov/.

Nichols, L. A., and R. Nicki. (2004). Development of a psychometrically sound Internet Addiction Scale: A preliminary step. *Psychology of Addictive Behaviors* 18: 381–84.

O'Dea, J. A., and S. Abraham. (2002). Eating and exercise disorders in young college men. *Journal of American College Health* 50: 273–78.

Orford, J. (2002). *Excessive appetites*, 2d ed. Chichester, UK: Wiley.

Orzack, M. H., and C. J. Ross. (2000). Should virtual sex be treated like other addictions? Pp. 113–26 in *Cybersex: The dark side of the force*, ed. A. Cooper. Philadelphia: Brunner-Routledge.

Pasternak, A. V., and M. F. Fleming. (1999). Prevalence of gambling disorders in a primary care setting. *Archives of Family Medicine* 8: 515–20.

Peele, S., ed. (1985). *The meaning of addiction: A compulsive experience and its interpretation*. Lexington, MA: Lexington Books.

Peele, S. (1995). *Diseasing of America*. San Francisco: Jossey-Boss.

Pendery, M. L., I. M. Maltzman, and L. J. West. (1982). Controlled drinking by alcoholics? New findings and a reevaluation of a major affirmative study. *Science* 217: 169–74.

Petry, N. (2002). How treatments for pathological gambling can be informed by treatments for substance use disorders. *Experimental and Clinical Psychopharmacology* 10: 184–92.

———. (2003). A comparison of treatment-seeking pathological gamblers based on preferred gambling activity. *Addiction* 98 (5): 645–55.

Philpot, M., N. Pearson, V. Petratou, R. Dayanandan, M. Silverman, and J. Marshall. (2003). Screening for problem drinking in older people referred to a mental health service: A comparison of the CAGE and AUDIT. *Aging and Mental Health* 7: 171–75.

Poikolainen, K. (1999). Effectiveness of brief interventions to reduce alcohol intake in primary health care populations: A meta-analysis. *Preventive Medicine* 28: 503–9.

Randall, C. L., J. S. Roberts, F. K. Del Coca, K. M. Carroll, G .J. Connors, and M. E. Mattson. (2002). Temporal sequencing of alcohol-related problems, problem recognition, and help-seeking episodes. *Addictive Behaviors* 27: 659–74.

Recovery Institute, The. (1998). The Road to Recovery: A Landmark National Study on Public Perceptions of Alcoholism and Barriers to Treatment.

Reiger, D. A., M. E. Farmer, D. S. Raie, B. A. Locke, S. J. Keith, L. L. Juidd, et al. (1990). Comorbidity of mental disorders with alcohol and other drug abuse. *Journal of the American Medical Association* 264: 2511–81.

Reis, J., and W. L. Reiley. (2000). Predictors of college students' alcohol consumption: Implications for student education. *Journal of Genetic Psychology* 161: 282–91.

Robins, L. N., D. H. Davis, and D. W. Goodwin. (1974). Drug use by U.S. enlisted Army men in Vietnam: A follow-up on their return home. *American Journal of Epidemiology* 99: 235–49.

Rosenker, D. C. (2002). Heroin reaches the well-to-do adolescent population. *Brown University Child and Adolescent Behavior Letter* 18: 3–4.

Rosenberg, H. (1993). Prediction of controlled drinking by alcoholics and problem drinkers. *Psychological Bulletin* 113: 129–39.

Rouse, S. V., J. N. Butcher, and K. B. Miller. (1999). Assessment of substance abuse in psychotherapy clients: The effectiveness of the MMPI-2 substance abuse scales. *Psychological Assessment* 11: 101–7.

Russell, M., S. S. Martier, R. J. Sokol, S. Jacobson, J. Jacobson, and S. Bottom. (1991). Screening for pregnancy risk drinking: Tweaking the tests. *Alcoholism: Clinical and Experimental Research* 15: 638–42.

Saladin, M. E., and E. J. Santa Ana. (2004). Controlled drinking: More than just a controversy. *Current Opinion in Psychiatry* 17: 175–87.

Sannibale, C., and W. Hall. (1998). An evaluation of Cloninger's typology of alcohol abuse. *Addiction* 93: 1241–49.

Saunders, J. B., O. G. Aasland, T. F. Babor, J. R. De La Fuente, and M. Grant. (1993). Development of the Alcohol Use Disorders Identification Test (AUDIT): WHO Collaborative Project on early detection of persons with harmful alcohol consumption. *Addiction* 88: 381–89.

Schneider, J. P. (2000). Effects of cybersex addiction on the family. Pp. 31–58 in *Cybersex: The dark side of the force*, ed. A. Cooper. Philadelphia: Brunner-Routledge.

Schottenfeld, R. S. (1994). Assessment of the patient. Pp.25–33 in *Textbook of substance abuse treatment*, ed. M. Galanter and H. D. Kleber. Washington, DC: American Psychiatric Press.

Schuckit, M. A. (1998). *Educating yourself about alcohol and drugs: A people's primer.* Cambridge, MA: Perseus Books.

Schuckit, M. A., G. P. Danko, E. B. Raimo, T. L. Smith, M. Y. Eng, K.K.T. Carpenter, et al. (2001). A preliminary evaluation of the potential usefulness of the diagnosis of polysubstance dependence. *Journal of Studies on Alcohol* 62: 54–61.

Schuckit, M. A., T. L. Smith, G. P. Danko, K. K. Bucholz, T. Reich, aand L. Bierut, (2002). Five-year clinical course associated with DSM-IV alcohol abuse or dependence in a large group of men and women. *American Journal of Psychiatry* 158: 1084–90.

Selzer, M. L. (1971). The Michigan Alcoholism Screening Test: The quest for a new diagnostic instrument. *American Journal of Psychiatry* 127: 1653–58.

Selzer, M., A. Vinokur, and L. J. van Rooijen. (1975). A self-administered short Michigan Alcohol Screening Test (SMAST). *Journal of Studies on Alcohol* 36: 117–26.

Shaffer, H. (1991). Toward an epistemology of "addictive disease." *Behavioral Sciences and the Law* 9: 269–86.

———. (1997). The most important unresolved issue in the addictions: Conceptual chaos. *Substance Use and Misuse* 32: 1573–80.

———. (1999). Strange bedfellows: A critical view of pathological gambling and addiction. *Addiction* 94: 1445–48.

Shea, S. C. (1999). *The practical art of suicide assessment: A guide for mental health professionals and substance abuse counselors.* New York: John Wiley.

Shewan, D., P. Dalgarno, A. Marshall, and E. Lowe. (1998). Patterns of heroin use among a non-treatment sample in Glasgow, Scotland. *Addiction Research* 6: 215–34.

Sivestri, T. J., D. Pollaci, and A. Genco. (2003). A four tier approach to AOD interventions at a college counseling center. *The Addiction Newsletter* 10: 12–13.

Skinner, H. A. (1982). The drug abuse screening test. *Addictive Behaviors* 7: 363–71.

Smaldino, A., ed. (1991). *Psychoanalytic Approaches to Addiction.* New York: Brunner/Mazel.

Smith, D. E. (1986). Cocaine-alcohol abuse: Epidemiological, diagnostic, and treatment considerations. *Journal of Psychoactive Drugs* 18: 117–30.

Sobell, L. C., and M. B. Sobell. (1990). Self-report issues in alcohol abuse: State of the art and future directions. *Behavioral Assessment* 12: 77–90.

———. (1993). *Problem drinkers: Guided self-change treatment.* New York: Guilford.

Sobell, M. B., and L. C. Sobell. (1973). Individualized behavior therapy for alcoholics. *Behavior Therapy* 4: 543–46.

Sokol, R. J., S. S. Martier, and J. W. Ager. (1989). The T-ACE questions: Practical prenatal screening detection of risk drinking. *American Journal of Obstetrics and Gynecology* 160: 863–70.

Staines, G. L., S. Magura, J. Foote, A. Deluca, and N. Kosanke. (2001). Polysubstance use among alcoholics. *Journal of Addictive Diseases* 20: 53–69.

Starace, G. (2002). New "normalities," new "madness." *British Journal of Psychotherapy* 19: 21–32.

Stein, L.A.R., J. R. Graham, Y. S. Ben-Porath, and J. L. McNulty. (1999). Using the MMPI-2 to detect substance abuse in an outpatient mental health setting. *Psychological Assessment* 11: 94–100.

Strong, D. R., R. B. Breen, H. R. Lesieur, and C. W. Lejuez. (2003). Using the Rasch model to evaluate the South Oaks Gambling Screen for use with nonpathological gamblers. *Addictive Behaviors* 28: 1465–72.

Substance Abuse and Mental Health Services Administration. (2002). *Results from the 2001 National Household Survey on Drug Abuse: Volume 1. Summary of National Findings.* Office of Applied Studies, NHSDA Series H-17, DHHS Publication No. SMA02-3758. Rockville, MD: U.S. Department of Health and Human Services.

———. (2003). *Drug abuse statistics.* Retrieved on January 20, 2004, from www.samhsa.gov/oas/occupation.htm.

Swadi, H. (1997). Substance Misuse in Adolescence Questionnaire: A pilot study of a screening instrument for problematic use of drugs and volatile substances in adolescents. *Child Psychology and Psychiatry Review* 2: 63–67.

Talmadge, J. (2003). Highlights from the 13th annual meeting of the American Association for Addiction Psychiatry. *Medscape Psychiatry and Mental Health,* 8. Retrived on February 13, 2004, from www.medscape.com/viewarticle/448468.

Tartarsky, A. (2002). *Harm reduction psychotherapy: A new treatment for drug and alcohol problems.* New York: Jason Aronson.

Tarter, R. E. (2002). Etiology of adolescent substance abuse: A developmental perspective. *American Journal of Addictions* 11: 171–91.

Thom, B., and C. Tellez. (1986). A difficult business: Detecting and managing alcohol problems in general practice. *British Journal of Addictions* 81: 405–18.

Tonigan, J. S., W. R. Miller, and J. M. Brown. (1997). The reliability of FORM 90: An instrument for assessing alcohol treatment outcome. *Journal of Studies on Alcohol* 58: 358–64.

Tracy, J. I., D. M. Gorman, and E. A. Leventhal. (1992). Reports of physical symptoms and alcohol use: Findings from a primary health care sample. *Alcohol and Alcoholism* 27: 481–89.

U.S. Deptartment of Health and Human Services: National Institute on Alcohol abuse and Alcoholism. (2000). NIH publication number 00–1583.

Vaillant, G. E. (1995). *The natural history of alcoholism revisited.* Cambridge, MA: Harvard University Press.

Vinson, C. (1997). Alcohol is not a dichotomous variable. *Journal of Family Practice* 44: 147–49.

Vinson, C. D., J. M. Galliher, C. Reidinger, and J. A. Kappus (2004). Comfortably engaging: Which approach to alcohol screening should we use? *Annals of Family Medicine* 2: 398–404.

von Ranson, K. M., M. McGue, and W. G. Iacono. (2003). Disordered eating and substance use in an epidemiological sample: II. Associations within families. *Psychology of Addictive Behaviors* 17: 193–202.

Wallace, J. M. (1999). The social ecology of addiction: Race, risk, resilience. *Pediatrics* 103: 1122–27.

Washington State Department of Health. (2002). *Substance abuse during pregnancy: Guidelines for screening.* Olympia, WA: Washington State Department of Health. Retrieved on January 28, 2004, from www.doh.wa.gov/cfh/mch/mchpublications.htm.

Washton, A. M. (1989). Cocaine abuse and compulsive sexuality. *Medical Aspects of Human Sexuality* 23: 32–39.

———. (2001). Why psychologists should know how to treat substance use disorders. *New Jersey Psychologist* (Spring): 10–13.

Washton, A. M., and M. S. Gold, and A. C. Pottash. (1985). Cocaine abuse: Techniques of assessment, diagnosis and treatment. *Psychiatric Medicine* 3: 185–95.

Wasilow-Mueller, S., and C. K. Erickson. (2001). Drug abuse and dependency: Understanding gender differences in etiology and management. *Journal of the American Pharmaceutical Association* 41: 78–90.

Wechsler, H., G. Dowdall, A. Davenport, and E. Rimm. (1995). A gender-specific measure of binge drinking among college students. *American Journal of Public Health* 85: 982–85.

Wechsler, H., and M. Kuo. (2000). College students define binge drinking and estimate its prevalence: Results of a national survey. *Journal of American College of Health* 49: 57–64.

Wechsler, H., and T. F. Nelson. (2001). Binge drinking and the American college student: What's five drinks? *Psychology of Addictive Behaviors* 15: 287–91.

Weegmann, M., and R. Cohen, eds. (2002). *The Psychodynamics of Addiction.* London, UK: Whurr Publishers.

Weinberg, N. M., E. Rahdert, J. D. Colliver, and M. D. Glantz. (1998). Adolescent substance abuse: A review of the past 10 years. *Journal of the American Academy of Child and Adolescent Psychiatry* 37: 252–61.

Weisner, C., and H. Matzger. (2003). Missed opportunities in addressing drinking behavior in medical and mental health settings. *Alcoholism: Clinical and Experimental Research* 27: 1132–41.

Welch, B. (2001). Keeping up: The need for continuing education. *Insight: Safeguarding Psychologists Against Liability Risks* 2: 1–5.

Wholey, D. (1984). *The courage to change: Hope and help for alcoholics and their families.* Boston: Houghton Mifflin.

Wilke, D. (1994). Women and alcoholism: How a male-as-norm bias affects research, assessment, and treatment. *Health and Social Work* 19: 29–35.

Willner, P. (2000). Further validation and development of a screening instrument for the assessment of substance misuse in adolescents. *Addiction* 95: 1691–98.

Wills, T. A., G. McNamara, D. Vaccaro, and A. E. Hirky. (1996). Escalated substance use: A longitudinal grouping analysis from early to middle adolescence. *Journal of Abnormal Psychology* 105: 166–80.

Wilsnack, R. W., N. D. Vogeltanz, S. C. Wilsnack, and T. R. Harris. (2000). Gender differences in alcohol consumption and adverse drinking consequences: Cross-cultural patterns. *Addiction* 95: 251–65.

Wilson, G. T. (1991). The addiction model of eating disorders: A critical analysis. *Advances in Behaviour Research and Therapy* 13: 27–72.

Winters, K. C. (1992). Development of an adolescent alcohol and other drug abuse screening scale: Personal Experience Screening Questionnaire. *Addictive Behaviors* 17: 479–90.

Wolford, G. L., S. D. Rosenberg, R. E. Drake, K. T. Mueser, T. E. Oxman, D. Hoffman, et al. (1999). Evaluation of methods for detecting substance use disorder in persons with severe mental illness. *Psychology of Addictive Behaviors* 13: 313–26.

World Health Organization. (1997). *Multiaxial presentation of the ICD-10 for use in adult psychiatry.* Cambridge, UK: Cambridge University Press.

Wurtzel, Elizabeth. (1994). *Prozac nation. Young and depressed in America: A Memoir.* Boston: Houghton Mifflin.

———. (2002). *More, now, again.* New York: Simon and Schuster.

Index

257

Swadi, H., 161
Symons Downs, D., 77
symptoms amplification, 110

T-ACE (screening instrument), 65–66
test strips for toxicology screening, 63
therapeutic alliance, 25
TICS (screening instrument), 66
tolerance: definition of, 5; as diagnostic
  criterion, 5–6, 15; in process
  addictions, 16; screening questions
  on, 65–66
toxicology screening, 62–64, 126–27
training. *See* education
trauma, history of, 100
treatment: assessment as means to,
  155–76, 198, 215–16; cognitive-
  behavioral approach to, 22, 24;
  diverse addictions benefiting from
  similar, 17; harm-reduction
  approach to, 23, 55–56, 127, 206–7;
  patient-led, 175, 185; pessimism
  about, 43–45; psychotherapy role in,
  19, 21, 23–26, 34–35, 60, 155,
  174–75, 194, 206; toxicology
  screening in, 62; twelve-step
  programs, 19–21
TWEAK (screening instrument), 65–66,
  116, 123
twelve-step programs: criticisms of, 25,
  230; overview of, 19–21; as relapse
  prevention, 24; success of, 17

underdiagnosis: of alcoholism in
  women, 112; ambiguities leading to,
  53–59; cross addictions and,
  145–47; cross tolerance and,
  142–43; denial and, 32, 47–53;
  education ineffective against, 40–41;
  factors in, 32–33, 36–60;
  polysubstance use and, 143–45, 214;
  prevalence of, ix–x, 31–32;

psychotherapy's reputation harmed
  by, 26; stereotypes and, 41–46; when
  substance effects mimic
  psychological symptoms, 147–54.
  See also addictions: hiddenness of
urine screens, 62–63, 126–27

Vaillant, G. E., 6
validity of screening instruments, 70–73
validity techniques for clinical
  interviewing, 107–10; behavioral
  incident questions, 109–10, 193,
  200–202; denial of the specific, 108,
  166; gentle assumptions, 107, 201;
  normalization, 109, 117, 166; shame
  attenuation, 108–9, 117, 166;
  symptoms amplification, 110
Vinson, C., 56

Wallace, J. M., 136, 138
Washton, A. M., 46
Wechsler, H., 128, 129–30
weight-control medications, 9
Welch, Bob, 50
Welch, Bryant, 36
Wholey, Dennis, 54
withdrawal: dangers of, 106, 169, 202;
  definition of, 5; as diagnostic criterion,
  5–6, 15; in process addictions, 16;
  protracted, masking addictions,
  151–52; psychological symptoms as
  misdiagnosis for, 96, 147–52
women: and alcohol, 112–15; buying
  addiction and, 79; and depression,
  112–13; and gambling, 82–83; and
  mental health treatment for
  addiction, 112–13; and shame over
  substance use, 117, 185
work, and signs of addiction, 98
Wurtzel, Elizabeth, 9, 220, 221, 237–38

young adults, 127–30

About the Author

Marilyn Freimuth has been on the faculty of the Fielding Graduate University for over sixteen years. She is also on the teaching faculty of the Alonso Center for Psychodynamic Studies. With her students, Dr. Freimuth has a number of ongoing research projects designed to improve the assessment of addictions and the integration of addiction assessment and psychotherapy. Her earlier research addressed psychotherapists' attitudes toward twelve-step programs and how a patient's experience with self-help programs can be incorporated into psychotherapy. She lectures on the assessment and treatment of addictions and is a practicing clinical psychologist and supervisor. After many years living and practicing in New York, she now resides in Wisconsin with her husband, Scott, and two sons, Ben and Lucas.